Constitutional Essentials

Constitutional Essentials

On the Constitutional Theory of Political Liberalism

FRANK I. MICHELMAN

Harvard University

OXFORD
UNIVERSITY PRESS

OXFORD
UNIVERSITY PRESS

Oxford University Press is a department of the University of Oxford. It furthers the University's objective of excellence in research, scholarship, and education by publishing worldwide. Oxford is a registered trade mark of Oxford University Press in the UK and certain other countries.

Published in the United States of America by Oxford University Press
198 Madison Avenue, New York, NY 10016, United States of America.

Library of Congress Cataloging-in-Publication Data
Names: Michelman, Frank I., 1936– author.
Title: Constitutional essentials : on the constitutional theory of political liberalism / Frank I. Michelman.
Description: New York, NY : Oxford University Press, 2022. |
Includes bibliographical references and index.
Identifiers: LCCN 2022006293 (print) | LCCN 2022006294 (ebook) |
ISBN 9780197655832 (hardback) | ISBN 9780197655856 (epub) |
ISBN 9780197655849 (updf) | ISBN 9780197655863 (online)
Subjects: LCSH: Constitutional law—Philosophy. | Constitutional law—Political aspects. |
Liberalism—Political aspects. | Legitimacy of governments. | Rawls, John, 1921–2002.
Classification: LCC K3165 .M53 2022 (print) | LCC K3165 (ebook) |
DDC 342—dc23/eng/20220608
LC record available at https://lccn.loc.gov/2022006293
LC ebook record available at https://lccn.loc.gov/2022006294

DOI: 10.1093/oso/9780197655832.001.0001

For the questioners, the explainers, and the defenders of liberal constitutional faith

Contents

Foreword xiii
List of Abbreviations and Short Names xvii

Introduction: An Entanglement of Missions for Constitutional Law 1
1. Rawls's Constitution-Centered "Liberal Principle of Legitimacy": A First Look 2
2. A Regulatory and a Justificatory Mission for Substantive Constitutional Law 3
3. Rawls: Justification-by-Constitution 6
4. Debates of the Lawyers 8
5. Plan of the Book 12

PART I. JUSTIFICATION-BY-CONSTITUTION

1. The Constitution as Procedural Recourse: Rawls's "Liberal Principle of Legitimacy" 17
   1. Public Reason to Constitution? 17
      1.1. Public Reason 17
      1.2. Constitution 19
   2. Constitution and Justification 20
      2.1. Justification: The Problem of Political Liberalism 20
      2.2. The Liberal Principle of Legitimacy (LPL); Justification-by-Constitution 21
      2.3. Who's This "We"? 22
      2.4. Reasonability for Constitutions 24
   3. The Constitution as a Procedure 25
      3.1. Procedure as Deflection 25
      3.2. Procedure Incorporating Substance 27
   4. *TJ* to *PL*: Justice to Justification 28
      4.1. The Constitution in *TJ*: "Imperfect Procedural Justice" 28
      4.2. The Constitution in *PL*: Justification ("Legitimacy") in Place of Justice 30

2. A Fixation Thesis and a Secondary Proceduralization: Constitution as Positive Law 33
   1. A Constitution in What Medium? 33
      1.1. A Dated Exegetical Question 34

1.2. Ambiguities of "Unwritten" 35
1.2.1. A Directive Constitution But Conventional (Not Legal)? 35
1.2.2. A Constitution Empirical (Not Directive)? 36
2. Constitution as Directive Code 37
2.1. Lecture VI of *PL* 38
2.2. The Second Procedural Turn: Institutional Settlement: Objectivity, Abstraction, Deferral, and Dependence on a Referee 41
3. Constitution as What Happens 44
3.1. Shadow Norms 45
3.2. Each Our Own Hercules? 46

3. Constitutional Essentials: A Singularity of Reason, or a Space of Reasonability? 51
1. A Scheme of Rights and Their Central Ranges 51
1.1. Between Thick and Thin: "Completeness" Without Repression 51
1.2. The Fallback to "Central Ranges" in a "Scheme of Liberties" 52
1.3. The Burdens of Judgment 54
1.4. Supreme Court as Referee 54
2. Liberal Justice Conceptions as a "Family": A Complication for the LPL? 56
3. The Idea of the "At-Least Reasonable" as Bridge 59

4. Constitutional Law and Human Rights: The Call to Civility 61
1. Domains and Constituencies of Political-Normative Discourses 62
1.1. Domains 62
1.2. Constituencies 64
2. Morality and Civility: Convergence or Division? 64
2.1. Moral Fault to Moral Obligation to Repair? 64
2.2. A Question of the Applicable (Sub)Morality? 65
2.3. Beyond Pragmatism, Relativism, and Popular Constitutionalism: Justification-by-Constitution 65
3. Civility a Moral Trump? 68
3.1. For Citizens at Large ("You and Me")? 68
3.2. For Courts of Law 69

5. Constitutional Fidelity: Of Courts, Citizens, and Time 71
1. Public Reason and Constitution: "Stricter" for Courts than for Citizens 71
1.1. Justification as to Means: "Guidelines of Inquiry" 72
1.2. Justification as to Ends: "Principles and Values" 73
2. Due Regard for the Constitution in Force 74
2.1. Application, Not Revision 74
2.2. "This" Constitution, or Its Family? 75
2.3. The Counter-Logic of the Proceduralist LPL 77
2.4. Aspiration for Citizens, Obligation for Courts? 78

3. Temporality 78
3.1. Dialectical Liberal Reasonability 79
3.2. Flashback: The Sequence of Stages in *TJ* 80
3.3. An Idea of Constitutional-Moral Progress? 82
3.4. Fixture and Project; Court and People 84
4. A Common-Law Constitution? 87

6. A Realistic Utopia? 89
1. Justification as Speculative Sociology 90
1.1. A State of Society 90
2. Elements 91
2.1. A Political Conception of the Reasonable 92
2.2. Burdens of Judgment (Including Raw Pluralism) 95
2.3. Liberal Political Toleration: The Idea of the At-Least Reasonable 97
2.4. The Idea of Democratic Openness 97
2.5. The Idea of a Constraint of Public Reason 98
3. Remainders 99

PART II. "THE CRITERION OF RECIPROCITY"

7. Legitimacy: Procedural Compliance or Ethical Attitude? 105
1. "The Idea of Legitimacy Based on the Criterion of Reciprocity" 105
2. Objective Constitutionality Displaced? 107
3. Reciprocity on the "Constitution" Level 108
4. On the Particular Statute Level, a Totalization of Public Reason? 109
4.1. Reciprocity as Aspirational 111
4.2. "The Proviso" 112
4.3. Borderline Uncertainty 112
4.4. Constitutional Proceduralism to Satisfy Reciprocity? 113

8. Offsets to Proceduralism 115
1. Alternative Readings 116
2. Whither Institutional Settlement? 117
3. Proceduralism Softened? 119
4. Whence the Democratic-Monist Alternative? 122

PART III. SOME CHRONIC DEBATES

9. Constitutional Application: Between Will and Reason 127
1. A Contradiction of Aims 128
2. Not a Digression: Rawls to Dworkin and Back 130
3. A Gap That Cannot Be Closed? 132
4. Originalism Either Way? 133

10. Justification-by-Constitution, Economic Guarantees, and the Rise of Weak-Form Review 137
1. Socioeconomic Rights in a Liberal Constitutional Conception 138
1.1. "SER" and "Social Minimum" as Constitutional Matters 138
1.2. A Standard Worry 139
2. Four Questions: From Justice to Justiciability 140
2.1. Social Minimum and Justice in the Basic Structure 140
2.2. Social Minimum and Legitimacy in the Political Order 142
2.3. Social Minimum as Constitutional Essential 144
2.4. Social Minimum and Judicialization 145
3. Constitutional Essentials and Transparency 146
4. "The Bind" 148
4.1. A "Best Efforts" Commitment 148
4.2. Discursive Cogency 148
5. Enter Weak-Form Judicial Review 150

11. Judicial Restraint (and Judicial Supremacy) 153
1. Three Axes of Judicial Restraint 154
1.1. Restrained as Reserved (Opposite: Free-Spoken) 154
1.2. Restrained as Tolerant (Opposite: Dogmatist) 156
1.3. Restrained as "Weak-Form" (Opposite: "Strong-Form") 157
2. Grounds for Judicial Restraint: Democracy and Legitimacy 158
3. Restraint for the Rawlsian Supreme Court 159
3.1. Reserved Court? ("Justiciability") 160
3.2. Weak(er) Court? 162
3.2.1. Short-Term Legislative Consultation 162
3.2.2. Strong-Form Interagency Constitutional Colloquy 163
3.3. Tolerant Court? 165
4. Summation: Rawls and Judicial Supremacy 168

12. Legal Formalism and the Rule of Law 173
1. Fixing Ideas 173
1.1. "The Rule of Law" 173
1.2. "Legal Formalism" 174
1.3. A Question: "Liberal Legalism" Applied to Rawls? 174
2. What the Rawlsian Liberal "Rule of Law" Principle Is Not 176
2.1. Higher Law in a Dualist System 176
2.2. "The Rule of Law" as Constitutional Essential 178
3. Formalist Remainders in Rawlsian Constitutional Rights 179
4. How Does Strong Democracy Finally Differ? 181

13. Constitutional Rights and "Private" Legal Relations 183
1. The "Horizontal Application" Question, Addressed to Rawls 183
2. Main Liberal Arguments Pro and Con Horizontal Application 185
2.1. On the Side of Horizontality 185
2.2. Against Horizontality 186

3. The Rawlsian Case for Horizontality 188
3.1. "Basic Structure" as Subject 188
3.2. Justificatory Function 189
3.3. Scheme of Liberties, "At-Least" Reasonability 191

14. Liberal Tolerance to Liberal Collapse? 193

Bibliography 199
Index 205

Foreword

In the year 2000, I offered reflection on a suggestion from Mark Tushnet that what ultimately matters for continued constitutional-democratic health in a country like the United States is not which sides Supreme Court majorities come down on in the kinds of "thick" legal-doctrinal wrangles composing the daily fare of that tribunal.[1] What rather really count, thought Tushnet, are the spirit and terms in which the core issues behind those wrangles are framed and discussed in the country's politics at large. No matter whether Tushnet himself, as expert constitutional lawyer or as political moralist, might see some or other adjudicative outcome as reflecting the better view of our constitutional law in place. As long as people credibly aspiring to the abstract liberal values of the American Declaration of Independence, or to American "fundamental guarantees of equality, freedom of expression, and liberty"—our "thin constitution," as Tushnet then would have it—could lean otherwise, adjudicative outcomes of otherwise would be no sign of a distempered world.[2] The American habit of submission in such matters to the dictates of the Supreme Court might count—Tushnet thought that it did count—as a setback to the exercise of democracy here for no good reason, but neither that habit nor a reversal of it should count as a dire threat to the survival of American constitutional faith.

Thusly did I report Tushnet's view.[3] It might, I went on then to say, be "more than some of Tushnet's liberal-minded readers will find they can swallow." I said I thought that "some" would *not* include John Rawls. Tushnet asks of us, I wrote, "about what John Rawls does in his most recent explanations of

[1] See Mark Tushnet, *Taking the Constitution Away from the Courts* (Princeton University Press 1999). Tushnet's examples at the time included judicial treatments of disputes over the criminalization of flag-burning, the permissibility of race-based affirmative action, and burdens on religion from otherwise valid and neutral laws.

[2] Tushnet, *Away from the Courts* 11. For Tushnet's more recent thought on rights in a thin constitution, see Mark Tushnet and Bojan Bugaric, *Power to the People: Constitutionalism in the Age of Populism* (Oxford University Press 2021) 13–18, 21–22.

[3] See Frank I. Michelman, "Populist Natural Law (Reflections on Tushnet's 'Thin Constitution')" (2000) 34 *University of Richmond Law Review* 461. Not long thereafter, I was reading Sanford Levinson to comparable effect. See Frank I. Michelman, "Faith and Obligation, or What Makes Sandy Sweat?" (2003) 38 *Tulsa Law Review* 651, 666–68; Sanford Levinson, *Constitutional Faith* (Princeton University Press 1988).

the idea of public reason."[4] I still do think that to be a make-able proposition. (It could depend on what the meaning of the word "about" is.) I promised then to treat the matter further in future work.[5] That work has since come in fits and starts, tucked into sundry articles and anthology chapters, here reconsidered and recombined in a consolidated treatment of the topic: call it constitutional faith in Rawlsian key.

Thoughts, ideas, and patterns of expression recirculate here from those prior works—not always, though, with just the same shades and tilts of meaning as they once held for me. The initial publications and their venues all are listed in this book's bibliography. My gratitude goes to the publishers, editors, and event-instigators who thus provided birthing space for them. Where chapters have drawn more focally from particular prior publications, those connections are specified and acknowledged in initial footnotes to the chapters in question.

This book could not exist but for extended conversations and exchanges I have enjoyed over the years with C. Edwin Baker (much too soon interrupted), Richard Fallon, Alessandro Ferrara, Oliver Gerstenberg, Johan van der Walt, and Steven Winter. Other friends, colleagues, and acquaintances (including two whom I have never met in person) to whom I stand indebted for critical readings of drafts or for stimulation from exchanges—some recent, some not so much—about topics treated in the book, include Jim Fleming, Tom Hickey, Karl Klare, Dimitrios Kyritsis, Silje A. Langvatn, Linda McClain, Robert Post, and Vlad Perju.

Take away judicial constitutional review. Leave the invocation and application of your country's constitutional mandate entirely to your parliament or your populace acting through juries, polls, assemblies, civic associations, social movements, and elections. Let the country's constitution in those ways be entirely "political," its constitutionalism entirely "popular." Democracy-based resistance still will come—it has come at times from some of my friends named here—against the very idea of fidelity owed by current democratic majorities to pre-scripted constraints on their politics, not freshly adopted or agreed to by them. The philosophy of political liberalism argues directly and profoundly to the contrary. The possibility, that philosophy maintains, in

[4] Michelman, "Populist Natural Law" 487.
[5] Ibid.

our times, of a society just and stable among persons free and equal rests on the hope of a *constitutional* faith, a public confidence shared and sustained in a liberally justification-worthy political framework law-in-place. A picture then begins to take shape of the political workings of a conforming constitutional democracy. May we possibly see it as a picture drawn from life?

Frank Michelman
Lexington, Mass.
January 2022

List of Abbreviations and Short Names

Several works of John Rawls have appeared in multiple editions. Abbreviations and short names in the footnotes refer to the following editions of frequently cited works of Rawls.

JAF	John Rawls, *Justice as Fairness: A Restatement* (ed. Erin Kelly, Harvard University Press 2001)
PL	John Rawls, *Political Liberalism* (Columbia University Press 1993)
"PRR"	John Rawls, "The Idea of Public Reason Revisited" (1997) 64 *University of Chicago Law Review* 765
"Second Introduction"	"Introduction to the Paperback Edition" in John Rawls, *Political Liberalism with a New Introduction and the "Reply to Habermas"* (Columbia University Press 1966) xxxvii–lxii
TJ	John Rawls, *A Theory of Justice* (Harvard University Press 1971)

Introduction: An Entanglement of Missions for Constitutional Law

We enter here upon a history of conversational traffic between the respective departments of philosophy and law in the old academy of liberalism, where lawyers hear much from philosophers, yes—and philosophers hear from lawyers, too, in what has fruitfully been a both-ways exchange.

Our philosophical protagonist is John Rawls. This book comprises a study of the rise and workings, within the Rawlsian political-liberal philosophy, of the idea of a country's higher-legal constitution as a public platform for the justification of political coercion. A study of Rawls on constitutionalism can help us, I believe, in scoping out and managing a cluster of constitutional lawyers' debates—interminable ones, it seems, in the constitutional-democratic precincts of our times—that I will catalogue later in this introduction. But conversely, I believe, those seeking the best and truest readings of Rawls might have something to learn from the controversies of the lawyers. My approach to Rawls has accordingly been that of a critically leavened (while no doubt broadly sympathetic) exegesis, while with the legal-discursive materials I take more of a diagnostic turn. My hope is that a treatment of these two discourses in relation to each other will prove an aid to both political-philosophical and legal-practical reflection.

We start with two exceedingly thin and vaporous definitions (they will thicken as we go along): for *constitutionalism*, an idea of the subjection of on-the-ground political government to a public and prior directive framework for the conduct of politics, antecedently established and beyond any incumbent government's power to alter at will; for *liberalism*, an idea of a politics geared to a proposition of the freedom and equality of persons severally imbued with lives of their own to live. The two notions—this right now is the point to be grasped—are conceptually discrete, moving in different planes, neither subsumed by the other. Granting (if we do) that any serviceable modern political order will necessarily, at any given time, have fixed in place some set of prescriptive institutional and processual forms (thus, a

Constitutional Essentials. Frank I. Michelman, Oxford University Press. © Frank I. Michelman 2022.
DOI: 10.1093/oso/9780197655832.003.0001

"constitution"), it won't be the government's liberal character (if it has one) that generates *that* need.[1] It's true, of course—and pivotal for this book—that *John Rawls* does draw a particular further implication of constitutionalism out of liberalism. But that particular Rawlsian linkage of the two ideas is synthetic not analytic, a matter not of conceptual explication but operational need given certain contingent facts about the world. To present, as Rawls does (and as we soon will begin to explain), a case for a liberal democracy's fall-back to a constitution for fulfillment of government by consent in conditions of reasonable pluralism is not to make liberalism "mean" constitutionalism. It is rather, to the contrary, to make liberalism *need* constitutionalism.

1. Rawls's Constitution-Centered "Liberal Principle of Legitimacy": A First Look

A democracy, Rawls wrote, "necessarily requires that, as one equal citizen among others, each of us accept the obligations of legitimate law."[2] By his term "legitimate" Rawls meant something distinct from an edict's acceptance-in-fact by a population as practically mandatory for them, and distinct even from its reception-in-fact by them as worthy and deserving of their allegiance and support. By "legitimate" law, Rawls meant to distinguish some quality in or of or about the edict to *justify reasonably* such a response from free and equal citizens, aware of continuing deep disagreement among them about the moral and other merits of that edict—something to justify such a reception of it by them, in the sight (say) of you and me looking on.

The possible basis for such justification was a matter of core concern in Rawls's liberal-democratic political philosophy. It was what he called—with typographically unmarked but unmistakable emphasis on the definite article—"the problem of political liberalism,"[3] meaning by that phrase the

[1] "A constitution"—in our sense of the "rules that specify the major institutions . . . of government . . . and how they are to interact . . . and so forth"—is "a conceptual necessity of every legal system." John Gardner, "Can There Be a Written Constitution?" in Leslie Green and Brian Leiter (eds.), *Oxford Studies in Constitutional Law, Vol. 1* (Oxford Scholarship Online: Sept. 2011) 1–2 (hereafter Gardner, "Written Constitution").

An apology here for my use of that odd word "processual." I use it here and then later in like contexts because I have another use in store for "procedural"—to characterize Rawls's evolving ideas of the place of a country's constitution in the justification of political coercion—which I want not to have confused with my meaning here. See *infra* notes 16, 22; Chapter 1, §§ 1.3, 1.4.

[2] John Rawls, "The Idea of Public Reason Revisited" (1997) 64 *University of Chicago Law Review* 765, 782 (hereafter in this book cited as "PRR").

[3] *PL* xx; see Chapter 1, § 2.1.

problem to which the turn in liberal thought he labeled "political," and pursued in his work in the years following publication of *A Theory of Justice*, is specially designed to respond.[4] We will be grappling here with the political-liberal philosophy's particular way of binding legitimacy to constitutionalism, through its placement on a country's constitution of a main burden of support for willing acceptance, across a population of supposedly free and equal citizens, of laws over whose moral and other merits they sometimes quite deeply disagree.

As what he names "the liberal principle of legitimacy" (again that unmarked emphasis), Rawls postulates that exercises of coercive governmental powers, by acts of political majorities over considered dissent from others recognized as no less fully free and equal, may properly be justified to those others, as long as taken "in accordance with a constitution the essentials of which [including "equal rights and liberties of citizenship"] all citizens may reasonably be expected to endorse."[5] There is obviously much in that formulation to unpack, work that will largely occupy Part I of this book. That work will surface sundry doubts and concerns sure to cross the minds of many readers about this constitution-centered proposal on political justification. We neither aim here nor expect to set those doubts all to rest. Somewhat to the contrary, a guiding interest here will lie in noticing how a pursuit of the proposal's implications for constitutional-democratic institutional arrangements and practices stirs up debates long familiar to us as lawyers in constitutional democracy.

2. A Regulatory and a Justificatory Mission for Substantive Constitutional Law

Those debates are hounded (so I suggest in this book) by puzzles and problems issuing from a duality of missions—"regulatory" and "justificatory," as I name them—that we lawyers in constitutional democracies routinely ascribe to our countries' respective bodies of substantive constitutional law. By "substantive," I mean the parts of constitutional law setting restrictions or

[4] I do not mean Rawls was alone in this pursuit. Among liberal-minded philosophers working similar lines, one perhaps thinks first of Charles Larmore. See, e.g., Charles Larmore, *Patterns of Moral Complexity* (Cambridge University Press 1987) 40–130, and *The Morals of Modernity* (Cambridge University Press 1996) 121–221.

[5] *PL* 217, 227.

requirements on the goals to be sought or effects to be wrought by acts of legislation and administration that no one doubts have followed to the letter the constitutionally prescribed institutional forms. We take for granted that an operationally serviceable modern political order will at any given time have fixed in place its set of organizational and processual forms for exertions of state powers, if not strictly legal in force than reliably customary. A general mission for these "structure" parts of constitutions—to enable the possibility of effective government—seems by and large to go without saying. That mission assignment does not so self-evidently hold for the substantive parts usually also found in constitutions legal or conventional. Those parts being not plainly necessary to the effective operation of a political and legal order, our thoughts roam to other reasons for including them.

According to what I name as their *regulatory* assignment, bills of constitutional rights are aimed by constitutional framers at constraint of oncoming governmental acts and policies in directions set by the framers. They work from an expectation of advance-design effects on political outcomes. A constitutional-legal guarantee of "the freedom of speech" is meant to bolster the likelihood that a condition definitively (if more or less abstractly) named by that expression will actually prevail. Such a linkage of predictive hope to semantic confidence has obviously occupied a central place in the wide tradition of constitutional-democratic thought. A liberal society will always have in view, for its substantive constitutional matter, a regulatory aim.

It might have additionally in view a further, *justificatory* aim. It will not have in view the justificatory aim alone without the regulatory because—a point to which I recur soon and then repeatedly throughout this book—the former entails the latter. "Justificatory ambition presupposes regulatory effect," so will go my slogan. Yet the two aims are not nearly the same. The regulatory aim is at any instant forward-looking in time: to constrain political outcomes yet to come in directions preselected by the constitution. The justificatory aim, by contrast, fixes on the moving present. Its concern is to supply a basis on which free and equal citizens, some of them finding deeply wrong and repugnant some of the laws right now issuing from the duly constituted authorities, can nevertheless freely and willingly accept those laws and be prepared normally to abide by them. *Regulation*-by-constitution roughly says: "We the constitution's progenitors are set on certain instructions for the conduct of government policy in this country. Allowing as we must for the likelihood of future legislative majorities sometimes disposed to deviate from these instructions, we act now to secure their efficacy in this country over times to come, by writing them into a higher-directive constitution." *Justification*-by-constitution roughly says: "Allowing as we must for the frequency and depth of expected disagreement in this country over sundry legislative policy choices and directions, it is still the case (so we claim) that everyone here will have prevailing reason to accept and respect as law the legislative outputs of our political order in force—not just because it is, in fact, an order and in force (and not either just in deference to its democratic institutional forms), but *given also* an assurance that those outputs issue in conformity to certain instructions of policy contained in this higher-normative constitution to which we are just now pointing."[6]

Now, the regulatory assignment—sometimes decorously named as "precommitment"[7] and sometimes not so flatteringly as "hegemonic preservation"[8]—is of course axiomatic bedrock for constitutional-democratic self-explanation. The justificatory mission, while surely manifest in practice—Americans, to take a clear example, think it highly germane to respond to accusations of the sheer viciousness or stupidity of some legislative act or policy that it has after all been (or predictably will be) judicially upheld as constitutional—perhaps lies more in the theoretical shadows for most of us most of the time. But both mission assignments to substantive constitutional law—the regulatory and the justificatory—are commonplace and indeed ineluctable in constitutional-democratic thought and debate. As Samuel Freeman wrote shortly prior to the publication of *Political Liberalism*, "citizens refer to [the constitution] to assess, justify, and criticize government action, as well as the demands citizens themselves place upon government trust."[9] Freeman there, recalling to readers what they could see going on around them, captured in a nutshell the idea of the constitution's

[6] Of course, our bipartite classification—"regulatory"/"justificatory"—does not in itself conjure up the full array of reasons and motives by which observers and theorists would variously explain the introduction into a country's legal practice of a layer of substantive constitutional law; that classification only sorts out these sundry possible aims along one axis of differentiation among them. See, e.g., Ran Hirschl, *Toward Juristocracy: The Origin and Consequences of the New Constitutionalism* (Harvard University Press 2004) 43–47 (advancing a "hegemonic preservation" thesis to explain constitutionalization of substantive rights); Dieter Grimm, "Integration by Constitution" (2005) 3 *International Journal of Constitutional Law* 193, 195 (advancing the thesis of an affectively "integrative" function for substantive constitutional law).

[7] See Stephen Holmes, "Precommitment and the Paradox of Democracy" in Jon Elster and Rune Slagstad (eds.), *Constitutionalism and Democracy* (Cambridge University Press 1988) 195.

[8] Hirschl, *Toward Juristocracy* 43–47.

[9] Samuel Freeman, "Original Meaning, Democratic Interpretation, and the Constitution" (1992) 21 *Philosophy and Public Affairs* 3, 9.

justificatory function.[10] (Freeman had then recently been a student of John Rawls. Perhaps the two had helped to cue each other on this point.)

3. Rawls: Justification-by-Constitution

It is John Rawls who has set out most extensively a philosophical scaffolding for assignment to a country's substantive constitutional law of a mission and a burden of political justification. Rawls tied his conception to Bruce Ackerman's depiction of a constitutional democracy's legal order as "dual" in structure, comprising both an "ordinary" law of legislative bodies and a "higher" law of the people.[11] Rawls's point, though, in endorsing this depiction, was a different one from Ackerman's. For Ackerman, the aim initially was explanation of how subjection of everyone to a mix of laws enacted by small assemblies of elected representatives, sprinkled with vetoes imposed by a minuscule handful of non-elected judges, can count as self-government by the people. (The people, Ackerman proposed in response, exercise their rule through their authorship of the constitution.[12]) For Rawls, the aim always was explanation of how subjection of free and equal dissenters to laws favored by majorities can possibly still be legitimate. Democracy, for Ackerman, means authorship by the people of the laws they live under. So does it for Rawls. But *legitimacy*, for Rawls, means the justifiability among free and equal fellow citizens of the force of popularly legislated laws with which some fraction quite fundamentally disagree; it means the nearest possible approach, in such conditions, to the liberal grail of government by consent. The two quests start out from different places. For Rawls, while government by current majorities would of course have to occupy a major part of the policy space in any democratically legitimate regime, it could not occupy all of it. Rather to the contrary, the question for him was how majoritarian forms of rule might *also* become or remain legitimate.

[10] "A democratic constitution," Freeman wrote,

> embodies a conception of the legitimate demands citizens may place upon each other through laws, and the rightful expectations they may have with respect to one another's and government's conduct. As the publicly recognized statement of these terms, the Constitution serves as the basis for civic reasoning and agreement.

Ibid.

[11] *PL* 233.

[12] See Bruce Ackerman, *We the People: Foundations* (Harvard University Press 1991) 6–7, 42–44; Bruce Ackerman, "The Storrs Lectures: Discovering the Constitution" (1984) 93 *Yale Law Journal* 1013, 1044–50, 1070–71.

For Rawls writing in *A Theory of Justice* (1971) (hereinafter often *TJ*), the idea of the constitution follows secondarily upon a conception of *justice*, a set of precepts for a fair scheme of distribution, among members of a human society, of the sorts of claims, relationships, and statuses in that society that the members reasonably, rationally, and primarily value and seek.[13] If democratic citizens could be supposed to converge upon such a conception and its precepts (and Rawls undertook in *TJ* to show that they could), then the right and legitimate democratic constitution would be one conducive to the fulfillment of justice according to that conception and those precepts.[14] In *Political Liberalism* (1993) (hereinafter often *PL*), the idea of the constitution again comes in as secondary to a prior, more basic idea. This time, though, that prior idea is not justice but rather *justification*. What could be the basis, Rawls now asked, upon which democratic citizens could possibly hope to justify to each other, as free and equal persons in relevant, reasonable disagreement, their coercive impositions—political majorities over dissenters—by votes touching fundamental matters over which the citizens are morally, philosophically, and religiously divided?[15]

An idea of the constitution as a procedure of justification came in as a crucial part of Rawls's answer. Reasonable citizens, in deep and reasonable disagreement about the justice or other merits of policies and laws enacted by majorities over dissent, could still agree, Rawls proposed, on acceptance of a set of higher directive principles for the conduct of government—"constitutional essentials," Rawls called them—for sorting disputed laws and policies into those that would and would not be admissible among them.

Now, in order to serve in that way—"procedurally," as I shall be saying[16]—as a response to occasions of otherwise intractable but reasonable disagreement over values and policies, among citizens free and equal, the

[13] See *TJ* 4. In this work, I cite to the original version of *Theory* published in 1971, because my account of Rawls's evolving views depends, in part, on comparison of the view from 1971 with positions taken later, in *Political Liberalism* (1993) and thereafter.

[14] See Chapter 1, § 1.4.1.

[15] See *PL* 136–37, 216–17; *JAF* 40–41 (all posing the same question in essentially identical terms).

[16] For fuller statement of the sense of "procedural" at work in this book, see Chapter 1, § 3. It is worth noting here how this sense of the "procedural" differs from the sense of a purely formal, content-independent, normative principle (Kant's categorical imperative, Habermas's principle "U," a bare cost-benefit function with all value parameters waiting to be filled in). A failure to draw this distinction may have been a cause of static in exchanges between Rawls and Habermas. See Chapter 1, § 3.2. For a wider canvassing of the senses of "procedural" applied to constitutions, see Frank I. Michelman, "Constitutionalism as Proceduralism: A Glance at the Terrain" in Emilios Christodoulidis and Stephen Tierney (eds.), *Public Law and Politics: The Scope and Limits of Constitutionalism* (Ashgate 2008) 141.

constitution would have to be a compendium of directives commonly cognized by all citizens, fixed in advance of their applications, which all as free, equal, and reasonable could be supposed to accept. By way of showing a realistic possibility that these requirements could be met in modern free societies with their inevitable divisions, Rawls undertook to explain (how far he succeeded will be a central and constant question for this book) (1) how an expectation of convergence by citizens on a set of core meanings—"central ranges of application," Rawls called them—for a short list of essential constitutional guarantees could suffice to meet the requirements, and (2) how a constitutional judiciary could be enlisted and trusted by citizens to know and internalize those convergent core meanings and ensure their prevalence in practice—thus, in Rawls's phrase, to "protect" the justification-sustaining constitutional higher law.[17] To this constitution-centered, justificatory construction as a whole, I will give the name of *justification-by-constitution*—the hyphens marking this as a term of art within this book. I will use this phrase in regard to both the construction's appearance in the philosophy of Rawls and (as I claim) its influence on legal-practical debates ongoing at present in constitutional-democratic arenas.

4. Debates of the Lawyers

Justification-by-constitution consists in claims of fulfillment of certain instructions already laid down in a publicly legible script—justificatory force presupposing regulatory effect. One might, accordingly, suppose that normally, at least, the two aims will coincide in practice, so that the pursuit of one is also the pursuit of the other. On closer look, though, one finds that in some respects and in some contexts the two pursuits are not obviously aligned. They sponsor sometimes divergent implications for institutional practice and our idealizations thereof. Their problematic entanglement in the thought and arguments of lawyers, judges, and legal scholars shows up, as I will maintain, in the persistence of debates over the point, the aims, and the preferred institutional specifications for modern constitutionalism, conducted over decades and centuries by spacious-minded lawyers and their political-philosophical and social-theoretic kibitzers, with no resolutions yet

[17] *PL* 233.

in sight but still within a wide tradition we can definitely know by the name of constitutional democracy.[18]

We can take, as a first illustrative example, debate over the necessity—either conceptual, as already built into the very idea of a differentiation of higher from ordinary law, or practical, as requisite for the higher law's fulfillment of its function in the polity—for a processual entrenchment of substantive constitutional law. By a "processual entrenchment," I mean a processual requirement for enactment or revision of the higher law beyond those in force for ordinary legislation.

Suppose you find in operation, in some country, a legal-systemic practice configured as follows. There is in place, as all agree, a written set of higher laws, including a substantive bill of rights, imposing terms of validity for all further legal operations of the state. Save for one slight detail soon to be noted, these higher laws stand subject to revision by the exact same authorities and processes as they themselves prescribe for enactment of ordinary, day-to-day legislation. In practice, that has allowed affirmative votes from simple parliamentary majorities (or even fewer votes than that, depending on the parliamentary quorum rules) to make and remake constitutional laws. There are no requirements for parliamentary supermajorities, successive-session enactments, or popular ratification. The one and only added processual hurdle for a constitution-level enactment is that the bill must announce in its title that it is of higher-law rank and import. Call that setup a weak processual entrenchment of the higher law. How, if at all, does it make any practical sense? For what good reason might anyone think of using it?

The case I pose is not purely imaginary. As some readers surely will see, I have approximately described what is in fact the case in Israel today, as it has been for many years past. Not, however, without vigorous debate about how it possibly *can* be the case. In the face of argument from many that Israel's

[18] Pratap Mehta lists as follows a set of basic ingredients for a "dominant paradigm of liberal constitutionalism":

> the entrenchment of individual rights to protect the basic freedom of individuals, the affirmation of at least the formal political equality of all citizens, the creation of institutional checks and balances, formally defined limitations on the power of government, and the preservation of institutions and practices that allow citizens to exercise political agency and engage in practices of political justification.

Pratap Bhanu Mehta, "Constitutionalism and Nationalism," Working Paper Presented at Online Conference in Honor of Mark Tushnet's Contributions to Comparative Constitutional Law, June 25, 2021. On a higher plane of abstraction, one may expect to see named as marks of liberal constitutionalism such highly general features as "representative democracy, judicial review, the civil service, . . . an independent judiciary [and] accountable government." Mark Tushnet and Bojan Bugaric, *Power to the People* (Oxford University Press 2021) 5.

so-called "basic laws"—some of them enacted (owing to quorum rules) by minorities of the full Knesset membership—cannot conceivably be deemed higher-ranking laws enforceable by courts against current parliamentary majority will,[19] the Israeli Supreme Court to date effectively maintains the contrary and the government complies.[20]

Weak entrenchment of that sort can be useful. It can provide a shield for laws containing particular state commitments for which no risk is acceptable of accidental displacement by "implied repeal."[21] The same device makes little apparent sense, however, as a general rule for constitutional amendment. At least that is so when we think strictly from the standpoint of a long-term regulatory function for substantive constitutional law. Use of weak entrenchment becomes more readily understandable, though, from the standpoint of a justificatory function. That function requires at all times the separate legibility of the higher law from the ordinary, and furthermore the security of the higher law from accidental or sub rosa alteration in the daily run of ordinary legislation. Without plain guardrails against confusion or conflation of the two ranks of laws, compliance with the higher could not stand as a justificatory test for the workings of the lower. Weak entrenchment meets those needs, and it does so—as might imaginably be a constitution-maker's preference for the country at hand at a given historical moment—while trusting parliamentary majorities, acting in the public spotlight, to move with due mixes of deliberation and dispatch to update the country's constitutional laws as needed.[22]

Opposite-tending implications of the regulatory and justificatory functions for substantive constitutional law are not confined the entrenchment question. As guides to exercises of power by voters, judges, and officials, the two can tug in opposite directions at various points in a country's constitutional career. We can start with the choice whether to have a "legal" constitution at all (as opposed to one that is purely "political" or

[19] See, e.g., Daniel Friedmann, *The Purse and the Sword: The Trials of Israel's Legal Revolution* (Oxford University Press 2016) 190–91.

[20] See United Mizrahi Bank Ltd. v. Migdal Cooperative Village, 49(4) P.D. 221 (1995) (Supreme Court of Israel); Rivka Weill, "Reconciling Parliamentary Sovereignty and Judicial Review: On the Theoretical and Historical Origins of the Israeli Legislative Override Power" (2012) 29 *Hastings Constitutional Law Quarterly* 457, 461, 499–500.

[21] As with the case, for example, of the United Kingdom's European Communities Act 1972, for this reason granted a qualified "constitutional" status by UK courts. See Gardner, "Written Constitution" (n 1) 2.

[22] We shall see later how, in matters constitutional as conceived by Rawls, trust in judgement by select bodies apart from the population of citizens at large cannot be avoided somewhere along the line. See Chapters 2, § 2.2, and 3, § 1.4.

"conventional"). And then next (if legal the constitution is to be) might come choices between a legal constitution that is strongly codified and one that is not (a "common law" constitution), and between one that is or is not strongly processually entrenched against alteration by the modes of ordinary legislative enactment; and then next, perhaps, the choice of whether to assign the legal constitution—codified or common-law, entrenched or not, as the case may be—for application (as with other laws) by an independent judiciary, or rather leave it (exceptionally among laws) to be construed and applied in other political venues of a working democracy; or, to put the latter question another way, whether a rejection of strongly judicialized constitutional control, in favor (say) of "popular" constitutionalism, is tantamount to a rejection tout court of the constitution's status as law.[23]

There come then questions of the proper topical coverage and content of constitutional law. Those might start with a question of how far framers rightly ought to go in cementing into constitutional law their own deepest convictions of the demands of political justice. They could run thence to more specific, familiar debates: Is the constitution to include substantive guarantees at all? If so, what is the appropriate level of generality at which to cast them? What about the extension of such guarantees beyond civil rights and liberties to "social" matters such as access to socioeconomic position and material goods? And then what about application of the guarantees to so-called "horizontal" relations among actors in civil society (not just to "vertical" relations between state power and civil society)?

Then we have debates over the conduct of judicial constitutional review (assuming we are to have this feature at all). Shall it be activist or restrained, strong-form or weak-form, and what exactly shall we mean by these terms? Shall we or shall we not provide expressly (by a "limitation" or "justification" clause) for proportionality testing or some other measure of allowance for prima facie legislative encroachments on constitutional guarantees? Either way, debates will come over how to decide, in disputable cases, what shall count as a prima facie encroachment—originalism, textualism, constructivism, "moral reading"—or over whether substantive constitutional law is preferably to be cast as a body of formal rules impervious to political and ethical currents and concerns of the day, or as a body of ductile principles

[23] The answer is not, as you may be thinking, self-evidently yes. See, e.g., Larry D. Kramer, *The People Themselves: Popular Constitutionalism and Judicial Review* (Oxford University Press 2004), 24, 227 (describing an early American view of the Constitution as surely law but a law whose applications are finally to be determined not by judicial delegates but by "the people themselves").

responsive to those currents. Which among these approaches best serves a value of constitutional fidelity, and what exactly is that value? The chapters to follow will look at how these debates—every one of them—reflect a duality of yearnings, in the constitutional-democratic imagination of our times and places, for both a regulatory and a justificatory service from substantive constitutional law.

5. Plan of the Book

As developed in the book's Part I, Rawls in *PL*, first published in 1993, took a distinctly proceduralist approach—one designed to fend off to the outer limit of possibility any final appeal to choice among substantive values in controversy—to the problem of the justification of controversial legislation among free and equal citizens. In a 1996 paperback reissue of *PL*, a newly interpolated second introduction brought on board an expanded view of what ought to count as an admissible political conception in liberal political argument, causing (as I will suggest) a non-negligible complication to the proceduralist approach of 1993, but not a departure from it—the main text of the book remaining otherwise intact from 1993.[24] That 1996 second introduction did also, though, contain the makings for what would, in company with other writings at about the same time and soon thereafter, open out to what has the look of a shift away from insistent proceduralism toward an openly ethical ground of liberal political justification. The putative shift, in terms I will be using, would be from justification "by constitution" (procedural) to justification "by reciprocity" (ethical).

I have mapped the book to reflect these developments over time in Rawls's ideas. Part I contains my presentation—in what you might call a strong reading—of the Rawlsian idea of a procedural justification for the rule and the force of laws enacted by democratic majorities over deep but still reasonable dissent, with the country's constitution in the place of the justificatory load-bearing procedure. I develop the proceduralist theme as we find it first in *TJ* and then, in modified form, in *PL* as issued in 1993, and

[24] See John Rawls, "Introduction to the Paperback Edition," in *PL* xxxvii–lxii. I later sometimes refer to this as Rawls's "Second Introduction." All references in this book to *PL* are to the original introduction and main text of the book as issued in 1993, which are preserved intact in the paperback edition of 1996.

then arguably further modified in view of complications springing from an expanded view of liberal reasonability tabled by Rawls in the second introduction of 1996.

Part II then brings on line some later writing of Rawls that might seem to herald a shift of focus from a public-procedural to an individual-ethical basis of political justification—from a proposition (say) for "legitimation-by-constitution" to one for "legitimation-by-reciprocity." I look to see whether what we have from Rawls at that point is best taken as announcement of such a shift or rather as clarification or further elucidation of positions taken previously. I conclude in favor of the latter reading. We take up resulting implications, some of them uncertain and some problematic, for the conduct of courts and citizens engaged in the application, production, and reception of constitutional law. These Parts I and II together make up the book's elaboration of Rawls's constitutional theory as finally I read it.

Part III then take us into some chronic debates in constitutional-legal practice, where we find reflections of tensions, both between the political-liberal project of justification-by-constitution and the regulatory service for which we also rely on constitutional law, and within the liberal justificatory project itself. My thesis and my hope throughout is that this probe into the Rawls-eye view of the issues at hand may bring from my cohort of constitutional lawyer-theorists some nods of appreciation for the Rawlsian endeavor.

One closing comment, now, with which to wrap up this introduction. The book's undoubted partiality of focus toward the "rights" part—largely (but not totally) neglecting the "structure" part—of constitutional law is not due to any thought of mine that "rights" and "structures" will always fall into cleanly separable piles, or that structural provisions of constitutions are any less crucially linked than the rights provisions are to a constitution's justificatory function—with consequential implications, then, for constitutional-structural practice.[25] It's just the way this book has turned out, for entirely other reasons.

[25] For impressive teaching on the relation of constitutional structural provisions to legitimacy concerns, see Madhav Khosla, *India's Founding Moment: The Constitution of a Most Surprising Democracy* (Harvard University Press 2020). Khosla provides an extended reflection on how the Indian Constitution's adoption of certain structural forms—corresponding, as Khosla says, to elements in contemporary liberal thought and including both commitment to a strongly codified constitutional law (compare this book's Chapter 2) and a model of representation "whose units [are] individuals rather than groups" (compare this book's Chapter 6)—were chosen by the framers with an eye toward conduciveness to "legitimation," by which Khosla means chosen for the sake of "how they would allow Indians to arrive at outcomes agreeable to free and equal individuals." Ibid, 21.

PART I

JUSTIFICATION-BY-CONSTITUTION

We face "the problem" (as John Rawls terms it in *PL*) "of political liberalism." A population of citizens, committed to affirmance of the freedom and equality of each, finds its members frequently dividing over right and good directions for government and public policy. What, then, can be the ground of justification for their reciprocating expectations of willing submission by all to laws with which some fraction—now one fraction, now another—quite deeply disagree? In *PL*, Rawls postulates in response (as "the liberal principle of legitimacy") that such expectations can be justified on the condition of the assured compatibility of the contested laws with "a constitution" that itself merits acceptance by reasonable and rational citizens. If the mode of production of the laws is accepted or acceptable as beyond reasonable complaint—so apparently runs, very roughly, the thought—then so must be the resultant legislative products.

It seems that by "a constitution" Rawls must mean here what that term normally signifies in the political tradition of constitutional democracy—that is, an antecedently established, publicly cognizable body of institutional forms and directives—a public mandatory normative framework for the conduct of government. But assignment to a country's constitution, thus conceived, of the justification-bearing load envisaged for it by the liberal principle of legitimacy carries particular implications for numerous matters of debate within that tradition. These include the range of topics to be addressed at the constitutional level; the levels of precision or abstraction at which to address them; the ones of the society's normative orders (legal? cultural/conventional?) to which the constitution most aptly belongs; the institutional modes of its effectuation; allowance (or not) for alteration over time of the meanings and applications of the constitution's terms, and the processes by which this may occur; and then also, not least in importance, the assumptions in regard to reasonability on the part of citizens that must inevitably infiltrate the debates.

1

The Constitution as Procedural Recourse: Rawls's "Liberal Principle of Legitimacy"

In the view of John Rawls, the idea of the justification of the force of law among free and equal citizens falls under a larger ideal of *public reason* for the conduct of politics in a modern, democratic society. It is with that larger ideal that our exposition begins.

1. Public Reason to Constitution?

1.1. Public Reason

Rawls locates his philosophical inquiry within a certain "public political culture," that of "a democratic society, and . . . the traditions of interpretation of its constitution and basic laws."[1] He reads that culture and that tradition through a moral-contractual lens, as a quest for fair basic terms of cooperation across populations of citizens conceived as severally free and equal—as each one a "self-authenticating source of valid claims."[2] Rawls thus draws the connection between what he sees as two fundamental political ideas in the constitutional-democratic tradition. We have the idea of persons as a severalty among whom each one is endowed with "moral powers" (to "have, to revise, and rationally to pursue a conception of the good" and to "understand and . . . act from . . . principles of justice"), and then we have the idea of society as a scheme of cooperation among them.[3] "Reasonable persons," Rawls posits, living within the political tradition of constitutional democracy,

[1] *JAF* 5; see *PL* 13–14, 223.
[2] Ibid, 32.
[3] Ibid, 299–304; *JAF* 18–19.

Constitutional Essentials. Frank I. Michelman, Oxford University Press. © Frank I. Michelman 2022.
DOI: 10.1093/oso/9780197655832.003.0002

"desire a social world in which they, as free and equal, can cooperate with others on terms all can accept."[4]

Yet a modern free society, Rawls further posits, inevitably is a home to persons and groups holding to a clashing plurality of moral, metaphysical, and religious orientations—the social fact, as Rawls names it, of "reasonable pluralism."[5] There arises, in the argument of Rawls, a resulting moral constraint on deployments by democratic citizens of their powers of mutual coercion through lawmaking. In a democracy, writes Rawls, "political power"—the coercive power applied by the state though its regime of laws—is "citizens' power, which they impose on one another as free and equal."[6] An ideal of public reason then says their actions are to be guided by "political" or "public" values only, meaning values so steeped in the public political culture that all citizens conscientiously can accept them as bearing properly on decisions of public policy, even as the citizens also reasonably differ over the how best to cast the balances for the matter at hand. "As reasonable and rational," Rawls writes,

> and knowing that they affirm a diversity of reasonable religious and philosophical doctrines, [citizens] should be ready to explain the basis of their actions to one another in terms each could reasonably expect the others to endorse as consistent with their freedom and equality.[7]

The public-reason ideal takes hold especially, Rawls maintains, when political actions touch on "fundamental" questions and concerns.[8] Exactly what makes a matter-at-issue a fundamental one to call the ideal of public reason thus imperatively into play is never, so far as I can see, expressly addressed by Rawls. It will turn out, as we go along, that we do not have to settle it, either. (In what follows, I shall sometimes use expressions such as "deeply controversial" or "deep objection" to signal an assumption that fundamental matters are in play.) At least in those cases, Rawls maintains, lawmakers and

[4] *PL* 50.

[5] See *PL* 36–37 (positing a "fact of reasonable pluralism"); ibid, xviii (taking as a premise that "a plurality of reasonable yet incompatible doctrines is the normal result of the exercise of human reason within [a] framework of . . . free institutions").

[6] *JAF* 40–41. "[P]ublic reason is the reason of equal citizens who, as a collective body, exercise final and coercive power over one another in enacting laws and amending their constitution." *PL* 214.

[7] Ibid. See ibid, 218.

[8] See ibid, 214–15.

citizens ideally exercise their shares of political power in accord with what they sincerely find to be the most reasonable balances of applicable public values.

1.2. Constitution

Nothing so far indicates a need for a separate body of substantive higher-level ("constitutional") rules or principles to oversee the contents of the "ordinary" or "ground-level" laws, the ones that directly regulate the conduct of officials and citizens. Such a higher normative compendium would have to be cast in terms on the whole more general and abstract than would be typical for those ground-level laws, given that its job is to rule some of the latter in and some of them out. ("On the whole," because quite concrete specifics are not categorically excluded from constitutional-democratic constitutions—say, "no killing as a punishment for crime.") But still its terms must also, on the whole, be more explicit or concrete than the general call to public reasonability. (If they were not, then the substantive constitution would be a redundancy; and why, then, introduce it at all?) Whatever the reasons for having the substantive constitution, they must start from perceptions of moral or practical advantage from an initial translation (so to speak) of the general call to public reasonability into terms *somewhat* more concretely declared as fitted to the historical and cultural circumstances of the society in question.

In any given country at any given time, such considerations (or some other historical contingencies) may possibly have called into force a body of constitutional directives thus mediating between generic reasonability and the legislative-policy ground level. In the case in which they have, those directives must of course then play their part in defining or delimiting which values are to count as applicable public values for assessments of ground-level, day-to-day legislation. Exactly what that part should be is a matter to be addressed at some length in chapters to follow. The point for now is that the ideal of public reason does not in itself prescribe the existence of *any* substantive constitution intermediating between the morality of public reason and ground-level legislation.

John Rawls himself can possibly be read to have allowed expressly that not every justly governed country's political practice must make a place for that sort of thing. Whether such makes the best reading of Rawls's text, and if so on what grounds, are questions to be taken up as we move our inquiry along.[9] For now, though, and until further notice, we assume the case of a constitutional democracy that does have such a substantive constitution in place. We do so because our aim for now is to bring out some implications of a particular kind of solution Rawls hopes that constitution might provide, if it is there, to the liberal problem of the justification of the coercive force of democratic law in the conditions of visionary pluralism sure to be affecting any modern democratic state.

2. Constitution and Justification

2.1. Justification: The Problem of Political Liberalism

Near the start of *PL* Rawls poses the question to which his work there will be addressed. "How is it possible"—Rawls thus states his leading question—"that there may exist over time a stable and just society of free and equal citizens profoundly divided by reasonable though incompatible religious, philosophical, and moral doctrines?"[10] Rawls calls that "the problem of political liberalism."[11] He then immediately follows on with what he sees as the same question "put another way." How is it possible, he now inquires, "that deeply opposed though reasonable [religious, philosophical, and moral] doctrines may live together and all affirm the political conception of a constitutional regime?"[12] Or take this formulation from a later work: "By what ideals and principles are citizens who share equally in ultimate political power to exercise the power so that each can reasonably justify his or her political decisions to everyone?"[13]

In order fully to feel the force of Rawls's query, you need to have also before you his distinctly liberal-tinted understanding of democracy. As liberal, Rawls conceives democracy as the vesting of political power—the power of rule—in citizens severally free and equal, acting consciously in concert.[14] Political power, "which is always coercive power," is in a democracy a power by which citizens collectively impose on citizens individually—by which

[9] See Chapters 2, § 2.1, and 8, § 4.
[10] *PL* xx.
[11] Ibid.
[12] Ibid.
[13] "PRR" 64.
[14] "In a democratic regime," Rawls writes, "political power is regarded as the power of free and equal citizens as a collective body." *JAF* 40.

the citizens as a body "impose on themselves and one another as free and equal."[15] But thence springs a question:

> [I]f the fact of reasonable pluralism always characterizes democratic societies and if political power is indeed the power of free and equal citizens, in the light of what reasons and values . . . can citizens legitimately exercise that coercive power over one another?[16]

2.2. The Liberal Principle of Legitimacy (LPL); Justification-by-Constitution

It is specifically in answer to that question that Rawls offers, in *PL*, the idea of a higher-normative prescript—a "constitution"—whose terms for the regulation of all further political actions in that country any citizen might reasonably call upon all fellow citizens to accept, even as all would understand that some outcomes allowed by those terms will certainly turn out repugnant—and far from trivially so—to some fraction of the citizens. To a question cast initially in terms of a putative convergence on "reasons and values," Rawls offers in response an institutional idea, that of the constitution as a table of terms for a procedural deflection of substantive disagreements. Subject to variations of wording that do not reach to our concerns in this chapter, the principle reads as follows:

> Our exercise of political power is proper and hence justifiable [among citizens free and equal] only when it is exercised in accordance with a constitution the essentials of which all citizens may reasonably be expected to endorse in the light of principles and ideals acceptable to them as reasonable and rational. This is the liberal principle of legitimacy.[17]

The liberal principle of legitimacy (LPL, as we shall familiarly call it) presents us with an institutional object-class, "constitution," of which some members do and some do not, in certain essential respects, meet a test of hypothetical reasonable acceptability spelled out (more or less) by the LPL. The LPL

[15] Ibid.
[16] Ibid, 41.
[17] *PL* 217. See ibid, 237; *JAF* 41.

then lets justification ride on the back of an actual constitution that meets the test. By hypothesis, in a well-ordered society, the constitution actually now in force in the country does meet the test; it is, as we shall say, a "justification-worthy" constitution (compare "a seaworthy ship").[18] Majorities justify to protesting dissenters their exertions of political power by pointing to the justification-worthy constitution-in-force, with which those exertions can be seen to comply. Citizens severally engaged with their shares in this power—through, say, their votes on ballot questions and in partisan elections—thus claim to be acting with *that* constitution in view. A supreme court acts as institutional protector of that extant constitutional pact, to which officials and citizens point by way of justification for their votes and other political actions.[19] We have, in sum, the political practice I call by the name of justification-by-constitution.

The LPL, please note, advances no direct claim about anyone's general moral obligation to comply with state law just *as* state law. The question of legitimacy, for Rawls, runs to justification of demands for compliance, not justification of refusals to comply. The question is one of the possible basis of justification among free and equal citizens for their everyday expectations of each other's normal readiness to comply with duly enacted laws. The LPL comes as Rawls's response to that question. Taking it thus as given, our aim will be to develop its implications for constitutional-democratic institutional arrangements and practices, and to match those up against assumptions and positions widely found in our familiar constitutional-legal discourses and debates.

2.3. Who's This "We"?

Preliminarily, we need a certain further specification regarding the exertions of power for which the LPL purports to stipulate terms of justification. *Whose* are those exertions? Most obviously, we have in view here coercive

[18] To be exact: As matters will develop later, reference to an extant constitution as justification-worthy in the sight of this or that political actor will have to mean approximately or nearly justification-worthy, depending on how controversies over application are resolved. The analogy is to Rawls resting some analyses on the assumption of a society that is "more or less" or "nearly" well ordered, meaning still subject to serious disputes over applications of principles of justice in a general conception of justice on which, and on its place and the place of public reasoning in political ordering, there is wide agreement. See *PL* 248–49.

[19] See *PL* 233; Chapter 2, § 2.2.

acts of lawmaking and legal administration that democratic citizen bodies may be said to own collectively through the doings of the governments and officials they deputize by their votes. The LPL says those collectively owned governmental acts are justifiable among free and equal citizens "only when" they comply with a constitution that itself meets certain terms of acceptability among reasonable citizens.

The test as stated is objective. It is not that you or I or anyone or everyone believes it to be satisfied but just that it be satisfied. No doubt that leaves many questions dangling, which it will be a main task of this book to address. To begin to address them, we can note that it is not *only* collectively owned acts of government that are up for justification *per* the LPL. Rawls quite specifically asks how citizens can legitimately exercise their coercive political power "over one another."[20] In a democracy, it appears, while political power is wielded by citizens collectively, its authorship is composed also of a distributive "we" who *severally owe each other* justification for our various inputs to that power's exercise.[21] As citizens in democracies—as constituents in electorates and participants in civil society—we are always choosing, from among proposed and pending governmental policies and acts, the ones we will to help promote and support, including only passively by our silent submission and implicit calls on fellow citizens to abide by them when duly enacted. For these para-governmental stances (so to call them) that we take and pursue as voters, candidates, activists, bystanders, and so on, we owe each other justification. "The ideal of public reason," Rawls says, applies to "citizens when they engage in public advocacy in the public forum . . . and for how citizens vote in elections when constitutional essentials and matters of basic justice are at stake."[22] And the ideal of public reason, remember, *is* an ideal of citizens explaining to other citizens the grounds of their political actions.[23]

So democratic citizens carry burdens of justification both collectively and distributively—collectively for governmental policies and acts and distributively for para-governmental stances and activities. In what follows in Parts I and II of this book, I read the LPL to cover both burdens. In either

[20] *PL* 214; *JAF* 40–41.

[21] In a subsequent follow-on to the LPL of *PL*, Rawls made the point completely explicit. "By what ideals and principles," he then phrased the question, "are citizens as sharing equally in ultimate political power to exercise that power so that each of them can reasonably justify their political decisions to each other?" "Second Introduction," xlvi.

[22] *PL* 215.

[23] See *supra*, § 1.1.

case, justification entails claims of the publicly assertable compatibility of a questioned act, policy, or stance with a justification-worthy constitution-in-force. The constitution supplies the society's performative stage for combined fulfillment of collective and distributive political-justificatory obligations. Viewed another way, the constitution stands as the society's manifest of the condition of *publicity* that according to Rawls prevails in any well-ordered society: the condition, that is, of standing under effective regulation by principles that "citizens accept and know that others likewise accept," and "this knowledge in turn is publicly recognized."[24]

2.4. Reasonability for Constitutions

According to the LPL of *PL*, a finding of a contested law's compatibility with a country's constitution supplies justification for your or my acts in support of that law. The constitution serves thus by virtue of its own presupposed reasonability when judged as the script for such a political-justificatory procedure. By hypothesis, the constitution's prescriptive content is such that those who accept and resort to it for such a purpose do conscientiously see their way clear to deeming it thus acceptable to everyone else in sight, or at any rate everyone for whose acceptance they have good moral reason to care. That might not include literally everyone, but it would have to include (say) everyone reasonable.

We can see right away at least a part of what "reasonable," here, would mean. (We will be filling out this idea as we move through later chapters, and will return later for a more complete rendition.[25]) Political liberalism falls back on a set of perceptions that everyone supposedly could and should share: a perception, first, of the very great moral and practical benefits to everyone of having some decent regime of law effectively in force;[26] a perception, second, of the persisting facts of conflicts of interests and value-laden disagreements that might be tolerantly respected on all sides;[27] and then a perception, third, of the commanding moral logic of a reciprocity of respect

[24] *PL* 66.

[25] See Chapter 6, § 2.

[26] See *PL* 301 ("There is no alternative to social cooperation except unwilling and resentful compliance, or resistance and civil war."); "PRR" 766 ("[A] reasonable doctrine accepts a constitutional democratic regime and its companion idea of legitimate law."); ibid, 782 ("[A] democracy necessarily requires that, as one equal citizen among others, each of us accept the obligations of legitimate law.").

[27] See "PRR" 805.

for *everyone's* quest for a life lived in dignity, according to aims and values that a person affirms for herself or himself in conditions of freedom. With that set of perceptions on board, we then posit the possibility of a publicly established test for the continued wide acceptability of the works of the regime in force. It would have to be a test to which each citizen could in good conscience point the others—each treating the others as equals in dignity and freedom—as a basis for reciprocating demands for a general disposition to comply with laws that issue in accordance with its terms. So when someone takes exception to a given policy to be carried out by law, reasonable citizens could feel themselves morally entitled to respond that the law or policy in question might be right or it might be wrong, it might be just or it might be unjust, but *it is not outside the constitution* and so it is in good moral order for us to call on each other for compliance with it.

3. The Constitution as a Procedure

3.1. Procedure as Deflection

To the question of the possibility of a legitimate democratic regime in conditions of reasonable pluralism, Rawls thus offers an institutional and a procedural response. *Procedures*, we may say, are a resort for groups of persons who find themselves divided over policies for their group but who even so prefer (or see no choice but) to stick together rather than go their separate ways. In the philosophy of Rawls, "society" (within a given territory) names such a group.[28] Faced with disagreements about their group's proceedings that could break their unity apart, the members find they still can agree on a deflection to a different question, for which they expect a publicly certifiable answer to be more readily at hand. That deflection is what I mean here by a "procedure." The initial question is what we label the "substance" of the disagreement. The substitute question then is the "procedure" the group accepts for getting past it.[29] I expect you to think here of a vote-count.

The idea of the procedural, as I use it here, is that of resort to a previously accepted platform of background or framework terms for getting past

[28] See *TJ* 4 (on the political idea of "society"); ibid, 109–112 (on "the circumstances of justice").

[29] See Frank I. Michelman, "Dilemmas of Belonging: Moral Truth, Human Rights, and Why We Might Not Want a Representative Judiciary" (1999) 47 *UCLA Law Review* 1221, 1234–36 (explaining this sense of procedure and its application to problems of legal controversy).

disagreements over matters on the collective table that all concerned share a wish to have resolved one way or another. In the LPL of *PL*, society's regnant body of constitutional law serves, in that sense, as stipulation of the terms of a procedure. The LPL's stated criterion for constitutional content ("which all citizens as free and equal can be expected to endorse in the light of principles and ideals acceptable to them as reasonable and rational") may or may not strike you as possible of fulfillment in any modern even moderately free society. Set aside that worry, though, for now (we take it up in Chapter 6), and assume that the condition is, in the case before you, fulfilled. The constitution's content is such that any citizen can look any other in the eye and say: Accepting the need for some system of social ordering by law, and given the special challenge of justification of the force of law among free and equal citizens in pluralist conditions, a system constituted by *just these* basic-level commitments and expectations (here pointing to the constitution) is sufficiently worth upholding to give each of us prevailing moral reason to accept presumptively as binding law whatever issues duly from the system.

The constitution, then, would be serving as a table of terms for a procedural solution to the special challenge of democratic political justification in the pluralized conditions of a modern free society. That table would be our recourse for a deflection of divisive questions of substance (does this law or policy merit the respect or rather the contempt of a right-thinking person?), to a different question (is this law or policy constitutional?) for which the answer is to be publicly apparent, or at any rate is to be ascertainable by means that are an order of magnitude less open to divisive dispute than are the deflected substantive disagreements.

On this understanding of the proceduralist cast of the LPL, consent precedes fairness as the keynote for justification. The bottom-line argument in support of the proposed procedure is that it has a supportable claim on the consent of all reasonable and rational parties concerned. Fairness might be a load-bearing term in *that* argument—in the realm of politics, the argument may run, consent to an overarching procedural framework is reasonably sought or attributable if and only if the procedure can be counted fair among free and equal citizens in conditions of reasonable pluralism—but that is a contingency of the argument's contained conception of reasonability, not its utmost axiomatic starting point. As it pertains to the aims and functions of constitutional law, Rawlsian proceduralism is in the last resort an upshot from the pursuit of the liberal grail of government by consent. Therein lies the stamp of its liberal character.

3.2. Procedure Incorporating Substance

Serving thus as a procedure does not mean the constitution's terms deal only with political processes (we vote and the majority rules) as opposed to political outcomes (prohibitions of the free exercise of religion are disallowed). Compliance with certain outcome-constraining terms can constitute a part of the procedural (deflected-to) displacement of the questions on which agreement is not be found. So it is with Rawls. "The political system," he writes, "would not be a just procedure if it did not incorporate" certain liberties.[30] Rawls's "essentials" for a justificatory load-bearing constitution are accordingly of "two kinds," comprising provisions for "the . . . structure of government and the political process . . . and equal basic rights and liberties of citizenship that legislative majorities are to respect."[31]

Responding to a call from Jürgen Habermas for a more rigorously procedural defense of liberal constitutional democracy than Habermas thought he could see in Rawls's writings,[32] Rawls later would defend both his conception's proceduralist credentials and that conception's incorporation of substantive basic and liberties. Those come, he said, to one and the same thing: Democratic laws are "legitimate, not because they are just but because they are legitimately enacted in accordance with an accepted legitimate democratic procedure";[33] but also, in politics (unlike in pure gambling), the acceptability and legitimacy of the procedure depend "on the justice of its likely outcome, or on substantive justice." "Any liberal view," Rawls wrote, must, in that way and to that extent, "be substantive."[34]

Rawls's LPL in *PL* thus stands in reply to a question we posed near the start of this book, about the need or reason for substantive constitutional law in a constitutional democracy. The reply proceeds, we may now say by way of summation, in four steps. First, citizens in any approximately well-ordered, complex modern society will necessarily be looking to one another

[30] *TJ* 197–98.
[31] *PL* 227.
[32] See Jürgen Habermas, "Reconciliation Through the Public Use of Reason" (1995) 92 *Journal of Philosophy* 109, 116, 126–27.
[33] John Rawls, "Reply to Habermas" (1995) 92 *Journal of Philosophy* 132, 175.
[34] Ibid, 170.

for a regularity of submission to day-to-day exertions of political power with which some fraction deeply disagree. Second, citizens in a democracy stand under moral obligation to justify to each other their calls for such a reciprocity of submission. Third, in conditions of reasonable pluralism, such justification must necessarily take the procedural form of a deflection to a set of "higher" or "framework" principles of political order. Fourth, the substantive parts of a constitutional-democratic country's constitution are to serve in a table of terms for the requisite deflection.

4. *TJ* to *PL*: Justice to Justification

That account in *PL* (vintage 1993) of the place and moral function of substantive constitutional law in a constitutional democracy does not exactly match the account we find in *TJ* (vintage 1971). In his introduction to *PL*, Rawls makes it a point to advise readers that some departures from the prior account would follow from a newly heightened sensitivity to the problem posed to democratic legitimacy by the fact of reasonable pluralism.[35] There has occurred, in consequence, a shift of the ground of legitimacy from justice to justification.

4.1. The Constitution in *TJ*: "Imperfect Procedural Justice"

Let us, then, shift our gaze back to *TJ*. Part One of that book takes up the question of standards for just distributional outcomes over "social primary goods"—rights and liberties, income and wealth, opportunities and the social bases of self-respect—in an all-encompassing scheme of social cooperation.[36] The search there is for a set of directive principles cast at a background or framework level of generality—the level, as Rawls says, of a society's "basic structure"—represented by the famous two principles of justice as fairness for which Rawls argues at length in Part One of *TJ*. Both principles address terms of distribution of social primary goods; but a table of the terms and measures for a fair distribution would not yet, Rawls thought, fulfill the mission of political philosophy while conceived "in abstraction from

[35] See *PL* xvi–xix.
[36] See *TJ* 62.

institutional forms."[37] Philosophy, Rawls thought, was obligated no less for a corresponding institutional conception—in schematic outline, not concrete detail—in keeping with those terms and conducive toward those measures.[38]

Accordingly, Part Two of *TJ* proceeds to the question of just political institutions, *given* that the principles of justice from Part One are now settled as the background or framework principles for substantive constraint of distributional outcomes.[39] The institutional question presses because given also is the inevitability of sincere and honest disagreement among citizens—"especially," Rawls writes in *TJ*, "when their interests are engaged"—regarding true applications of the substantive principles to later-arriving concrete laws and policies.[40] A complete conception of political justice draws a connection from its substantive principles for the basic structure to some feasible institutional arrangement, itself consonant with justice, for proceeding in the face of conflicting opinions about the applications of the principles.[41] That arrangement would comprise, then, in Rawls's terms in *TJ*, a "just constitution."[42]

But what, exactly, are we to understand by the word "just" as thus applied by Rawls in *TJ* to constitutions and constitutional arrangements? It does not mean "purely procedurally" just. It does not say that the constitutional arrangement is to merit acceptance—in the way that a coin-flip or a simple majority vote arguably often does[43]—as an outcome-blind, fair way among party-equals to resolve disputes over collective policies for which no outcome-sensitive criteria are in view.[44] Rather, in *TJ* a just constitution is one that (1) itself conforms to settled principles of fairness among recognized equals in the guidance of collectively binding choices (say, a principle of equality of political liberty), and beyond that (2) is best designed to deliver legislative outputs, and only such outputs, as really and truly count as correct or permissible implementations of the other given background principles.

That is what Rawls expressly says in *TJ*. "First," he writes, "the constitution is to be a just procedure satisfying the requirements of equal liberty."

[37] Ibid, 195.

[38] See also Chapter 6, § 1 (on the idea of a "realistic utopia").

[39] See ibid, 198 ("I assume that the . . . principles of justice already chosen define an independent standard of the desired outcome.").

[40] Ibid, 195–96.

[41] Ibid, 196.

[42] Ibid, 197.

[43] See, e.g., Jeremy Waldron, *Law and Disagreement* (Oxford University Press 1999) 113–16.

[44] "Pure procedural justice obtains when there is no independent criterion for the rights result: instead there is a correct or fair procedure such that the outcome is likewise correct or fair, whatever it is, provided that the procedure has been properly followed." *TJ* 86.

And then second, the constitution "is to be framed so that of all [such] arrangements that are feasible, it is more likely than any other to result in a just and effective system of legislation."[45] Ideally, the constitution would be a just procedure arranged to insure a just outcome, where the range of just outcomes is already defined by an independent criterion such as *TJ*'s substantive principles of justice provide.[46] That is not, however, an achievable end, because any feasible political procedure is sure to yield some erroneous outcomes. The "best attainable" constitutional scheme will be an "imperfectly just" procedure, meaning by that term a procedure we count on "to yield the correct results not always but most of the time."[47]

Before now shifting our gaze back from *TJ* to *PL*, we will need to be a bit more precise about the makeup of these "correct results" toward which we want our just constitution in *TJ* to be conducive. The idea is not that for any choice among competing legislative policies there will always be a single one that is uniquely favored by a correct application of the background principles of justice. (If that were the case, they would not be background principles, nor would they be principles for a democracy.) It is rather that some policies will be decisively ruled out by a correct application of the principles. A just constitution in *TJ* is one that will, as reliably as possible, work toward an exclusion of policies that a correct application of the background principles rules out.[48]

4.2. The Constitution in *PL*: Justification ("Legitimacy") in Place of Justice

We are now in a position to ask: In the LPL of *PL*, is the constitution's place still in that same sense that of an imperfectly just procedure, one whose workings are more or less guaranteed to mimic correct applications of principles of justice already settled? To that question, our answer must be that it is not, or

[45] Ibid, 220–21.

[46] See *TJ* 197.

[47] Ibid, 198. See ibid, 85–86 (explaining how, where there is a procedure-independent criterion for correct outcomes but no feasible procedure sure to lead to them, we may settle for an "imperfectly just" procedure—meaning one that is reasonably expected to yield the right results "not always but . . . most of the time").

[48] We may note here that such an aim for the constitution can encompass so-called "positive" guarantees (regarding, say, provision for everyone's basic material needs) as well as negative prohibitions. In the former case, a check for compliance may entail critical inspection not just of legislative enactments but also of legislative agendas past and recent. See Chapter 10.

anyway not exactly. There has been an intervening complication in the social circumstances to which the constitution is being asked to respond. That new complication is the fact of reasonable pluralism. In consequence of that complication, the question of a disputed legislative policy's compatibility with an agreed set of background principles can no longer be treated, among free and equal citizens, as controlled by a uniquely correct application of the principles to rule in or out a contested legislative policy. Reasonably acceptable answers to the compatibility question will now themselves often be plural in number. The need for an institutional device of reconciliation of conflicting opinions arises, now, not only from clashes of interests and other humanly unavoidable causes of slippage in applicative debates, but as well from clashes of reasonable, comprehensive moral and philosophical outlooks, for which any constitutional-procedural solution must then also make due allowance. One could almost say that it's as a signal of this departure in *PL* from the prior wisdom of *TJ* that "legitimacy" replaces "justice" as the name of the quest to which the constitutional-procedural arrangement must answer.

2

A Fixation Thesis and a Secondary Proceduralization: Constitution as Positive Law

In search of a moral warrant for calls among a country's citizens for everyone's willing submission to the enactments of legislative authorities in that country, regardless of sustained objection on the part of some citizens to the moral or other merits of some of those enactments, John Rawls proposes that the terms of the country's constitution in force may possibly be such as to answer to the need. I ask you now to draw your mental picture of the constitution Rawls here has in view.[1]

1. A Constitution in What Medium?

What does it look like? Is it the kind of constitution Americans know, a canonically scripted fixture in a country's body of positive laws? (A constitution "in the formal sense," as some theorists would say?[2]) Did Rawls, then, by his statements of the liberal principle of legitimacy ("justifiable *only* when in accord with a constitution . . ."), render his stance adverse to that of (say) those Britons who today still resist or decry an introduction into their country's political practice of positive-legal limitation on the sovereignty of Parliament?[3] The work in *PL* contains a sign that possibly he did not wish or mean to do so; but did he do so all the same?

[1] This chapter is partly drawn from my "'Constitution (Written or Unwritten)': Legitimacy and Legality in the Thought of John Rawls" (2018) 31 *Ratio Juris* 379.

[2] See Joel I. Colón-Rios, "The Constitution of Puerto Rico" in R. Albert, S. O'Brien, and S. Wheatle (eds.), *The Oxford Handbook of Caribbean Constitutions* (Oxford University Press 2020) 391.

[3] See, e.g., Richard Bellamy, *Political Constitutionalism* (Cambridge University Press 2007).

Constitutional Essentials. Frank I. Michelman, Oxford University Press. © Frank I. Michelman 2022.
DOI: 10.1093/oso/9780197655832.003.0003

1.1. A Dated Exegetical Question

PL's statements of the LPL are not the only ones Rawls penned at about the same time. In *Justice as Fairness: A Restatement* (hereinafter sometimes *JAF*), the LPL appears as follows:

> Political power is legitimate only when it is exercised in accordance with a constitution (written or unwritten) the essentials of which all citizens, as reasonable and rational, can endorse in the light of their common human reason. This is the liberal principle of legitimacy.[4]

In the place of "constitution" in the *PL* versions of the LPL, the *JAF* rendition uses "constitution (written or unwritten)." If by a "written" constitution, we take Rawls to have meant the American codified model I strongly suspect you have up to now been picturing in your own head, what then would follow for "unwritten?" If "constitution (written or unwritten)" in *JAF* signifies acceptance there by Rawls of the possible sufficiency, to bear the load of the justification of the force of democratic law, of something that is identifiable as a country's constitution but varies from the standard model of the written-down, codified legal constitution, then how exactly does it vary?[5]

I thus pose the question in strictly exegetical terms, having mind that the pursuit of it in that form will take us into constitutional-theoretic matters of independent interest. And indeed it will not finally be on historical-exegetical but rather on constitutional-theoretic grounds that I will arrive, in this chapter, at a doubt that Rawls, writing in *PL*, could well have thought that anything too drastically at odds with the standard model could satisfy his constitution-centered proposition on political justification. We will consider later whether some moderately qualified departure may have been the direction toward which his later thought was tending, but that further consideration will rest on some exegetical considerations involving post-1993 Rawlsian texts not yet before us.

[4] *JAF* 41.

[5] If or insofar as the two texts—*PL* and *JAF*—might be in some such respect at odds, presumably the more recent text should rule. *PL* first appeared in print in 1993. The manuscript for *JAF*—so that book's editor advises—was mainly completed by 1989, but underwent some limited revision thereafter, prior to publication in 2001. See *JAF* xii ("Editor's Foreword"). If we wanted to read one book's version of the LPL as meant by Rawls to supersede (as opposed to simply echo) the other's, the dating information at hand would leave us guessing which would be the superseding work.

1.2. Ambiguities of "Unwritten"

The standard model of a constitution envisages a *basic law* for the country, a fixed corpus of positive-legal prescripts for the conduct of the country's politics. Theory immediately suggests two ways in which the LPL's "constitution" might deviate radically from that, for which "unwritten" might plausibly serve as marker. First, the constitution in view might be composed of prescriptive social norms (like those, say, of common courtesy) not considered to have the institutionally sanctioned force of law but only the action-guiding effects (such as those may be) of conventional understandings among the members of society. Second, we might have in view, by "constitution," nothing at all to be taken as directive or prescriptive but merely a set of observable, apparently dependable regularities in the conduct of a country's politics. Those two possibilities for "unwritten" we will consider and reject in this chapter.

A third possibility, more closely aligned to the standard model but still variant from it, is that Rawls had in mind by "unwritten constitution" that part of a country's regnant constitutional law that consists of doctrinal elaborations of canonical texts, now in force as judicial precedent in the manner of common law: thus, a legal constitution arguably classifiable as written, but not in fully codified form.[6] We take up that possibility later, in Chapter 5.[7] A fourth possibility, deserving of serious attention but plausible for consideration only after a good deal of our book's intervening work has been completed, is that "or unwritten" in the *JAF* version of the LPL refers not at all to a constitution actually in force, but rather to a *possible* or idealized constitution that the citizen defending a coercive political act would find fitting to the country—a "constitution *in mente*," as I will name it when we get back to this idea in Chapter 8.[8]

1.2.1. A Directive Constitution But Conventional (Not Legal)?

The following definitions are crude in some respects, question-begging in others, but adequate, I believe, for the work to follow. By the term *social norm*, I mean something beyond an empirically observable regularity of coordination in some space of social interaction. I mean by this term a *rule or standard*

[6] For arguments pro and con treating a constitution thus encased in a body of judicial-precedential constitutional law as "written," see John Gardner, "Can There Be a Written Constitution?" in Leslie Green and Brian Leiter (eds.), *Oxford Studies in Constitutional Law, Vol. 1* (Oxford Scholarship Online: Sept. 2011) 18–20 (hereafter Gardner, "Written Constitution").

[7] See Chapter 5, § 4.

[8] See Chapter 8, § 4.

for conduct in such space that is (1) apparently recognized and accepted as such by an effective preponderance of agents in that space aware of its acceptance there by others, and (2) observed with dependable regularity by them, at least partly owing to awareness of preponderant acceptance of it across the group. By a *legal norm*, I mean a rule or standard of conduct that has recognition in the operations of the state's legal system and its contained institutions. For many social norms there exist substantially overlapping legal norms (*do not steal*), but not by any means for all of them (*tip your restaurant server*).

A norm is *constitutional* when and insofar as its directive content goes to the manner and form of exertions of the primary legislative powers of the state, or to the permitted or required aims and effects of such exertions.[9] Constitutional norms can be legal norms or they can be social norms only. No doubt there can be constraints on the conduct of a country's politics (with a content we would call "constitutional") that are real enough to experience but that take effect only by and through social practices, forms, and forces that are not of the legal-institutional ilk. Constitutional constraints of that kind are sometimes labeled "conventional," in contradistinction to "legal."[10] Might Rawls's "constitution (written or unwritten)" in *JAF* have signified his acceptance there of the possible sufficiency, to meet the needs of the justification of the force of democratic law, of a body of constitutional-directive norms subsisting purely as convention outside the law?[11]

1.2.2. A Constitution Empirical (Not Directive)?

The term "constitution," which the standard model takes to refer to a directive code for the conduct of a country's politics, can also refer to certain persisting, observable regularities in that conduct or major institutional aspects of it.[12]

[9] Covered as well would be exertions of the state's administrative powers, insofar as the system may be supposed to include a rule (written or unwritten) requiring authorization by primary law, or consistency with primary laws, for any coercive administrative action.

[10] Norms conventional-not-legal at birth can be transformed over time into legal norms by courts treating them as such, see Gardner, "Written Constitution" (n 6) 5–6, but that fact has no direct bearing on our analysis here.

[11] The question here should be kept distinct from that of whether the complete directive content of subsisting positive constitutional law is or possibly could be contained within a canonical written text—whether some part of it must not rather always necessarily subsist as (let us call it) constitutional common law. See Samuel Freeman, "Original Meaning, Democratic Interpretation, and the Constitution" (1992) 21 *Philosophy and Public Affairs* 3, 6–7 ("It is an institutional fact that there are many significant practices, institutions, and procedures that are part of our constitution—because they are publicly recognized, followed, and enforced—that are not set forth in the document bearing the name 'the Constitution.' "); Chapter 5, § 4.

[12] See Dieter Grimm, *Constitutionalism: Past, Present, and Future* (Oxford University Press 2016) 3 (hereafter Grimm, *Constitutionalism*).

(The term is sometimes thus used quite aggressively. In a famous dictum, "the constitution is no more and no less than what happens."[13]) The regularities would be, as such, in the most radical sense, unwritten. (They might be written up by a scientific observer, but the write-up would be a description or simulacrum of them, not the regularities as such.) Might Rawls perhaps have meant to say, by his "(written or unwritten)" in *JAF* that the fact of there being observably in place a cluster of such empirical regularities, whose combination happens to be such as can be found satisfactory for the purpose by all citizens reasonable and rational, would satisfy the LPL's prescription for justification by constitution?

Our work to follow in this chapter proceeds in two major steps. At the first step, we suppose that Rawls undoubtedly meant by "constitution" something prescriptive, a commonly legible code of directives for the conduct of state power ("constitution as directive code"). The question, then, is whether, in order to fulfill the justificatory program of the LPL, the directive content must subsist in the institutionalized medium of law and not (merely) customary understanding. We answer, at this point, that it seems this content would normally, for Rawls, have to subsist as law.

At the second step, we take up the thought that Rawls might possibly have meant, by "unwritten," a constitution in the descriptive as opposed to the prescriptive sense of that term ("constitution as what happens"). We find some reason to entertain such a reading, but end up having to reject it.

2. Constitution as Directive Code

Grant everything we have said so far about the "constitution" in the Rawlsian LPL. It contains substantive parts; these parts are to serve in a table of terms for a procedural response to the special challenge of democratic political justification under reasonable pluralism; that table is to be our recourse for a deflection of intractably divisive questions of choice among competing legislative policies to a different question for which the answers are to be publicly apparent, or at any rate are to be ascertainable by means that are measurably less open to divisive dispute than are the deflected substantive disagreements. Does anything there preclude the thought of that constitution

[13] John Griffith, "The Political Constitution" (1979) 42 *Modern Law Review* 19.

subsisting as a purely customary-conventional normative corpus? Defenders of conventional-not-legal constitutionalism rightly claim that there is no reason in theory, nor is there any proof in history, that a constitution in that guise cannot serve adequately a democratic society's *regulatory* needs or desires for basic-level steering of the oncoming stream of political outputs. The question here, though, will be whether the same holds in regard to the Rawlsian idea of *justification*-by-constitution, to free and equal citizens, of the force of ordinary law. Accepting that a purely conventional constitution might *regulate* politics effectively, it still might not work properly to *justify* the politics it regulates. Justification-by-constitution, as I now will suggest, apparently presupposes a kind and degree of fixation and publication of the constitution's prescriptive contents, and of advance public settlement of their meanings-in-application, that sounds more in ideas of law than of pure custom.

2.1. Lecture VI of *PL*

It seems that "constitution" in the LPL must signify a body of directives for the ground-level conduct of politics, the terms of which are such that (1) citizens see in common what are those terms, and (2) any citizen reasonably disposed can find those terms acceptable by any other so disposed as a framework for politics going forward, despite a virtual certainty that from that framework will issue some outcomes that one or another fraction of reasonable citizens will find to be morally, philosophically, or religiously repugnant. As long as—so the thinking goes—outcomes are guaranteed to fall within bounds of a good-faith adherence *to those terms*, such repugnancies should not be such as to warrant cessation of cooperation by any citizen both reasonable and morally conscientious. Now, that description of the body of directives in question seems bound to call up immediately in the minds of readers the idea of a body of laws in a positive-legal order.

In Lecture VI of *PL* we have ample indication that it did so in the mind of John Rawls, for there it quite plainly is what we have called the standard model—the image of a codified legal constitution with a bill of substantive rights, under administration by a court of law—that Rawls is picturing as the justificatory load-bearing "constitution" of the LPL. Only (if at all) as an afterthought does Rawls there (perhaps) advert to the possible service in that role of a lawmaking regime ("parliamentary supremacy")[14] unbound by any substantive legal constraint and subject only to whatever limits might be at work in the medium of convention.

Lecture VI of *PL* is entitled "The Idea of Public Reason." It starts off with an exposition of that idea as prescriptive for the form and content proper to arguments and persuasions among "equal citizens who, as a collective body, exercise . . . coercive power over one another in enacting laws and amending their constitution."[15] The Lecture then turns to explaining how "it can be either reasonable or rational, when basic matters are at stake, for citizens to appeal only to a public conception of justice and not to the whole truth as they see it."[16] It does so in the terms I have presented previously.[17] And that, then, is the exact point where Rawls issues his statement of the LPL in Lecture VI.[18]

After then introducing certain limits to application of the public-reason ideal, and elaborating some on the content of public reason, Lecture VI picks up again the theme of the constitution as it figures in the LPL. In a passage mainly devoted to the substantive "essentials" to be included in a justificatory load-bearing constitution,[19] Rawls excludes from that category those parts of a society's founding principles of justice addressed to fairness in distributions of wealth and income. Those are ill-suited to the justificatory purpose because, Rawls says, of inevitable reasonable uncertainty and debate over the policies and actions required for their satisfaction, as compared with the classic liberal, mainly negative, "basic rights and liberties," about whose satisfaction at any moment, Rawls thought, "it is far easier to tell."[20]

That then led Rawls into a discussion of the special role of the American Supreme Court as the "highest judicial interpreter" of the higher law, in a regime sustaining both a "higher law of the people" and an "ordinary law of legislative bodies." In such a "dualist" constitutional democracy, Rawls wrote, a supreme court fits in as "one of the institutional devices to protect

[14] *PL* 234; see John Rawls, "Reply to Habermas" (1995) 92 *Journal of Philosophy* 132, 157–58 (hereafter Rawls, "Reply").

[15] *PL* 214.

[16] See ibid, 216–17.

[17] See Introduction, § 3, and Chapter 1, § 2.1.

[18] See *PL* 216–17.

[19] See ibid, 227–30. Compare "PRR" 767 n. 7 (confirming that the question of "constitutional essentials" in *PL* is that of "what political rights and liberties, say, may reasonably be included in a written constitution, when assuming that the constitution may be interpreted by a supreme court, or some similar body.").

[20] *PL* 227–30. We pursue this matter further in Chapters 3 and 10.

the higher law."[21] Accordingly, the constraint of the ideal of public reason—to have reasons for support of potentially coercive political actions that all reasonable and rational citizens can accept as rightly applicable to the case at hand—would apply in a specially constrictive way "to the judiciary and above all to the supreme court in a constitutional democracy with powers of judicial review." The judges, Rawls wrote, are especially bound to "explain and justify their decisions as based on their understanding of the constitution and the relevant statutes and precedents."[22]

Everything up to here in Lecture VI points straight at what I have called the standard model of a written legal constitution—with which (we might add) the American Rawls was not only most familiar but most closely engaged as interpreter and critic.[23] But then came an afterthought. "Some will say," Rawls wrote,

> that parliamentary supremacy with no bill of rights at all . . . offers firmer support for the values that higher law in the dualist regime tries to secure. . . . Judged by the values of a reasonable political conception of justice, [this regime] may be superior to a dualist regime in which these basic questions are settled by the higher law.[24]

Such a claim, Rawls hastened to add, would not be subject to rejection by the philosophy of political liberalism "as such."[25] *John Rawls*, we gather, might be disposed to doubt it on empirical-pragmatic grounds, but the philosophy he espoused could not, on principle, reject it.

But then what, exactly, is the claim which the philosophy could not reject? It might, from the text, be simply a pragmatic claim that a constitutional

[21] *PL* 231–33. On Rawls's behalf, anticipating possible objections, I note he is careful here to say "one of" the requisite institutional devices. He does not suggest that a single court can possibly sustain this burden alone without co-participation not just from lower courts but from other political and social institutions including an executive branch and sundry government agencies, academic and journalistic professions, and so on. Everything Rawls has to say about a special role and special obligations of the Supreme Court seems sufficiently supported by the premise of a country's reliance on it as a *main, leading*, exceptionally visible, exemplary institutional servant in this role of protector of the higher law.

[22] Ibid, 216. We take up this proposition, of a special judicial obligation of fidelity to law, for further examination in Chapter 5.

[23] See, for example, his discussions of the American Supreme Court's work in cases under the free-speech and general-liberty guarantees of the U.S. Constitution, *PL* 340–63; "*Commonweal* Interview with John Rawls" in Samuel Freeman (ed.), *John Rawls, Collected Papers* (Harvard University Press 1998) 615, 617–19.

[24] *PL* 234–35.

[25] Ibid, 235; see Rawls, "Reply" (n 14) (calling the question "one of constitutional design").

norm of parliamentary supremacy unbound by higher law (but possibly, then, still guided by convention), can and does, at some times in some countries, work out better than a judicially administered higher-legal code would do for the cause of the liberal values of freedom and equality represented by the Rawlsian conception of justice as fairness.[26] Quite a few constitutional scholars these days so suspect or believe (not all of them British).[27] It is another question, though, whether a constitution of legally unconstrained parliamentary supremacy can provide the *justificatory* service envisaged by the LPL. Seemingly, it cannot not do that on Rawls's terms—which include among the essential provisions in a justification-bearing constitution the "basic rights and liberties of citizenship that legislative majorities are to respect"[28]—unless attended by highly reliable, customary-conventional substantive limitations.

We may suppose, then, that such was Rawls's assumption while making his concession to the possible superiority of a legal regime of parliamentary supremacy. On that assumption, would the concession have been well warranted? With that question, exegesis now turns to face normative theory.

2.2. The Second Procedural Turn: Institutional Settlement: Objectivity, Abstraction, Deferral, and Dependence on a Referee

It seems that a script for a procedural deflection from concrete political disagreements must itself be an object of socially convergent perceptions. A supposition of objectivity—"publicity," in a more Rawlsian turn of phrase—attends upon any constitutional platform serving in that capacity.[29]

[26] Compare *PL* 235 ("[T]he content of a political conception of justice includes the values of public reason by appeal to which the merits of the three kinds of regime [parliamentary supremacy, permanently entrenched basic rights, dualist democracy] are to be judged."); ibid, 240 (indicating that any defense of "a constitutional scheme with judicial review" must advert to "historical circumstances and conditions of political culture").

[27] See, e.g., Louis M. Seidman, *On Constitutional Disobedience* (Oxford University Press 2012) (hereafter Seidman, *Constitutional Disobedience*); Mark Tushnet, *Taking the Constitution Away From the Courts* (Princeton University Press 1999); Robin West, "Constitutional Culture or Ordinary Politics: A Reply to Reva Siegel" (1996) 94 *California Law Review* 1465 (hereafter West, "Constitutional Culture").

[28] *PL* 227.

[29] See *PL* 66 (understanding by "publicity" the condition in which society is effectively regulated by principles that "citizens accept and know that others accept," and "this knowledge in turn is publicly recognized").

We can hardly avoid picturing that platform as a text or text-like object, the terms of which are made visible in the public space where everyone can point to them and agree that, yes, *that* is the country's constitution.

The script for a procedural deflection seemingly must meet a further pair of requirements, delicately balanced—presenting as we might say, a Goldilocks problem. Not only are the outward terms (the words or signs) of the text to be on public view, those signs are to carry a commonly shared core of significations or applications. Those common-core significations are to be such as to support the claims of citizens to each other of the worthiness of any conforming regime for continued support. To that end, as Chapter 3 will treat at further length, they must not be too thin; they have to say something beyond vaporous or trivial about matters people care deeply about. But neither may they be too thick. They must stop short of foreclosure of questions of fundamental import to some citizens, over which reasonable citizens divide. They will have to be cast, then, at accommodating levels of abstraction.[30] That strategy, though, comes with a price, or call it a puzzle. How does it not just kick the can of disagreement down the road? A procedural device for getting past ground-level divisions has as its premise that questions of compliance with the procedure will not themselves be so exposed to divisive disagreement as to render bootless a deflection from the one set of issues to the other. The requisite spareness of the scripted constitutional essentials puts that premise in jeopardy. Sooner or later, hard cases arrive, to the resolution of which the body of substantive constitutional norms, spare enough to pass the test of universal-reasonable acceptability, cannot be applied without potentially divisive disagreement.

The LPL takes as a premise that some possible constitutional text can say enough without saying too much. *Given* that premise (Rawls's defense for it will come in Chapter 3), we have seen nothing yet to disqualify from justificatory-procedural service a constitution of convention. Objectivity? A constitution of convention can meet that demand. Citizens and scholars find their own words and sentences by which to describe and affirm the conventions-in-force that they see, and in the resulting communicative milieu they sustain a sense that they all see sufficiently the same thing in substance. There is nothing impossible in that. Neither too thin nor too thick? Why may not essentials cast in the less formulaically frozen medium of

[30] See *PL* 232 ("The principled expression of higher law is to be widely supported," and so "it is best not to burden it with many details and qualifications.").

convention comply at least as well as those cast in the more formalized medium of law? Kicking the can of disagreement down the road? A procedural pact might do better in customary-conventional than in formal-legal dress to sidle its way past that difficulty. Debates over applications may then be less doctrinally cut-and-dried, less adversarial, less one-right-answerish, less conclusively now-and-evermore, less victor-and-vanquished, less divisive.[31] The net effect might be, as Paul Craig has pointed out, "a constitutional order that is similar to, and equally efficacious as, its written constitutional cousin."[32]

But the constitution-of-convention solution will not do, unless it can meet the expectation of convergence on *applications of* the constitutional essentials to rule contested laws and policies in or out, which we have seen to be a part of any procedural solution to the problem of justification. Now, an apparent attraction of procedural solutions—in the sense of my use of that term in this book[33]—is that they do not require that constituents must always converge in their own first-person judgments about answers to questions of compliance with the accepted procedure. Constituents might rather find good enough reason to converge on a dedicated institutional service, whose judgments regarding such questions could themselves be trusted to fall within the bounds of a reasonable balance of the public values bearing on the case—not infallibly, but with a frequency sufficient to qualify those judgments as publicly authoritative for justification-sustaining purposes.

We may call this the second turn of proceduralization (deflection from ground-level disagreement is the first turn) in Rawlsian justification-by-constitution. The institutional service need not take the particular form of a law-court (it could be, say, a committee of the parliament responsible for constitutional review of pending legislation and legislative agendas), but the argument now is leaning strongly toward a need for *some* such trusted institution, in order finally to block the kick-the-can objection to a diplomatically abstract constitutional-procedural anticipation of ground-level

[31] See Seidman, *Constitutional Disobedience* (n 27) 141–42; Jeremy Waldron, "The Core of the Case Against Judicial Review" (2006) 115 *Yale Law Journal* 1346, 1383–85; West, "Constitutional Culture" (n 27) 1476.

[32] Paul Craig, "Written and Unwritten Constitutions: The Modality of Change" in Sam Bookman, Edward Willis, Hanna Wilberg, and Max Harris (eds.), *Pragmatism, Principle, and Power in Common Law Constitutional Systems: Essays in Honour of Bruce Harris* (forthcoming). https://papers.ssrn.com/sol3/papers.cfm?abstract_id=3897906 [13] Craig is, however, at pains to distinguish this quasi-written, convention-rule order from an order, still exemplified by the United Kingdom, in which the truly "animating constitutional principle" is that of parliamentary supremacy. See ibid, [13–16].

[33] See Chapter 1, § 3.1.

political disagreement. If so, then a directive constitution strictly of convention, not law, cannot do the trick. At least it cannot if, as many would hold, a submission to institutional settlement is what defines the border dividing off the directive medium of law from that of convention.[34] If speaking at all as a directive code, then, the Rawlsian justification-bearing constitution would have to speak in the medium of law.

That is not, however, a logically airtight conclusion. Constitutional conventions do, after all, at least in concept, present socially real and palpable reasons for action. Given an imaginable sufficiency of public convergence on their content and application, they will work as effective constraints on politics. Under imaginably favorable conditions, their wide recognition across society could satisfy the Rawlsian condition of publicity for a well-ordered society: that is, that the society is effectively regulated by principles that "citizens accept and know that others accept," and "this knowledge in turn is publicly recognized." That is what Rawls would seem to have been allowing for in what I called previously, in section 2.1, his "afterthought."

An afterthought, though, is still how I say we should treat it. Granting as true all that has just been said, still the convergence does have to be sufficient and sufficiently palpable, the conditions do have to be favorable, and the facts of reasonable pluralism and burdens of judgment do seem to set up contrary headwinds—all pointing toward institutional settlement as a normally requisite term in the constitutional procedural pact for justification-by-constitution, and so all helping to explain why Rawls through the bulk of Lecture VI of *PL* apparently supposes that the justificatory load-bearing constitution in force would be a legal one in the "protection" (as Rawls puts it) of a supreme court.

3. Constitution as What Happens

We turn now to the thought that the constitution of the LPL might subsist not in any directive medium, whether of law or convention, but rather only as a cluster of empirically observable regularities of political conduct, sufficiently

[34] See, e.g., Neil MacCormick, "Institutional Normative Order: A Conception of Law" (1997) 82 *Cornell Law Review* 1051 (distinguishing law from politics, on the one hand, and morality, on the other, as "institutional normative order"); Henry M. Hart, Jr. and Albert M. Sacks, *The Legal Process: Basic Problems in the Making and Application of Law*, ed. William N. Eskridge, Jr. and Philip P. Frickey (Foundation Press 1995) 3–4 (principle of institutional settlement).

clear and firm to sustain the acceptability of the regime they compose to free and equal citizens in the light of political reason and reasonability.

3.1. Shadow Norms

As applied to political units, writes Dieter Grimm, the term "constitution" can bear either of two senses. "Constitution" in a prescriptive or normative sense refers to a directive concerning "the establishment and exercise of political rule." "Constitution" in a descriptive or empirical sense refers to "the nature of a country with reference to its political conditions."[35] In the first instance, "constitution" means something that speaks; in the second, something that mutely *is*.

Grimm's second instance can be extended to take in observable regularities of political practice affecting matters of constitutional import. In a given country at a given time, there may be sensibly in place a cluster of such regularities, recordable (say) by a visiting anthropologist, without reference (yet) to anything normative or obligational. (In the classification introduced by a young John Rawls, the anthropologist's compilation so far would fall under a "summary" conception, not yet a "practice" conception of social rules.[36]) But then, in her striving to form a report of what she sees, the anthropologist finds herself cooking up the raw data into some set of hypothetical framework norms—shadow-norms, as we might call them—for the conduct of politics in that country. Her resulting shadow-normative set might or might not be such (if they were actual norms) as to give free and equal citizens, divided by reasonable pluralism, sufficient reason to abide by the legislative outcomes. If and only if the raw data set is reasonably constructible into a shadow-normative set that does meet the test, the LPL is satisfied.

Could that or something like it be what Rawls had in mind by "unwritten constitution" in the LPL of *JAF*? It would leave us, if just barely, on the empirical-descriptive side, not the normative-prescriptive side, of Grimm's dichotomy of significations for "constitution." Our justificatory load-bearing object would then consist not of a commonly cognized directive instruction-set, but of a commonly observable, manifold "what happens."[37] Legitimacy

[35] Grimm, "Constitutionalism" (n 12) 3.
[36] See John Rawls, "Two Concepts of Rules" (1955) 64 *Philosophical Review* 3.
[37] My following discussion takes it that the manifold is, indeed, "commonly observable," at an apt level of graininess and as pre-filtered for all through one and the same deeply embedded, culturally

would depend not on the manifold's conformity to some pre-given directive text that we judge to meet a test of universal reasonable acceptability, but on the manifold's reasonable availability to construction as *one* directive constitution (among some indefinite number of plausible constructions) that would meet the test.

The difference may seem slight to the point of vanishing, but perhaps it is not. The possibility to be considered is this: A country's "constitution" thus empirically understood can work as a procedural deflection from disagreements over the moral and other merits of concrete laws and policies (1) without any public convergence on a canonical collation of verbal signs or the core significations thereof (evading the Goldilocks problem) and (2) without necessary final dependence on resort to institutional settlement (evading the deferral problem).

3.2. Each Our Own Hercules?

Go back to the LPL of *PL* as set out in Chapter 1, section 2.2. For the words "in accordance with a constitution" substitute "in a political practice." You still have a procedural deflection from ground-level disagreement. A citizen—you or I—looks out at the entire, ongoing conduct of politics in our country: its institutional and cultural forms, conventions, thoughtways, laws, legal interpretations—the "governmental totality," as I once named it.[38] We have some sense, as well, of animating spirit and motivations. We put to what we see the question put by the LPL to whatever scripted constitution might be currently in place in the country: Are you, O Practice, such that I can in good conscience say, to fellow citizens in revolt against some law or policy, that it might be right or it might be wrong, it might be just or it might be unjust, but it issues from this practice, which I judge to meet a test of acceptability for this purpose to reasonable and rational citizens? (Note that the practice to which we put the question might assign some part to a written

entrenched "conceptual scheme" or "language." (See, e.g., Hilary Putnam, *Realism with a Human Face* (Harvard University Press 1990) 28, 34 ("[W]e treat people two hundred years ago as having referred to what we call plants . . . even though we disagree with [them] over the essential attributes of plants. Without . . . discounting certain differences in belief . . . , we could not say the most common words of the language have kept even a part of their reference fixed across two hundred years.").

[38] Frank I. Michelman, "Ida's Way" (2003) 72 *Fordham Law Review* 345, 347.

constitution with judicial review, but it also might not, and that could be a variable that would weigh in our assessment.)

Of course, we would each of us be engaged there in substantial constructive work. Each sorts the dots in the aggregate mass of the "what happens" into shadow-normative patterns and trend-lines. We extrapolate shadow-normative guides and principles. We make some kind of start, at least, toward cooking the raw data into a shadow-normative political theory. We will each be as Ronald Dworkin's Judge Hercules (only the social practice we thus rationally reconstruct won't be confined to law). Of course, there will be plenty of room both for choice among more-or-less plausible constructions—a duck for you, a rabbit for me, a hedgehog for him—and for differing assessments of this or that construction's meeting (or not) the acceptability test of the LPL. We will each accordingly have to bring to the data what Dworkin called our "theory of institutional mistakes."[39] In the result, citizens will be no likelier to converge on their Practice constructions than on their applications, in hard cases, of the sparely stated ledger of substantive guarantees in a scripted constitution. Are not the deferral and kick-the-can objections then back before us?

They are not. Avoidance of them lies in this picture's displacement of *him* (Hercules J.) by *each*. I say to you, by way of justification of my connivance in the force of some law you are detesting: "Look: the law you detest conforms to *that*, and *that* is something that our common human reason should find acceptable for the justificatory purpose at hand." Saying "*that*," I point to something that I claim you see the same as I do. If that something consists of a set of instructions, my premise has to be that the instructions not only read the same to you as to me but that they "mean" to both of us purely and simply what they "say"—and the Goldilocks and deferral problems are off and running. If, by contrast, the "*that*" to which I point is a mass of data points open to public observation, then, while that predigested mass satisfies the requirement that what I point to is the same to your observational powers as it is to mine, my only further premise is that the mass is reasonably open to construction into *some* reasonably and rationally acceptable shadow-normative constitution (compare: into some mammalian shape or other). Why should it matter, then, whether your construction of "it" as acceptable (or not) differs

[39] Ronald Dworkin, "Hard Cases" (1975) 88 *Harvard Law Review* 1057, 1097–1101. That is, each will have our own idea of how best to organize the data into the major trends (regression lines) that best (and consistently) explain the bulk of them, and which data points, accordingly, are to be discarded as accidents and outliers ("mistakes").

in material respects from mine (whether your mammal is the same as mine, as long as we both are seeing a mammal)? As long as an influential preponderance of citizens continue to arrive at constructions they variously can find to meet the test of universal reasonable acceptability, our exercise of political power can move ahead as if fully justified. We require no institutional settlement of differences. The justificatory load-bearing "constitution" need not be of the stuff of norms, or hence of law.

Tempting as it may be, *as a reading of John Rawls* that will not do. The giveaway is in my "*as if* justified." What I have just offered up could possibly be seen as an early step along the way toward the kind of socially self-aware convergence on a distinct political-moral conception—an assemblage of "political ideas and values"— that defines, for Rawls, a true political community, but it is not yet nearly the thing itself.[40] It does not satisfy the publicity condition Rawls posits for a well-ordered society, in which not only is the society "effectively regulated by public principles of justice," but "citizens accept and know that others likewise accept those principles, and this knowledge in turn is publicly recognized."[41]

With that and previous conclusions before us, we proceed, pending further notice, on the understanding that "constitution" in the LPL of *PL* signifies a specifically marked-off body of positive laws that are *basic*, *scriptural*, *relatively ascertainable*, and *institutionally settleable* (with apologies for that ungainly coinage). *Basic*: The laws of the constitution set terms of validity—of recognition as binding law by courts and other legal authorities—for any further legal operations of the state and its legislative organs. *Scriptural*: The constitution is a collation of canonically worded prescriptive sentences, laid down in advance and fixed until duly revised or replaced. Everyone can point to one and the same collation—fixed (so to speak) in the public space—and agree that *that* is what is presently and for some indefinite future time to count as this country's set of constitutional essentials. *Relatively ascertainable*: Correct applications of the essentials are "more or less visible on [their] face" and will not too often be "open to wide differences of reasonable opinion."[42] *Institutionally settleable*: A designated institutional body's

[40] Compare *PL* xlii–xliii, 146–48.

[41] *PL* 66. See, for a fuller treatment, James Gordon Finlayson, *The Habermas-Rawls Debate* (Columbia University Press 2019) 184–85. Our congeries of shadow-normative constructions is not yet even what Rawls calls a "modus vivendi" (as opposed to a political-moral consensus), in which bodies of citizens agree (for now) on one and the same constitutional stipulation but only out of strategic calculations on the part of each that it's (for now) the best deal for its own concerns that it can hope to get at acceptable cost in social peace and so on. See ibid, 121–23.

[42] *PL* 229. See *PL* 232 ("[The citizen body fixes once and for all certain constitutional essentials.").

answers to interpretative questions carry the force of law unless and until duly institutionally revised. These elements of publicity, objectivity, fixation *pro tempore*, ascertainability, and institutional resolvability of constitutional terms are what enable the constitution to serve us *procedurally* to justify controversial exertions of political power that are found to conform to its terms.

3
Constitutional Essentials: A Singularity of Reason, or a Space of Reasonability?

Justification-by-constitution works by a deflection of divisive questions of legislative policy and value (does this law or policy merit the respect or rather the contempt of a right-thinking person?), to a different question (is this law or policy constitutional?) for which the answer is to be publicly apparent, or at any rate is to be ascertainable by means that are an order of magnitude less open to divisive dispute than are the deflected substantive disagreements. It thus offers itself as a procedural response to the special challenge of democratic political justification in conditions of reasonable pluralism. It is true, of course, that the Rawlsian constitutional essentials are in some part substantive in content; but still they work as part of what remains overall a procedural device.

1. A Scheme of Rights and Their Central Ranges

1.1. Between Thick and Thin: "Completeness" Without Repression

But then we have our Goldilocks dilemma. A justification-bearing constitution's terms of assurance will have to be not too thin, but also not too thick. *Not too thin*: The roster of justification-bearing constitutional essentials must be sufficiently thick with commonly shared signification to render both mutually coherent and widely persuasive the claims of citizens to each other of the worthiness of any conforming regime for continued support. The terms in that roster must compose, in the terminology of Rawls, a "complete" political conception, meaning "the values specified by that conception can be balanced or combined, or otherwise united" to give "a reasonable public answer to all, or nearly all, questions involving the constitutional

Constitutional Essentials. Frank I. Michelman, Oxford University Press. © Frank I. Michelman 2022.
DOI: 10.1093/oso/9780197655832.003.0004

essentials and questions of basic justice."[1] Only thus, after all, can the constitution serve *procedurally* as a platform of political justification.[2]

Not too thick: But still, in order to sustain the regime's acceptability to all reasonable and rational citizens, those terms will have to stop short of express and conclusive foreclosure of questions over which citizens reasonably divide (and which some or all reasonably count as fundamental), leaving those questions for future continuing examination in the democratic political venues of daily life. To that end, in the view of Rawls, the roster of justification-supporting constitutional essentials is to be kept short and its items cast at accommodating levels of abstraction.[3] The challenge, then, is to cater for a completeness at all times, but never at any time a surplusage, of publicly settled meanings-in-application for the constitutional essentials.

1.2. The Fallback to "Central Ranges" in a "Scheme of Liberties"

Rawls offers explanation for how this challenge can possibly be met. Among free and equal citizens, any justificatory load-bearing constitution will include guarantees respecting certain liberties under abstract names such as "conscience" and "property." But since the liberties thus named can all without strain be extended in ways that will bring them sometimes into conflict, "the institutional rules which define these liberties must," as Rawls writes, "be adjusted so that they fit into a coherent scheme of liberties secured equally for all citizens."[4] The scheme, then, will require unification by some known, single, overall governing aim that can adequately guide the adjustments and curtailments (of which guarantees? in which particular respects?) as needs become manifest in courses of events.[5] It seems an expression of this unifying aim for the scheme of liberties would itself fit aptly as a term of the reasonably and rationally acceptable constitutional pact. Rawls does not himself

[1] *PL* 225.

[2] See "PRR" 777 ("[U]nless a political conception is complete, it is not an adequate framework of thought in the light of which the discussion of fundamental political questions can be carried out.").

[3] See *PL* 232 ("The principled expression of higher law is to be widely supported," and so "it is best not to burden it with many details and qualifications.").

[4] Ibid, 295.

[5] Compare "PRR" 778 ("[W]e are required . . . to work to the basic ideas of a complete political conception and from there to elaborate its principles and ideals and to use the arguments they provide. Otherwise public reason allows arguments that are too immediate and fragmentary.").

advance that suggestion, though. Section 2 will show us a possible reason why not.

Rawls does himself defend for this purpose a guiding aim to secure for each citizen the social conditions of a full and adequate development and exercise, over a complete life, of certain moral powers of the "reasonable" and the "rational."[6] What the warrant might be for this claim is a question to be taken up later.[7] The point to see for now is that the liberties listed in the underlying conception are never reasonably to be understood as (each one) "absolute";[8] rather they all stand subject to being institutionally adjusted as experience may show is required to hold them together as a unified expression of political ends and values. Exposure to such institutional adjustment of the named liberties does thus become, in effect, an additional key clause in the deal.

But then we have a problem. As one horn of our Goldilocks dilemma (we said), the substantive terms of a justification-bearing constitution in the LPL must at all times carry a core of commonly agreed meanings, sufficient to render coherent and persuasive the claims of citizens to each other of the worthiness of any conforming regime for continued support. Is that requirement compatible with attachment of a "subject to institutional adjustment" codicil to the constitution's requisite terms of guarantee?

I do not find in Rawls's works a direct answer to that query, expressly framed (as here) as one for the justification-bearing constitution of the LPL of *PL*. We can infer his likely answer, though, from his treatment of a parallel query posed in regard to the scheme of basic liberties in an underlying liberal conception of justice, from which a particular society's constitutional essentials are to be fashioned.[9] That scheme can sufficiently maintain its normative frame-setting position in the society's political life, Rawls suggests, under ongoing adjustment of the respective extensions of its component liberties, as long as we can assume that (1) there resides within each component guarantee some widely agreed, fixed core of meaning or "central range of application," and (2) there is just about always "a practicable scheme of liberties . . . in which the central range of each is protected."[10] Supposing those conditions satisfied in the main, we can then understand

[6] See *PL* 291, 333.
[7] See *infra* § 2; Chapter 6, § 2.
[8] *PL* 295.
[9] See ibid, 294; Chapter 1, § 4.1.
[10] *PL* 297–98.

the justification-bearing constitution of the LPL to include, as one further stipulation, a guarantee that all institutional adjustments of the extensions of the liberties will so far as possible "preserve intact" the central range of application of each.[11] The problem then would stand minimized, if not totally solved.

1.3. The Burdens of Judgment

Except, that is, for one further wrinkle. Owing in part to the intrinsic reasonable contestability of the issues, but especially when given the visionary pluralist conditions posited by Rawls, applicative disagreements among reasonable citizens cannot be expected to stop at the water's edge. Owing to what Rawls calls "burdens of judgment" inevitable in a free society, such disagreements will extend even to setting the respective bounds of the central ranges of the justificatory load-bearing constitution's named essential guarantees.[12] As explained by Rawls, these socially endemic obstacles to agreement include (a) difficulties in assessing evidence, (b) disagreement over weights to be assigned to competing considerations, (c) ambiguities in political and moral concepts, (d) conflicts arising from different life experiences and perspectives, (e) incommensurability of relevant competing considerations, and (f) the difficulty of accommodating all recognized goods in a single political system.[13]

1.4. Supreme Court as Referee

Here is not the place for full consideration of the key position of the burdens of judgment in the Rawlsian proceduralist conception of justification-by-constitution. That will come later, in Chapter 6. For now, the point is simply this: The social fact of these impediments to full agreement, among reasonable citizens, on the core coverages of essential constitutional guarantees apparently necessitates instead—as a further procedural workaround, a "second proceduralization," as I have elsewhere called it[14]—a convergence of citizens

[11] Ibid, 296.
[12] See "PRR" 804–05.
[13] *PL* 54–58.
[14] See Frank I. Michelman, "Legitimacy, The Social Turn, and Constitutional Review: What Political Liberalism Suggests" (2015) 3 *Critical Quarterly for Legislation and Law* 183, 195.

on an institutional service whose judgments regarding such questions are trusted by all to fall within the bounds of reasonable acceptability. It is with a view to fulfilling this role of trusted service that Rawls defends the use of courts as authoritative public arbiters of the fulfillment of the constitutional essentials.[15] It is not that Rawls assumes the requisite institutional service must necessarily be a law-court, or that any court alone can sustain the full burden of justification-by-constitution. Rather, Rawls finds no cause to upend assignment to a court of a central role in such service, when once that has become a settled part of a country's political practice.

Rawls takes that choice to be a reasonable one in line with the constitution-centered proposition on legitimacy.[16] It seems that he here could almost have taken a leaf from the famous plurality opinion in the *Casey* case (on constitutional limits to regulation of abortion), proclaiming our Supreme Court's mission to "call[] the contending sides of a national controversy to end their national division by accepting a common mandate rooted in the Constitution."[17] "Almost," I say, taking care to save room for a signature Rawlsian wrinkle. We do not, Rawls explained, suppose that the judges agree any more than citizens do "in the details of their understanding of the constitution." What rather is required is that the judges

> [are], and appear to be, interpreting the same constitution in view of what they [severally] see as the relevant parts of [an underlying] political conception. . . . The [Supreme Court's] role as the highest judicial interpreter of the constitution supposes that the political conceptions the judges hold and their views of the constitutional essentials locate the central range of the basic freedoms in more or less the same place. In these cases at least its decisions succeed in settling the most fundamental political questions.[18]

Note the hedges: "more or less," "at least," "most fundamental." Why these wiggle-room reservations?

We make a start, here, at dealing with these questions. (It will take more than one chapter to cover the job.)

[15] See *PL* 235–37, 240.

[16] See ibid, 234, 240.

[17] Planned Parenthood of South-Eastern Pennsylvania. v. Casey, 505 U.S. 833, 867 (1992) (plurality opinion).

[18] See *PL* 237.

2. Liberal Justice Conceptions as a "Family": A Complication for the LPL?

PL, initially published in 1993, was republished in paperback form in 1996. Keeping the book's main text from 1993 unrevised, Rawls did also, however, include a new "Introduction to the Paperback Edition."[19] Among a number of new emphases, Rawls there introduced the idea of a "family" of somewhat differing but all-of-them reasonable liberal conceptions of justice.[20] A society, Rawls now wrote, can be reasonably well-ordered in the constitutional-democratic tradition while reflecting, in its political arrangements, any one of an indefinitely numerous family of underlying liberal conceptions of justice. The family members have in common that they each pick out certain "rights, liberties, and opportunities" to which they assign a special priority.[21] But there can be "different and incompatible" reasonable such schemes of rights and liberties, and conscientiously reasonable citizenship therefore cannot demand more of you or of me than that we draw our resolutions of fundamental political matters from reasons consorting with that member of the family which is for you or for me "the most (more) reasonable."[22] For *John Rawls*, that member continues to be the conception he calls justice as fairness and develops at length in the unaltered main text of *PL*; but other liberal-minded thinkers, as Rawls now expressly allows, can and do reasonably differ.[23]

Recall, now, our pending solution to the problem posed by the insertion of a "subject to institutional adjustment" clause into the justificatory load-bearing constitution of the LPL.[24] We could insert, we said, a further clause to the effect that no such adjustment would invade a central range of application of any of the liberties guaranteed by the constitution. That solution would depend, we said (following Rawls), on fulfillment of two conditions: (1) that there is a practicable scheme of aptly adjusted liberties that protects the central ranges of each, and (2) that the ranges treated as central by this scheme are ones on which all reasonable views converge. Regarding condition (1), Rawls has offered historical experience as evidence of satisfaction, or at least

[19] See ibid, xxxvii–lxii ("Second Introduction").

[20] For more extended discussion of the new emphases, see Silje Aambo Langvatn, "Legitimate But Unjust; Just, But Illegitimate: Rawls on Political Legitimacy" (2016) 42 *Philosophy and Social Criticism* 132–53.

[21] *PL* xlviii.

[22] Ibid, xlix–l.

[23] See ibid, lvix. See also, on these same points, Rawls, "PRR" 773–75.

[24] See *supra* § 1.2.

of the possibility thereof, for at least some schemes of liberties we would count as reasonably justification-bearing.[25] Regarding condition (2), the Second Introduction's admission of a family of reasonable but conflicting underlying liberal justice conceptions poses a complication.

The hitch comes with the need, affirmed by Rawls, to supply an underlying normative conception by which to guide reciprocal adjustments of the ranges of the liberties listed in a constitution, as required to maintain them as a unified, coherent scheme.[26] As we have noted, the criterion advanced by Rawls is to keep the liberties, in combination, conducive to the development and exercise by citizens of certain powers of moral agency.[27] Thus, for example, the basic liberty to hold personal property will have as its core mission the assurance to each citizen of "a . . . material basis for a sense of personal independence and self-respect," sufficient to allow for the development and exercise of these agency powers. That liberty, then, will be open to possible institutional curtailments in respects deemed to fall outside that core: denial of inheritance rights, perhaps, or a move to socialized ownership of some of the means of production.[28]

Yet those might be curtailments to which other liberal views of the moral basis for property rights—say, a "classical liberal" view[29]—might take exception. And the troubling question, then, is whether *any* guiding criterion that you or I or John Rawls might propose will not be subject to liberally reasonable disagreement in conditions of pluralism. If we ask from whence Rawls draws the agency-powers criterion for intra-schematic adjustment of the outer reaches of the various liberties, the answer will be: from a certain conception of the person "as political," or "as citizen," embedded in an idea of justice as the pursuit of fair terms of social cooperation among persons free and equal, put forth and defended by Rawls in *PL* under the name of justice as fairness.[30] Defended by him, that is, as "the most reasonable" conception, for such a purpose, to be drawn from the broad historical tradition of constitutional democracy. The most reasonable, that is (as we now must add), among other, conflicting (but still reasonable) liberal conceptions. And then if, for others, the most reasonable conception is one that conflicts in one or another

[25] See *PL* pp. 297–98.

[26] See *supra* § 1.2.

[27] See *PL* 293, 297.

[28] *PL* 298. See generally William A. Edmundson, *John Rawls: Reticent Socialist* (Cambridge University Press 2017).

[29] See, e.g., Richard A. Epstein, *The Classical Liberal Constitution: The Uncertain Quest for Limited Government* (Harvard University Press 2014).

[30] See *PL* 18–19, 29, 34; "PRR" 799–800.

respect with Rawls's or yours or mine, where does that leave the hypothesis of a convergence across all reasonable conceptions on the central ranges of the basic liberties?

That is the complication, and you can perhaps glimpse from here the crux of a Rawlsian riposte. It lies in a distinction Rawls draws between what citizens variously will see as "most" reasonable and what they all can see as "at least" reasonable. A "most reasonable" conception, for you or for me or for John Rawls, might or might not fall within the set of "at least reasonable" conceptions for any and all of us and our fellow citizens inhabiting a wide historic tradition of constitutional democracy. The LPL of *PL*—read it again and you'll see[31]—stipulates for a convergence of reasonable citizens on the at-least reasonability of a currently regnant set of constitutionally essential basic liberties. Note—a point whose full importance will come clearer later—that there's no contradiction there with talk elsewhere from Rawls of an underlying political conception that would qualify as "most reasonable *for us*," meaning all of us of the constitutional-democratic tradition.[32] Rather, the implication is that what is "most reasonable for us" will be a conception by which reasonable and rational citizens justifiably call on each other for willing compliance with a constitution in force as long as they severally can count that constitution as at-least reasonable among free and equal citizens in conditions of pluralism.

That said, admission of a plurality of conflicting at-least reasonable constitutional conceptions must doubtless have the effect of narrowing the scopes of the widely agreed central ranges of the respective liberties. Yet *some* scopes of widespread endorsement could perhaps be expected to remain. "Property" (to continue with this example) might still always cover an immunity against a naked divestment from you, without compensatory payment and for no reason that can qualify as public, of a land-parcel you lawfully acquired by arm's-length purchase and now use as your not immodestly luxurious home.

There is, to be sure, a fair question about how far we can pare down the scopes of the widely endorsed central ranges and still have a sufficiently robust constitutional backstop for justification. Rawls will have more to say in response to that worry, but we do not go there yet.[33] Right now we want to nail down a further key role, in Rawls's constitutional-democratic conception, for the idea of the at-least reasonable.

[31] See Chapter 1, § 2.2.

[32] See, e.g., *PL* 28; John Rawls, "Kantian Constructivism in Moral Theory" (1980) 77 *Journal of Philosophy* 515, 519.

[33] See Chapter 6.

3. The Idea of the "At-Least Reasonable" as Bridge

The LPL, in keeping with the wider tradition of constitutional democracy in which it locates itself, anticipates a constitution that is, as I will say, programmatically democratic—in which, for example, a guarantee of everyone's fair access to the political liberties will figure as a constitutional essential. The LPL does not itself expressly and specifically stipulate for a constitution that is *originally* democratic, itself issuing from a course of democratic politics. John Rawls does himself, however, so contemplate—again, it would seem, in keeping with the wider tradition as he understands it.[34] Further pointing strongly in that direction is the consideration, surely non-rejectable by Rawls, that there are competing reasonable conceptions of what day-to-day democracy operationally requires,[35] from which it seems we would need an originary democratic warrant for whichever choices our own constitution is read to support, in order finally to nail down the claim that we are governed democratically.

Take it for now that authorship of their country's basic-law constitution is, for that or some other reason, deemed a necessary condition for the claim of a country's people to be self-governing. Then the "constitution" that figures pivotally in the Rawlsian LPL, read within the constitutional-democratic tradition, cannot be thought just to drift into our midst, heaven knows whence. It is, by constitutional-democratic understanding, a historically generated expression of a political will. That supposition of historical authorship then must figure crucially in the country's warranted acceptance of it as supreme law legitimate and legitimating.[36]

But then if and insofar as we thus would rely on popular authorship of the country's constitution to support the claim to popular self-government, that constitution must always and necessarily have, for us, the character of a mandate already and expressly laid down by politically circumstanced

[34] See, in this regard, Rawls's spirited rebuttal to a complaint from Jürgen Habermas that political liberalism elides or suppresses the originary aspect of democracy, John Rawls, "Reply to Habermas" (1995) 92 *Journal of Philosophy* 132, 165 (confirming that "whether the modern liberties are incorporated into the constitution is a matter to be decided by the constituent power of a democratic people"). See also *PL* 231–32 (distinguishing between "ordinary" law whose authority rests in acts of duly authorized officials and the constitutional "higher" law whose "higher authority [is that] of the will of We the People").

[35] Take as a live example our ongoing debates over the permissibility of the regulation of "hate speech" (or of the absence thereof) in contemporary democracies. See Mark Tushnet and Bojan Bugaric, *Power to the People: Constitutionalism in the Age of Populism* (Oxford University Press 2021) 11B12 (deeming both sides to be reasonable in a broad framework of liberal democracy).

[36] See *PL* 231–32.

human agents. That mandate must gain its bindingness on us now at least in part by force of its reputed intentionality as the dictate (say) of a democratically kosher constitutional assembly. Now, that intentionality on their part plainly and simply is not the same thing as a dictate of the contemporaneous common reason of those who are from day to day subject to the force of the laws issuing from the constitution in question. The two may happily happen to coincide in our particular case, but of that there can be no guarantee. And so for the LPL of *PL* constitutional bindingness-as-law will have to be both and simultaneously a matter of external (third-person) decisional fact (what I can see that an agent whose entitlement to rule I recognize has, as it happens, decided we are to do), and a matter of an internal (first-person) judgment of reason (what I can right now see that reason confirms we should do).

The apparent Rawlsian proposition of my ability to accept as *at-least* reasonable a substantive resolution of constitutional law that I do not find to be *the most* reasonable has the merit of explaining how I can simultaneously hold to both the third-person and first-person judgments in regard to a given constitutional-legal application. Within the bounded space of at-least reasonable liberal political conceptions would lie multiple schemes of constitutional essentials, differing and in some respects conflicting, any one of which a reasonable citizen could and should be able to accept as sufficient to serve procedurally as a platform of justification for compliant legislation. As long as we can find that to be the case, both the third-person and first-person judgments—both the pull to authority and the pull to reason—can possibly be realized simultaneously by any and all reasonable citizens. The constitution I freely and willingly accept as our country's procedural platform for the justification of contested ground-level laws is one that I both (1) perceive externally to be owing historically to the people and (2) judge internally to fall within the space of at-least reasonability for constitutions. Parallel perceptions and judgments then could hold for other reasonable citizens, still going strictly by our assumption (remember Rawlsian "publicity"[37]) that all would share the same perception of what that laid-down constitution *is*—which is what, by the argument of Chapters 2 and 3, the supreme court as protector of the people's constitution is there to ensure.

[37] See Chapters 1, § 2.3, and 2, §§ 2.2 & n. 29, 3.2.

4

Constitutional Law and Human Rights: The Call to Civility

As my contribution to a recent volume on *Human Rights, Democracy, and Legitimacy in a World of Disorder*, I took up a question about the connection (or lack of it) between two fields of discursive contention respectively known as "human rights" and "constitutional law." In what follows, I track closely the resulting paper.[1]

"The zeal to embody the whole truth in politics is incompatible with an idea of public reason that belongs with democratic citizenship."[2] So advises John Rawls. We easily see what Rawls is saying with that sentence. Just because you hold a conviction that a certain political-normative proposition is both true and important doesn't mean you necessarily should try to have it written into your country's constitutional law. But that proposition of self-restraint is not itself self-evidently true. On what ground does Rawls utter it? Is it that we are all prone to error, and he is beseeching you to consider that you may be mistaken? Is it that your conviction might pertain to some matter too specific or concrete or transitory, or otherwise unfit for constitutional attention or fixation? I think the ground finally is neither of those, but something else, something prior to them.

[1] See Frank I. Michelman, "Human Rights and Constitutional Rights: A Proceduralizing Function for Constitutional Law" in Silja Voeneky and Gerald Neuman (eds.), *Human Rights, Democracy, and Legitimacy in a World of Disorder* (Cambridge University Press 2018) 73.
[2] "PRR" 767.

Constitutional Essentials. Frank I. Michelman, Oxford University Press. © Frank I. Michelman 2022.
DOI: 10.1093/oso/9780197655832.003.0005

1. Domains and Constituencies of Political-Normative Discourses

1.1. Domains

Take this as an exemplary case to pose the question I have in view. You are settled in the conviction that a right of marriage equality for same-sex couples is truly and certainly a human right. Your country's body of constitutional law currently does treat some rights as specially protected, but not that one. Do you then stand under plain moral obligation to direct your share of political franchise in your country toward reversal of that omission?

I will use the term "constitutional law" here to mean a discretely identified, written-down body of basic positive laws (together with established judicial precedents for applying them in cases initially uncertain), setting terms of validity for any and all subsequent state legal operations, including first of all the issuance of ordinary laws by the constituted legislative bodies. I make this stipulation for reasons of expository convenience. The questions I pose can arise within practices of "political" or "common-law" constitutionalism,[3] but the arguments will run more cleanly by supposing a practice that treats as constitutional only those putative norms of framework law contained in, or officially and formally derived from, a written-down body of legal-normative materials expressly so designated. I suppose at the start that the constitutional law of your country, as it stands right now, leaves ordinary lawmakers free to decide either way about marriage equality. I further suppose that in your mind there are norms of right and wrong that apply to governments exerting power over citizens and others, regardless of what the applicable constitutional law might say. The category "human rights" takes in the ones of those norms that might sometimes require states to deviate from otherwise permissible and even commendable choices of laws, policies, and practices, in deference to certain specially favored interests, needs, or claims attributed to persons just as such. So to be clear: I speak here of what Gerald Neuman calls "suprapositive" norms[4] and Ronald Dworkin calls moral "background" norms that might or might not ever, in any given territory, be made into positive law.[5] By a "human right" I mean a norm we affirm on grounds and

[3] See Chapter 2, § 2; Chapter 5, § 4.

[4] See Gerald L. Neuman, "Human Rights and Constitutional Rights: Harmony and Dissonance" (2003) 55 *Stanford Law Review* 1863, 1868–69.

[5] See Ronald Dworkin, *Taking Rights Seriously* (Harvard University Press 1977) 93.

for reasons that do not essentially refer to norm-setting actions by political authorities anywhere. I am supposing here that such is what *you* mean by a human right. And my further supposition—just to set up the argument—is that *you* would include in that favored category the claims of persons everywhere to be able freely to conclude a state-recognized marriage (wherever those exist) with a partner of choice regardless of sex.

I don't mean you necessarily reach this conclusion as a strictly private excogitation. It will be fine for my purposes if, like Jeremy Waldron, you understand and value the pursuit of human rights as a common enterprise that binds together the people of the world,[6] and so your conclusions in regard to human rights take on board both that consideration and all the further considerations pro and con adduced by philosophical debates and political resolutions around the globe of which you are aware. The morality of human rights may be, in those respects and in your view, a quite complex and to some extent socially guided affair. Having paid whatever heed to world opinion and debate you think is demanded by a complex global morality of human rights, it is *that morality*, as finally resolved, whose effectuation (or not) in the positive laws of your country is what gives you concern.

But please also notice, then, that for you to view marriage equality as truly and surely a human right does not mean for you necessarily to insist on a distinct item on "marriage" in whatever lists of human rights you might find in books of political philosophy, or in public instruments like the ICCPR[7] and the ECHR.[8] You will not necessarily fault such a listing just as soon as you see that it lacks an entry devoted specifically to marriage or same-sex partnerships.[9] What you will, though, in such a case require is that the whole, combined array of more abstractly stated itemizations ("dignity," "liberty," "equality," "privacy," "association," "family life") is understood to carry with

[6] See Jeremy Waldron, "Human Rights: Universalism or the Integrity of a Common Enterprise" (2016) New York University School of Law Public Law & Legal Theory Research Paper Series, Working Paper No. 16–48, available at http://ssrn.com/abstract=2848611.

[7] See International Covenant on Civil and Political Rights, Dec. 16, 1966, S. Exec. Rep. 102–23, 999 U.N.T.S. 171 ("ICCPR").

[8] See Convention for the Protection of Human Rights and Fundamental Freedoms, Nov. 4, 1950, Europ.T.S. No. 5; 213 U.N.T.S. 221 ("European Convention on Human Rights").

[9] So, for example, you will not necessarily object to a philosophy proposing that the single ultimate human right is a "right to justification," see Rainer Forst, *The Right to Justification* (Columbia University Press 2002) 81 ("[W]hat is foundational is an individual basic right *to justification*. . . .") or a right to be treated by government "with equal concern and respect," see Ronald Dworkin, *Justice For Hedgehogs* (Harvard University Press 2011) 330 (hypothesizing that "all political rights are derivative from that fundamental one").

it a right of marriage equality, when and as that application comes up for consideration.

1.2. Constituencies

I have so far left unspecified whether the "you" in my scenario might possibly be a judge of law, as distinct from a common citizen. Suppose we did have before us the case of the judge. And let us for the moment take it to be common cause among constitutional democrats that no, judges of law are not normally free to direct their special shares of political authority toward a reading into their country's constitutional law of their own subjectively favored human-rights convictions (not precisely matching any there might be that citizens in a constitutional democracy must be supposed to hold in common). It seems my scenario can only, then, envisage a common-citizen "you."

2. Morality and Civility: Convergence or Division?

2.1. Moral Fault to Moral Obligation to Repair?

Take "moral fault" to mean any feature in a body of constitutional law whose correction would even slightly improve the constitution from a standpoint of morality.[10] The constitutional law of your country currently leaves ordinary lawmakers free to decide either way about marriage equality, and you sit holding a vote to cast pro or con a pending constitutional amendment to bar any legal conditioning of marriage on the genders of the partners. If we add to the picture your settled embrace of a human-rights conception that demands personal freedom of choice of a marital partner, does not that then add up to a finding by you of a moral fault in your country's constitution as it now stands? And would not morality in this setting oblige you to do your bit to make your country's constitution the morally best it can be? And are

[10] As opposed, that is, to the stricter sense of a fault so grave as to sink the constitution below some floor of bare tolerability *faute de mieux*. See, e.g., Richard H. Fallon, Jr., "Legitimacy and the Constitution" (2005) 118 *Harvard Law Review* 1787, 1798 (defining a regime's or a constitution's "minimal" moral legitimacy as "a threshold above which [the regime is] sufficiently just to deserve . . . support . . . in the absence of better [realistic] alternatives").

we not then left with an ironclad moral mandate for you to cast your vote in favor of the amendment?

2.2. A Question of the Applicable (Sub)Morality?

My expectation is that many readers, maybe most, will instantly answer with a "no" or at least a hesitation to say "yes." Those who do so hesitate may perhaps be thinking or intuiting that there are here in play two moralities—of human rights and of the conduct of politics—and the two are non-identical in directive content, so as sometimes to force on citizens a choice (itself a moral one) of which to follow.[11] My aim here will be to develop a line of thought to explain and support such a view. The key to it is the political-liberal idea of a justificatory function for substantive constitutional law, developed in the preceding chapters of this book. Placed in the context of our thought experiment, I think this idea will draw nods of sympathy or provisional assent from many readers. I want to see how far it will support resistance against a sweeping subjection of a citizen's attitude toward political obligation to dictation from a taken-as-true morality of human rights.

2.3. Beyond Pragmatism, Relativism, and Popular Constitutionalism: Justification-by-Constitution

We will have in view here, then, a certain kind of objection against a conflation of the morality of human rights with the moral criticism of constitutional law. We can call it a proceduralist objection, by way of keeping it distinct from certain others it may accompany and with which it may easily be confused. The proceduralist objection is not, in the first place, a merely pragmatic concession to supposed political realities (say, a calculation of costs from the pursuit of hopeless causes), but rather aspires to acceptance as a part of a robust full conception of rightness or justice in politics. Nor is this to be taken as a "relativist" objection, a concern about whether a claim as concrete as marriage equality could truly be a basic right of everyone

[11] I do not mean to be addressing here a meta-ethical question about whether the very idea of the moral excludes unresolved internal divisions. It is just easier to write of two competing "moralities" (instead of "sub-moralities"), while specifying that decision of which takes precedence in the case at hand is itself a moral question.

everywhere, regardless of country-by-country differences of society and culture. Nor, finally, is this a strictly democracy-based objection, to putting courts of law into position to decide matters whose resolution more justly or fitly belongs to parliamentary or popular forums.[12]

Let us ask: Why should it occur to anyone ever to aim a complaint of moral fault against (merely) *constitutional* law, when—as, for example, was until recently true in the United States—it is not *that* law that makes the choice to refuse admission of same-sex couples to state-recognized marriage, but rather it is ground-level legislation that constitutional law freely allows to go either way as political majorities may from time to time decide. No doubt you may have a moral complaint against ground-level laws that make the wrong choice, but what exactly can be your gripe with a constitution that leaves the choice to ground-level democratic lawmaking? (Consider that your country's constitution might have been one of those that contain no substantive parts at all—a perfectly workable arrangement that many countries historically have adopted. Would your moral complaint still hold in that case? Does the complaint run against resolutely substance-free constitutions, or only against constitutions that protect some rights but not a right of marriage equality?)

Well, you might feel you do have a moral complaint against any constitution that does not include special protection for all true human rights (and so that would cover constitutions having no substantive parts at all)—because, you say, constitutions morally ought to do whatever they can to bring about a fulfillment of human rights. An expectation of benign effects of that kind, from a body of aptly crafted, substantive constitutional law, has occupied a central place in the wide tradition of constitutional-democratic thought—even as it has also sometimes been a topic of doubt and debate.[13]

If that were your reason for objecting to a constitution's omission of protection for a right of marriage equality, you would be judging from what I have called in this book a regulatory conception of the service that constitutions—their substantive parts—are meant to provide in the overall workings of a country's political and legal affairs. In terms of the regulatory conception, the

[12] See, e.g., Jeremy Waldron, "Jeremy Waldron, dissenting" in Jack M. Balkin (ed.), *What Obergefell v. Hodges Should Have Said: The Nation's Top Legal Experts Rewrite America's Same-Sex Marriage Decision* (Yale University Press 2020) 281 __ (presenting objections to an adjudicatively determined extension of constitutional protection to a right of same-sex marriage).

[13] See Richard H. Fallon, Jr., "The Core of an Uneasy Case for Judicial Review" (2008) 121 *Harvard Law Review* 1701, 1704–15 (reviewing "outcome-related" reasons for resort to institutionally enforceable constitutional rights, and related scholarly controversy).

closer the fit between the constitution's substantive parts and your ideal conception of human rights, the better the constitution must be.

Or rather—and here starts the rub—the better it must be in *your* estimation, but maybe not in the estimation of all your fellow citizens who share with you a regulatory conception of the service of constitutional law, among whom there may be some whose ideal conceptions of human rights are deviant from yours (say, as quite decidedly *not* encompassing a right of marriage equality). If you will bend so far as to grant that some such moral disagreements might be sincerely held on all sides, then you should see how the regulatory conception leaves us with a nontrivial problem on our hands.

Recognition of the rub of inevitably recurrent moral disagreement in modern liberal societies has led some thinkers toward a complementary conception of the work of substantive constitutional law, the one this book has been calling both a justificatory and a proceduralizing conception. In this line of thought, such societies stand in need of a public code of basic forms and rules for the conduct of politics, on the basis of which a process of social ordering by majoritarian lawmaking can then proceed on terms of evident due regard for presumptively equal capacities of free citizens for responsible engagement with morally fraught matters of public law and policy. In the proceduralizing view of its service to our politics, a country's body of constitutional law is to serve as that code. Any substantive parts would accordingly have to be sufficiently thin or abstract to avoid foreclosures of matters of moral moment on which agreement does not yet exist throughout the population of citizens.[14]

Some will go further to say this proceduralizing view of the constitution's service to civic ordering must lead to extreme caution about including *any* substantive protections in constitutional law. Others (like John Rawls) oppositely say that a constitution serving this function must certainly include something in the way of substantive guarantees—no less (if also no more) than will allow each citizen to look the others in the eye and say we should all be able to agree that the system with just these guarantees in place is sufficiently worth upholding to give each of us prevailing reason to insist on each other's dispositions in general to conform to the laws that issue from it.

That latter position—John Rawls's—is the one to occupy us now. We want to see how it would handle the question of inclusion of marriage equality as a constitutional right. Suppose the answer it would give turns out to be

[14] See Chapter 3, § 1.1.

something like "it depends," or (see Chapter 5) "maybe at some point in time but not necessarily yet." If you feel drawn—as I think many readers will be—to both the regulatory and the proceduralizing views of constitutional function, and if you are otherwise also the *you* whose human-rights convictions I attribute in this chapter, that might all leave you feeling caught in a crossfire of justice (the regulatory view) and expediency (the proceduralizing view).

3. Civility a Moral Trump?

3.1. For Citizens at Large ("You and Me")?

But are considerations of morality and expediency so cleanly separable here as that question assumes? A failure of justification-by-constitution is not—or so it may be contended—a merely prudential or pragmatic mishap. Such a failure strips a country's citizens, you and me, of recourse to publicly assertable grounds for a regularity of uncoerced compliance with our country's laws by everyone. It seems that should not be a morally tolerable outcome for a people who claim to prize each person's free development and exercise of his or her moral powers, and on that very ground to find a moral necessity in the support of civil government and the force of legitimate law (but then only on terms that everyone as reasonable can find acceptable).[15] It seems a pursuit of that condition must be a part of what we owe to fellow citizens as a matter of basic recognition and respect. And then that commitment, too—that "intrinsically moral duty" of "civility," as John Rawls calls it,[16] that obligation of respect toward fellow citizens as presumptively free and equal, reasonable and rational—must itself qualify as a part of the background morality against which constitutions are to be rated as morally better and worse. That is what reliance on the constitution for a proceduralizing service seemingly must come to, from a moral point of view. Morality cannot

[15] Compare Arthur Isak Applbaum, *Legitimacy: The Right to Rule in a Wanton World* 104 (Harvard University Press 2019) 104. "A moral agent," Applbaum remarks,

> cannot possibly give up a commitment to internal freedom. . . . External freedom [is a precondition for] internal freedom, for without bodily integrity and liberty of thought and expression, self-governing action is not possible. . . . The offer of legitimate government—that is, the offer of institutions in which we are free enough to be authors of procedures and collective actions and that realize and protect the freedoms that make us free enough to have the capacity to be authors—is an offer we cannot refuse.

[16] "PRR" 769–70. See ibid, 797; *PL* 217–18, 226, 236, 242, 253; *JAF* 90, 92, 117.

then figure, at least not in any simple way, as a ground for stiffly nonnegotiable demands in democratic politics. (The philosophy of political liberalism, writes Rawls, "applies the principle of toleration to philosophy itself."[17])

So there *you* are—settled in the view of marriage equality as a true human right, and pledged to steer your country's constitution in the direction of moral perfection—about to cast your vote pro or con a constitutional amendment to make marriage equality a mandatory premise for any and all ground-level legislation on marriage. Can you say *without a further thought* that you will vote "yes"? Only, it would seem, by rigorously fencing out from your idea of a morally excellent constitution any and all thought of the proceduralizing—or some might say the civilizing—service of a body of substantive constitutional law.

3.2. For Courts of Law

Does a like answer then hold for the judges faced with deciding whether your country's constitution's clauses on liberty and equality do already mandate marriage equality, when the courts to date have ruled oppositely? However it may be with citizens voting on proposed constitutional amendments,[18] courts of law carry neither charge nor license to make over, in the pursuit of moral perfection, the given constitution of their country. On that fixed point in the constitutional-democratic tradition, our most avid moral readers concur. The courts, they say, are commissioned to search out the best account of "the commitments of our constitutional order."[19] That leaves the courts, though, still facing questions of where civility stands among commitments in that best account, and of how a constitutional commitment to civility might figure among those to be weighed by judges of law engaged in constitutional review of apparently oppressive legislation.

[17] *PL* 9–10; see John Rawls, "Justice as Fairness: Political Not Metaphysical" (1985) 14 *Philosophy and Public Affairs* 231, 240 ("method of avoidance").

[18] I merely note here that the question of substantive limits on the exercise of powers of amendment is a controversial one. See, e.g., Alessandro Ferrara *Sovereignty Across Generations: Constituent Power and Political Liberalism* (forthcoming 2023 from Oxford University Press); Walter F. Murphy, "Merlin's Memory: The Past and Future Imperfect of the Once and Future Polity" in Sanford Levinson (ed.), *Responding to Imperfection: The Theory and Practice of Constitutional Amendment* (Princeton University Press 1995) 163–77.

[19] James E. Fleming, *Fidelity to Our Imperfect Constitution: For Moral Readings and Against Originalism* (Oxford University Press 2015) 80. Compare William W. Van Alstyne, "Interpreting This Constitution: The Unhelpful Contributions of Special Theories of Judicial Review" (1983) 35 *University Florida Law Review* 209.

Those are hard questions. Neither can be dealt with in a sentence. They await further treatment later. But I am ready at this point to say this: A "yes" answer to the first question (civility a term in the constitutional compact?) may still leave room for a "no" response to the second (civility in judicial review?).

5

Constitutional Fidelity: Of Courts, Citizens, and Time

Constitutional fidelity is these days a contested idea, and I mean in countries falling squarely in the constitutional-democratic tradition.[1] While few in our midst would set that idea totally at naught, pundits do differ widely over its proper force and reach in the politics of a democracy. My interest in this chapter runs to a proposition from John Rawls that a liberally well-ordered constitutional democracy requires of its judges a different and stricter kind of constitutional fidelity than it does of citizens at large engaged in political action. We want to see how that possibly can be so, given the constitution's procedurally pivotal position, as assigned by Rawls, in the justification of democratic political power.[2]

1. Public Reason and Constitution: "Stricter" for Courts than for Citizens

In a Rawlsian well-ordered constitutional democracy, laws and policies touching fundamental political questions, controversial as they may be and remain among citizens, are nevertheless perceivable by all as consonant with some at-least reasonable balance of principles and values, themselves in line with some at-least reasonable political conception of justice.[3] Restrictions correspondingly follow on the kinds of reasons and reasoning to which, ideally, citizens turn for justification to each other of political acts affecting the

[1] See, e.g., Michael J. Klarman, "Antifidelity" (1997) 70 *Southern California Law Review* 381.
[2] Portions of this chapter are drawn, with some revision, from my "The Question of Constitutional Fidelity: Rawls on the Reason of Constitutional Courts" in Silje A. Langvatn, Mattias Kumm, and Woiciech Sadurski (eds.), *Public Reason and Courts* (Cambridge University Press 2020) 90, with other portions drawn from Frank I. Michelman, "Human Rights and Constitutional Rights: A Proceduralizing Function for Constitutional Law" in Silja Voeneky and Gerald Neuman (eds.), *Human Rights, Democracy, and Legitimacy in a World of Disorder* (Cambridge University Press 2018) 73.
[3] See Chapter 3, § 2, Chapter 6 § 2.3.

Constitutional Essentials. Frank I. Michelman, Oxford University Press. © Frank I. Michelman 2022.
DOI: 10.1093/oso/9780197655832.003.0006

essentials of the constitution in force. Such restrictions lie near the core of what Rawls calls an ideal of public reason.[4] They apply to officials and citizens generally;[5] but, Rawls says, they apply "in a special way," "more strictly," to "judges in their decisions" and "above all to a supreme court in a constitutional democracy with judicial review"—than to democratic citizens engaged in political action.[6] We want to see how and why this might be so.

1.1. Justification as to Means: "Guidelines of Inquiry"

Demands of public reasoning fall into two parts, corresponding to the common syntactic form of a justificatory explanation for a political act. Such explanations typically will (1) posit some goal supposedly approached through the act or some commitment or other value supposedly served by it; and (2) show how the act is expected to work out for the furtherance of that goal or the fulfillment of that value. We could say roughly that (1) supplies the explanation's major premises—"service to goal *G* (or fulfillment of value *V*) qualifies as a reason supporting a political act of this kind")—while (2) introduces minor premises consisting largely of claims about how things work in physical nature and society.

Let us just briefly peer more closely at (2). In order to qualify for what Rawls calls a "public" basis of justification for a contested law or policy, any claims regarding physical and social consequence must draw from "plain truths . . . widely accepted or available to citizens generally"—"beliefs found in common sense, and the methods and conclusions of science when those are not controversial."[7] Connections then drawn from such beliefs to anticipated social outcomes must rest on accepted standards of evidence, modes of inference, and so on.[8] It seems these "guidelines of inquiry," as Rawls calls them, must apply alike to justificatory explanations offered by anyone putting an oar in the waters of legislative action and debate, be that an official,

[4] See Chapter 1, § 1.

[5] "Public reason," Rawls writes, "is a view about the kind of reasons on which citizens are to rest their political cases in making their political justifications to one another when they support laws and policies that invoke the coercive powers of government concerning fundamental political questions." "PRR" 795. This ideal "applies to citizens when they engage in political advocacy in the public forum . . . and when they vote" on "questions concerning constitutional essentials and matters of basic justice." *PL* 252–53.

[6] "PRR" 767–68, *PL* 216.

[7] *PL* 224–225.

[8] See ibid, 224.

candidate, voter, influencer, or court. Saying so does not exclude our holding high court judges to a special standard of care and scrupulosity in the examples they set to citizens at large of adherence to the guidelines of inquiry.[9] In doing so, we would be confirming an identity, not a difference, in the guidelines ideally applicable to the court and to citizens.

1.2. Justification as to Ends: "Principles and Values"

What might still, however, vary as between courts and citizens are the ideal limits on the stocks of substantive principles and values from which they respectively draw the major premises in public justificatory explanations. Rawls seemingly holds these limits to be tighter for the supreme court than for citizens at large. The justices ideally strike their balances all and only from such values as they find to be expressed through the constitutional law in force, of course including its scripted scheme of basic liberties. "In a constitutional democracy with judicial review," Rawls writes, "the justices have to explain and justify their decisions as based on their understanding of the constitution and relevant statutes and precedents."[10] That seems surely right for a specially entrusted judicial protector of a constitutional-procedural pact.

Rawls then immediately goes on to say that political acts of other state branches need not be justified in the same way.[11] Nor need the acts of citizens at large when acting pro or con a contested law or policy. What rather then applies is a looser criterion of "reciprocity"[12]—a readiness of each to conduct their respective political acts in accord with whatever political conception of justice each may regard as most reasonable, as long as that conception is made up out of political values that the reasoner sincerely regards as ones that "others as free and equal also might reasonably be expected reasonably to endorse."[13] But why should there be this loosened standard for citizens? It doubtless is true, as Rawls says, that a supreme court, as trusted protector of a constitutional-procedural pact-in-force to which citizens point as justification for collaboration in the force of law, must visibly be bound to fidelity to *that pact*.[14] But then must not the same hold equally among the citizens who

[9] See ibid, 216, 231, 236 (calling the supreme court an "exemplar" of public reason).
[10] Ibid, 216; see ibid, 236–37.
[11] See ibid, 216.
[12] Ibid, xliv, 49–50.
[13] Ibid, l; see ibid, 218; "PRR" 773, 797.
[14] See ibid, 237; Chapter 3, § 1.4.

do the pointing? That pact, after all, is one for an *established* framework for politics and policy choice—by hypothesis, in a well-ordered society, one that is acceptable, *qua* framework, among any and all free and equal, reasonable and rational citizens. That is why—it would seem—whoever among them takes whatever share in the country's politics does so under obligation of due regard for *it*.[15]

2. Due Regard for the Constitution in Force

2.1. Application, Not Revision

The public-reason ideal applies to judges, officials, and citizens at various stages of constitutional time. At the stages where democratic citizens notionally assemble to choose the contents going forward for their country's body of constitutional laws—those contents as they are to stand until the next event of constitutional resettlement—the ideal requires of each participating citizen an abstention from pursuit of any term that cannot fit what that citizen sincerely can find to be a constitution that all could regard as *a* reasonable—if not necessarily in the eyes of everyone the only or the most reasonable—ordering of public values for a constitutional framework.[16] At the times when courts face decision of the constitutionality of committed or pending ground-level legislative and administrative actions or agendas, the ideal requires of each judge a search for correct or reasonable applications of the public values for which they find the constitution-in-force to speak. But then not likewise, too, for citizens? At least we will have to say that, for citizens engaged in day-to-day exercises of their shares of legislative and other political powers, the public reason ideal requires action *with due regard to* that constitution. Is due regard by judges, then, a stricter requirement than due regard by citizens?

It is a commonplace of constitutional-democratic thought that we grant to citizen bodies an exclusive moral title to bring about changes to their country's body of basic or constitutional laws. That is a title in which judges, as such, claim no part; rather, judges acting in their judicial capacities purport to apply in good faith the people's constitution as it currently stands. Rawls

[15] See Chapter 1, § 1.2.
[16] See *PL* 226–27.

expressly concurs.[17] But we detect also in his thought an endorsement of a further, less obvious sort of difference in the constitutional fidelities respectively owed by citizens and by judges—a difference, I mean, in the strictness of fidelities owed to the constitution *as it stands* during the periods between legally cognizable events of constitutional alteration by citizen action. Rawls apparently envisages, for those periods, a fidelity constraint that is tighter for judges deciding disputes at law than for citizens acting as litigants, voters, political organizers, and otherwise as agitators for political causes.

2.2. "This" Constitution, or Its Family?

The difference takes hold when applications of the undoubted standing terms of the constitution-in-force come under dispute. Take a currently pending example from the United States. Some states have recently extended their antidiscrimination statutes to prohibit and penalize commercial refusals to deal on the basis of a customer's perceived LGBQT status or identity. Our country's constitution, written well in the past, contains express guarantees respecting each person's liberties of association, expression, and religion—and additionally, through established judicial precedent, respecting liberty in matters of conscience beyond religion and decisional freedom in matters deemed intensely personal. It also guarantees the equal protection of the laws. Does the combination of those guarantees prohibit (or does it, perhaps, require) application of the new statutes to purveyors of wedding-related goods and services engaged in faith-based refusals to serve or supply same-sex lawful weddings?

In the view of Rawls, any judge's or citizen's defensible answer will have to ground itself in some political conception of justice that is broader than the constitution in force, in some sense subsuming and informing that constitution. For *judges* (it is different for citizens), that straightforwardly means a justice conception that the judicial answerer finds the constitution's guarantees in combination to express or represent.[18] No doubt that still leaves room for divisions of views, and those divisions may run deep. Judges starting out from somewhat differing, reasonable political conceptions of justice may correspondingly differ in their findings (say) in regard to the deepest point

[17] See *supra* § 1.2.
[18] See *PL* 237.

or aim of the First Amendment's free-speech clause. If some say it is to implement a scheme of discursive democracy[19] while others say it is to secure individual self-realization,[20] the differing sides may not only be pointing towards conflicting conclusions in a pending case on regulation of expression but dividing, so to speak, over the whole containing constitution's DNA.[21] Disputes among such views will hardly ever, though, arise on a blank slate. Readers of the country's legal history to date will usually find therein a prior deposit of legal constructions bearing on the case at hand. (Some of those, of course, may be passé, overtaken by others that more recently have held the ground over a stretch of time leading into now.) So understanding, the justices of a supreme court ideally

> try to develop and express in their reasoned opinions the best interpretation of the constitution they can, using their knowledge of what the constitution and constitutional precedents require. Here the best interpretation is the one that best fits the relevant body of those constitutional materials, and justifies it in terms of the public conception of justice or a reasonable variant thereof.[22]

That can stand as Rawls's summary statement of due regard by justices of the supreme court for the constitution in force.

For citizens, it seems due regard may take a looser shape. Like judges, citizens are to answer constitution-applicative questions with reference to a political conception of justice containing or subsuming the constitution in force. For them, however, the containing or subsuming conception need not be *the one* that the standing body of constitution law—precedents and all—is best read to implement. It need only be one *belonging to the same family* of reasonable political conceptions as that to which the standing constitution is reasonably found to belong. For the citizen engaged in actions affecting matters of constitutional import, due regard for the country's standing constitution means due regard for a family of reasonable political conceptions it is reasonably taken to represent. A judge does not have that same latitude for selection among guiding political conceptions. For a judge, the guiding

[19] See Robert Post, *Citizens Divided: Campaign Reform and the Constitution* (Harvard University Press 2014).

[20] Martin H. Redish, "The Value of Free Speech" (1982) *University of Pennsylvania Law Review* 191, 193.

[21] And compare the property-right example in Chapter 3, § 2.

[22] *PL* 236.

conception is to be *the one* she honestly finds to be represented by the whole body of constitutional law currently in place in the country. In the terms introduced by Ronald Dworkin, we might say that Rawls's judges are more tightly bound than are his citizens to the dimension of "fit" (to concrete historical constitutional practice) in constitutional interpretation.[23]

2.3. The Counter-Logic of the Proceduralist LPL

The LPL of *PL* posits a practice of politics in which democratic citizens, looking for willing compliance by all with coercive laws with which some deeply disagree, accept a political-moral obligation to justify those expectations to dissenters on terms the latter as fellow citizens can accept. They fulfill that obligation by showing that the contested laws after all do comply with the country's constitution in force—supposed, in a Rawlsian well-ordered constitutional democracy, to be such as citizens reasonably can call upon each other to accept as setting the basic terms for their political order, even as all understand that some resulting coercive laws will be ones that they or others will find deeply repugnant.

Inevitably, though, there will be disagreements about the constitutional compatibility of the contested laws. In order that every such occasion will not signify to the political losers a rupture of the constitutional-procedural pact, some stipulation for a space of tolerable disagreement over applications of the constitution's terms must itself be one of those terms, and so must trust in the country's supreme court's resolutions of contests over application to fall within that space of tolerability or "at-least" reasonability.[24] All of that has been the burden, by way of explication of the LPL of *PL*, of Chapters 2 and 3 of this book.

Now, in order for this scheme of justification to hold together, it seems the pact the judges act to protect must be the exact same one as that to which the citizens point by way of justification. And how, then, do we reconcile that deduction with an allowance—as I have suggested Rawls makes—of a looser

[23] The distinction I here find Rawls taking between the fidelity obligations of citizens and judges also calls to mind John Gardner's differentiation between "the constitution" and "constitutional law" as "rival objects of interpretation." John Gardner, "Can There Be a Written Constitution?" in Leslie Green and Brian Leiter (eds.), Oxford Studies in Constitutional Law, Vol. 1 (Oxford Scholarship Online: Sept. 2011) 20–21.

[24] See Chapter 2, § 2.2; Chapter 3, § 1.4.

license to citizens than to judges to stretch the envelope of constitutional interpretation?

2.4. Aspiration for Citizens, Obligation for Courts?

Consider this as a possible simple answer to my question. For citizens at large, public reason may stand as an aspirational ideal of good citizenship, but it cannot stand as a civically binding obligation without contradiction of the first principle of justice as fairness, with its guarantees of equal liberties of conscience, expression, and association.[25] For those exercising the judicial office, by contrast, binding obligation follows easily with acceptance of that office.

That undoubtedly is an accurate report of Rawls's view, and it does truly convey a sense in which the call to constitutional fidelity applies more strictly to courts than to citizens. It is not, however, a sense responsive to our question in this chapter. Our question has not been about an institutionally binding obligation of citizens in constitutional democracies; it has been from the start about how judges and citizens ideally do conduct themselves in a well-ordered constitutional democratic society.[26] Rawls undoubtedly means to say that citizens ideally will press for policies in accord with what they variously see as the liberal constitution most reasonable for their society, whereas judges ideally are more tightly bound to legalistic readings (let us call them) of the constitutional law now in force.

3. Temporality

In the hypothesis—in the narrative (so to speak)—of justification-by-constitution, citizens, coming to constitutional applications with differing deeper conceptions of what their country's constitutional law most reasonably ought to say, are destined for intractable good-faith disagreements over which of the reasonably arguable applications of constitutional law are the

[25] See "PRR" 769. ("This duty [of civility, to abide by public reason in the exercise of political franchise], is an intrinsically moral duty. I emphasize that it is not a legal duty, for in that case it would be incompatible with freedom of speech.").

[26] See *PL* 252–53; "PRR" 765.

most reasonable. The same of course holds for those citizens who become judges. But because—in what I have called the narrative's "second procedural turn"[27]—the judges are to serve as the system's trusted arbiters of the citizens' disagreements, *their* judgments cannot be products of votes among judges caught up in, and acting upon, those same disagreements. Those judgments will have to be more visibly and tightly bound to legalistic readings of the constitutional law now in force. That really does explain "stricter for courts" as a deduction from the ideal narrative of justification-by-constitution.

3.1. Dialectical Liberal Reasonability

It also sets up a dialectical process of long-term adaptive modulation in a citizenry's grasp of their justification-bearing constitutional essentials.

We noticed in Chapter 3 how Rawls, at the point of the republication of *PL* in 1996, introduced the idea of a family of somewhat conflicting but all-of-them reasonable liberal conceptions of justice, thus complicating our exposition of the LPL.[28] Along with that, as we now can add, came an observation from Rawls about temporal change. Not only, Rawls observed, does the substantive content of constitutional-democratic public reason—"the principles, ideals, and standards that may be appealed to"—range at any given time over a family of liberally reasonable but sometimes conflicting conceptions of justice, but this family's own political-moral DNA—what Rawls calls the "reason" that's both common and distinctive to the family[29]—itself changes over time, and it does so in very consequence of the family's range, at any moment, over partially conflicting conceptions that then become grist for public debate. Intra-familial conceptions being all mutually cognizable by family members as parties to one and the same family quarrel, that sense of outermost reasonability undergoes revision "as a result of their debates with one another"—as, for example, "social changes over generations . . . give rise to new groups with different political problems."[30] "New variations" appear from time to time, and "it is important that this be so; otherwise the claims of

[27] See Chapter 2, § 2.2; Chapter 3, § 1.3.

[28] See Chapter 3, § 2.

[29] See *PL* 212 (remarking that a political society, like a family, "has a way of formulating its plans, of putting its ends in an order of priority, and of making decisions accordingly. The way a political society does this is its reason. . . .").

[30] "Second Introduction" lii–liii; see "PRR" 775.

groups or interests arising from social change might be repressed and fail to gain their appropriate political voice."[31]

A justificatory load-bearing constitution, in short, is not armored against temporal stress. Over the course of historical time, as a country's conditions undergo change, so may widespread societal understandings of the innermost essences of its constitutional guarantees. New legislative initiatives call forth new and possibly modulated judicial responses. Those responses may themselves then exert a steering effect on the next run of legislative initiatives. The process over time may end in a somewhat reconfigured consolidation of core understandings of constitutional guarantees, and of attendant constitutional doctrine, from where the courts and the country had left them sometime back. "The ideal of a just constitution is always something to be worked toward," Rawls was to write, post-*PL*, in response to prompts from Jürgen Habermas.[32] But he had in fact already anticipated this dialectical outlook on constitutional-legal content, as far back as his work in *TJ*, where it appeared as an aspect of what Rawls then called "the four-stage sequence."[33]

3.2. Flashback: The Sequence of Stages in *TJ*

Rawls introduced in *TJ* the idea of a notional succession of stages of saturation of more and more concretely decisive content into the country's framework law. A "constitutional" stage of relatively abstract constitutional-essential scripts is succeeded by a "legislative" stage of concretizations of those, in statute law or in judge-made constitutional-legal doctrine, and then by a stage of application of the resulting laws and doctrines to cases. At each stage, the lawgivers and law-appliers are idealized as working from the kinds of information about their society and its affairs, ranging from the highly general to the increasingly specific, on which we would want lawgivers at that stage to focus their reasoning.[34] Thus, given the constitution's proceduralizing

[31] Ibid. We have there the Rawlsian version of Barry Friedman's mediated popular constitutionalism. See Barry Friedman, "Mediated Popular Constitutionalism" (2003) 101 *Michigan Law Review* 2596, 2599 ("[O]ur system is one of popular constitutionalism in that judicial interpretations of the Constitution reflect popular will over time.").

[32] John Rawls, "Reply to Habermas" (1995) 92 *Journal of Philosophy* 132, 154 (hereafter Rawls, "Reply"). Rawls thus responded to an objection from Habermas that his conception allows a constitution wrought by "theory" to settle forever all that really matters in the field of rights, thus precluding the citizenry from developing their constitution actively "as a project." Jürgen Habermas, "Reconciliation through the Public Use of Reason" (1995) 92 *Journal of Philosophy* 109, 128.

[33] *TJ* 195–201.

[34] See ibid; Rawls, "Reply" (n 32) 152.

function as laid out in Chapters 1 and 2, we would most certainly want constitutional lawgivers to know about—so that they will anticipate—the inevitability in societies like ours of recurrent reasonable moral and other disagreement about the most concrete specifications of the system of basic liberties. Just as surely, we would not want lawgivers at that stage engaged in predicting concretely the shape of such disagreements to come, or the identities or alignments of the parties to them, or the order or time of their appearance. Such predictions could serve as fodder for strategic choices antithetical to the aim of the resulting constitution's wide acceptability to reasonable citizens.[35] Things are different, though, at the legislative stage. Given the need for situatedly apt legislation, the legislature simply must be allowed to be in receipt of a great deal of information barred from the constitutional stage. And this we can safely allow—so runs the theory—*given* the constitution's prior assurance of legislative due regard for its more abstract basic-rights commitments.

Rawls called the succession of stages a "sequence," but the twist is that the sequence moves by flashback. It would be, Rawls wrote, by "moving back and forth between the stages of the constitutional convention and the legislature" that "the best constitution [would be] found."[36] Responses to social learning at a later stage might at any time flash back to modify the country's grasp of the gist or the scope of a prior-stage abstract principle or norm of right. Legislation reflective of the later learning would react back upon the constitutional script, keeping that script up to speed in its service as the body of basic assurances underwriting justification for the submission of free and equal, reasonable and rational citizens of that country to the coercions endemic in a ground-level rule of law.

Consider, now, this recent rumination from judges of an American intermediate appellate court, responding to a same-sex couple's claim to read the US Constitution's scripted constitutional essentials on liberty and equality as a mandate for same-sex marriage equality, issued at a time when that application had never up to then been made by US courts—and had, in fact, been refused by the US Supreme Court.[37] "Not long ago," wrote those judges,

[35] See *TJ* 200 (ruling out information at any stage that "is likely to give rise to bias and distortion and to set men against one another").

[36] Ibid, 198.

[37] In a ruling made subsequent to that time, our Supreme Court has reversed that position and has found a constitutional right of marriage equality. See Obergefell v. Hodges, 576 U.S. 644 (2015).

> American society took for granted the rough correlation between marriage and creation of new life, a vision under which limiting marriage to opposite-sex couples seemed natural. Not long from now, if current trends continue, American society may define marriage in terms of affirming mutual love, a vision under which the failure to add loving gay couples seems unfair.[38]

At the times when the US Constitution's bill of substantive guarantees was written down and ratified (1790–91 and 1866–68), a Rawlsian listener could hear those judges saying, concretization of a right of same-sex partners against exclusion from state-recognized marriage would have been wildly unfit for inclusion in a body of constitutional law designed for legitimation-support. Evolving social facts might at some later time open the way to such inclusion, through some modulation of public perceptions of marriage and concomitantly of the moral gist and scope of application of our Constitution's scripted essentials on liberty and equality. In such event, American state legislatures would then be expected, or even constitutionally obliged, to confirm this development by altering their laws on marriage in response to this altered understanding of the central ranges of some American constitutional essentials.

3.3. An Idea of Constitutional-Moral Progress?

The judges who so wrote did also take the position that it could *only* be electorally accountable legislatures, not politically insulated courts, on whom it would be incumbent to make the key finding of a shift in public understandings that would bring the same-sex marriage claim within those modulating central ranges. On that point, those judges faced a sharp dissent,[39] and in fact their view did not prevail when the matter later came again before the US Supreme Court. But that is not the debate that interests me here.

I want rather now to ask: On what basis might either a legislature or a court determine whether this or that shift in public opinion, supposing it appropriately confirmed, is to be given such a flashback constitutional effect? There

[38] DeBoer v. Snyder, 772 F.3d 388 (6th Cir., 2014) *reversed*, Obergfell v. Hodges, 576 U.S. 644 (2015).

[39] See *DeBoer* at 421 (Daughtrey, J., dissenting).

could be and have been any number of public-opinion shifts to which we would not dream of giving such effect. Of some, we might say that they register not as clarifications but as deviations from the American basic-liberties value system; of countless others, that they are simply beside the point. What is it about *this* public-opinion shift that makes it constitutionally pregnant? What makes it an occasion, as Rawls would say, for a development in constitutional law that "brings the constitution more in line with its original promise"?[40]

To the question thus framed, it seems only one answer can be found. We work here in the grip of an idea of a substantive moral foundation always already in place—or, to put the claim a bit more tendentiously, an idea of moral progress.[41] An idea, I mean, of an upward path of clarification of a founding American idea of basic liberty, the arc or telos of which is at least occasionally accessible to glimpse by at least some in our midst.[42] Dim, thin, or fleeting the glimpses may be, but not so dim or thin that they cannot occasionally secure a finding on a question such as whether extension of basic-liberty and equal-protection coverages to same-sex marriage is or is not a step along the true American path of libertarian ascent.

To be clear: I have said "progress," but I do not mean by that to impute to anyone an idea either of linearity or of uniformity of perception of the track of altered understandings over time. That track, in anyone's view of it, may show any number of false leads, reversals, and recalibrations of whence we have come and where we are headed. I say only that an idea of a justification-supportive constitution necessarily imports into the mind of any practitioner, at any given moment, a perception or an intuition of a "prior or more general moral or political theory that underlies" the constitution, or

[40] *PL* 238 (describing a limit on what can count as a proper constitutional amendment, as opposed to a breakdown or displacement of the extant constitution).

[41] See James E. Fleming, *Fidelity to Our Imperfect Constitution: For Moral Readings and Against Originalism* (Oxford University Press 2015) 80–81 (describing while commending a "philosophic" approach to judicial constitutional interpretation, in which judges progressively "strive for the true meaning or best account" of our "ends-dedicated scheme of . . . rights phrased more often than not as referring to general goods and principles"); ibid, 121 (describing a "common law" version of the process as one that "works the Constitution pure, striving for greater coherence, integrity, and perfection").

[42] Rawls wants to allow that the arc can become apparent over time. "The successful practice," he writes, "of [the American Constitution's] ideas and principles over two centuries place restrictions on what can now count as [a proper] amendment, whatever was true at the beginning." *PL* 239. "Successful" is the giveaway. It must carry an implication of nonnegotiable truth at the beginning—an "original promise" (or else Rawls, *per impossibile*, would have slipped here into equating justification-bearing constitutional law with law that is empirically "successful" in keeping the populace in line).

an "implicit moral or political logic" that inheres in it.[43] I do not say the logic must be either stable over time or identical across practitioners.

3.4. Fixture and Project; Court and People

If and insofar as we join with Rawls in holding to the idea of a constitution's service as a country's public procedural pact on justification of the force of the ordinary laws, political legitimacy in (say) the United States stands presently conditioned on fulfillment *now* of our constitution's guarantees respecting liberty and equality. If fulfillment now really does entail extension to cover a right of marriage equality, then a failure of the effective powers-that-be to comport themselves accordingly would be a failure to keep the pact, and hence a pro tanto damage to legitimacy.

So again we face a dilemma, this time between fixture and learning in our applications of the scripted, substantive essentials of a justification-bearing constitutional pact. That script—we have seen this over and over—has to carry meanings at any moment already fixed in the public space. Yet those meanings cannot be fully static and still bear the final weight of justification, if reasonable understandings of the point of constitutional guarantees undergo modulation in the sweep of time and change. It is by way of combined response, then, to not just one challenge but to two of them—the challenges from reasonable disagreement (extending even down to the level of underlying justice conceptions) and from temporality—that, as I now suggest, one might understand John Rawls to have endorsed the fine distinction I began this chapter by suggesting, between the constitutional fidelities required of judges and citizens, respectively, in a well-ordered constitutional democracy.

We would read Rawls to envisage an institutional division of labor between the supreme court and the people, in a dialectically structured project of justification-worthy constitutional maintenance over time. Rawls's reasonable citizens are heirs to a broad constitutional-democratic tradition. They have an acculturated general sense of when a law or policy begins to grate on a liberal democracy's scheme of constitutional guarantees. That

[43] Jack M. Balkin, "History, Rights, and the Moral Reading" (2016) 96 *Boston University Law Review* 1425, 1434–35 (describing sympathetically the conception of James Fleming).

sensibility sees and feels and responds to actions on large public questions, such as marriage equality or (say) the license of the police to crack open our cell phones. "The politically constructed bounds on which the Supreme Court issues its rulings" thus "change over time."[44] Rawls wants to have the people, chiming in with pressures and votes directed to such actions, to do so in consideration of *their* views of the most reasonable balances of the political values that *they* draw from the historical tradition of constitutional democracy.

Take the case of a citizen for whom, in all sincerity, the balance of such values weighs heavily against some term or terms in the constitution in force that up to now have been judicially held to preclude a law that she finds to have the support of a balance of applicable public reasons. (As examples to consider: in the United States of 1857, adjudicated constitutional preclusion of legislation by Congress to exclude slavery from territories of the United States outside the boundaries of any state of the United States;[45] or, in the present-day United States, adjudicated constitutional preclusion of legislation by states to require all public and private pregnancy-services providers to post accurate factual information regarding the availability of abortion-related services.[46]) In company with Abraham Lincoln, Rawls would not block that citizen from continued agitation in support of that law (and so of a reversal of position by the Supreme Court).[47]

The idea, I think, is that citizens pressing sundry views within a broad space allowed by the constitutional-democratic tradition can compose a constant force-in-waiting for provocation of updated adjustment of the scheme of constitutional guarantees in force in their country, so as always to be dragging it toward its fully justification-worthy state.[48] The people would not be that constant force-in-waiting if required to steer their deliberations formally and strictly (not to say woodenly) by past-established constitutional law and precedent. The judges, by comparison, are to stand somewhat more firmly by that stock because they are the system's visible anchor to windward,

[44] Richard H. Fallon, Jr., "Judicial Supremacy, Departmentalism, and the Rule of Law in a Populist Age" (2018) 86 *Texas Law Review* 487, 513.
[45] See Dred Scott v. Sandford, 60 U.S. (19 How.) (1857).
[46] See NIFLA v. Beccera, 585 U.S. __, 138 S. Ct. 2361 (2018).
[47] On Lincoln's view, see Chapter 11, § 3.2.1.
[48] See "PRR" 774–75; Silje Aambo Langvatn, "Legitimate But Unjust; Just, But Illegitimate: Rawls on Political Legitimacy" (2016) 42 *Philosophy and Social Criticism* 145–46.

its representation of the element of fixture that must necessarily inhere at all times in any procedural pact, in order that it be a pact at all. And still the judges working under agitation from citizens variously responding, from within a somewhat extended family of reasonable political conceptions, can sometimes see how the seed of a required new adjustment—one that citizens in pluralist conditions can (now) accept as at least reasonable, if not (all of them) as the most reasonable—is already planted in the previously settled material. A just constitution, as Rawls eventually would write, is never "fully realized. In Habermas's terms, it is a project to be carried out."[49]

In summation, then, of the findings of this chapter and its predecessors: The "constitution" at the fulcrum of the LPL of *PL* essentially includes, in addition to its scripted table of constitutional essentials, clauses and codicils on (1) adjustment of the respective scopes of the substantive essentials so as to maintain them in a coherent scheme,[50] (2) a space allowed for reasonable disagreements over applications of the essentials, (3) a trusted device of institutional settlement of the borders of that space of allowance,[51] and (as now we can add) (4) an ongoing dialectical process of progressive modulation of the scheme and its component central ranges, in which the people, disagreeing, have their part.[52]

In the sight of public reason, writes Rawls, the offices, respectively, of citizen and judge are "analogous,"[53] meaning not identical. "[A]s judges are to decide [cases] by legal grounds of precedent and recognized canons of statutory construction and other relevant grounds, so citizens are to reason by public reason and to be guided by the criterion of reciprocity, whenever constitutional essentials and matters of basic justice are at stake."[54] That is

[49] Rawls, "Reply" (n 32) 152. Rawls is here responding to a complaint from Jürgen Habermas that justice as fairness puts "the philosopher" into the people's rightful place, in a democracy, as constitutional author, see Habermas, "Reconciliation through Reason" 119–21, 128. Silje A. Langvatn presses the case that having in force a justification-supportive constitutional-procedural pact was not ever, in the view of Rawls, in itself a sufficient condition for a political regime's legitimacy. Additionally required by him was always, in her view, an element of authorship of that pact by the people subject to it. See Langvatn, "Legitimate But Unjust" 137.

[50] See Chapter 3, § 1.2.

[51] See Chapter 2, § 2.2; Chapter 3, § 1.4.

[52] My reading here can fit with Alessandro Ferrara's reading of Rawls to ascribe constituent power to a succession of generations running back to the foundations and forward into the future (as distinguished from the "living segment of the people"), see Alessandro Ferrara, Sovereignty Across Generations. Constituent Power and Political Liberalism (forthcoming 2023 from Oxford University Press). As organ for that trans-generational people, Rawls, on my reading, proposes an ongoing interlocution between a supreme court and the living segment of society.

[53] "Second Introduction" lv.

[54] Ibid.

how it can be the case that "the idea of public reason applies more strictly to judges," but that "the requirements of public justification for that reason are the same."[55]

4. A Common-Law Constitution?

In Chapter 2, canvassing what Rawls might have envisaged as the "unwritten" option in "constitution (written or unwritten)" in the *JAF* version of the LPL, we mentioned the possibility of a constitution that is vocally directive (not dumbly empirical), and furthermore is directive in the medium of law (not merely convention)—but of law not fully codified, a "common-law" constitution. We postponed until a later point any further consideration of that possibility. That point now has come.

Suppose a complete absence from a country's legal tradition of any sovereignly enacted text that is deemed to contain, or uniquely to represent, the constitution. What and all there is, in place of that, is an ever-accumulating body of judicial rulings, on matters of constitutional import, hinged by the judges to nothing but the prior accumulation as they find it rolling along, worked and reworked by generations of judges into more or less systematized bodies of precedent and doctrine. All of this would be prescriptive stuff, constitutional and legal. It would also be, in a certain well-worn sense, "unwritten."

We are now in a position to see how a case for assigning this sense of "unwritten" in Rawls's "constitution (written or unwritten)" might unfold in three steps. At a first step, we find that Rawls undoubtedly meant by "constitution" a directive code, not (merely) an impression of "what happens."[56] At the second, we find that the code must subsist in the institutionalized medium of law and not (merely) social-normative understanding.[57] At the third step, we see that a common-law conception of the legal constitution dovetails neatly with the fixture/project dialectic we have now found to be deeply sunk in Rawls's idealization of a constitutional democracy. Codified—in that sense "written"—as the Rawlsian constitution may be at some historically recollected moment of origin, it is also destined to come, over time, to look

55 "PRR" 768.
56 See Chapter 2, § 3.2.
57 See Chapter 2, § 2.2.

more like common law than code law—becoming, in that sense "unwritten." A codified constitutional text, if there is one, will not ever be disregarded, but its provisions will come increasingly, over time, to be treated, in the words of David Strauss, "more or less the same way as precedents in a common law system."[58]

[58] David Strauss, "The Supreme Court 2014 Term—Foreword: Does the Constitution Mean What It Says?" (1985) 129 *Harvard Law Review* 1, 4–5. Strauss thus describes what he finds to be the case with American constitutional law—justifiably so, Strauss further finds, as an accommodation of interests in "sovereignty," "adaptation," and "settlement." Ibid, 13, 53. My argument in this chapter would place Rawls and Strauss in accord.

Looked at from the other side, we have the case whose possibility Paul Craig asserts, of an "unwritten constitution" resembling a written one in its acceptance by all concerned as bounding "ordinary legislative power . . . by . . . structural and rights-based precepts that are enforced, inter alia, by courts." Paul Craig, "Written and Unwritten Constitutions: The Modality of Change" in Sam Bookman, Edward Willis, Hanna Wilberg, and Max Harris (eds.), *Pragmatism, Principle, and Power in Common Law Constitutional Systems: Essays in Honour of Bruce Harris* (forthcoming) https://papers.ssrn.com/sol3/papers.cfm?abstract_id=3897906 [2].).

6
A Realistic Utopia?

Our work so far has consisted in a close interrogation of John Rawls's proposition in *PL* for justification-by-constitution and its condensation there as "the liberal principle of legitimacy."[1] Having shown that proposition's motivation from pursuit of a liberal ideal of government by consent in challenging conditions—"the problem of political liberalism"[2]— we traced out from there a corresponding prescriptive model for a dualist democracy under a legally institutionalized body of framework law—a "constitution"—consisting partly of substantive guarantees.

Our implication of positive-legal constitutionalism from the LPL has issued, in this Part I of the book, in terms of a distinctly proceduralistic reading of Rawls's intentions. (That reading will undergo some reconsideration in Part II, but mainly will there be sustained.) Our exposition, in Chapters 3, 4, and 5, of a corresponding institutional conception has turned up along the way a number of causes for worry or doubt that still hang unresolved. It remains for us now to reprise these unresolved issues, with a view to mustering such response to them as the Rawlsian materials themselves can offer or suggest. To be clear: I take my business here to be an address to these issues on terms internal to a Rawlsian guidance for the project of liberal constitutional democracy. Defense of that project against external dangers and threats now abroad in our world lies largely beyond the scope of this work. Except, I should add, for a word at the end in response to suggestions that promotion of a distinctively tolerationist, "political liberal" version of the project has itself been a contributing cause to the dangers, and possibly in that respect has been misguided.[3]

The still pending internal issues, as I see them, come down to three in number. Two of them pivot on the political-liberal idea of reasonability in

[1] See Chapter 1, § 2.2.
[2] See Chapter 1, § 2.1.
[3] See Chapter 14. See also Frank I. Michelman, "Concluding Reflections: A Liberal Limit to Constitutional Thinness" in Alessandro Ferrara & Frank I. Michelman, *Legitimation by Constitution: A Dialogue on Political Liberalism* 170 (OUP 2021).

Constitutional Essentials. Frank I. Michelman, Oxford University Press. © Frank I. Michelman 2022.
DOI: 10.1093/oso/9780197655832.003.0007

politics. These are: (1) the Goldilocks challenge to present at any given moment a body of substantive constitutional law that is thick enough to sustain the weight of justification and yet reasonably and rationally acceptable to everyone reasonable;[4] and (2) an unresolved tension between acceptance of a plurality of differing reasonable liberal political conceptions and hopes for normal consensus on the "at-least reasonability" of contested applications of substantive constitutional essentials.[5] In addition to those concerns with the idea of political reasonability, we also have (3) an unresolved tension between justice and civility as the morally mandatory ultimate pursuit for the Rawlsian ideal citizen or judge engaged in constitutional-legal contention.[6] Responses in Rawlsian spirit to these issues all must take, as I will suggest, a common form: Where each can be stated in terms of a conceptual gap that cannot be closed, we can still seek the means in political practice to limit cases falling into such gaps or otherwise to smooth over or offset their potentially destabilizing effects on our politics and their moral quality.

1. Justification as Speculative Sociology

1.1. A State of Society

It is not as if Rawls proceeds in blindness to these challenges. His liberal principle of legitimacy envisages a society of free and equal citizens conducting their politics in mutually accredited submission to a publicly established framework law ("constitution"). What's required is that they all can find that framework law sufficiently complete ("thick") to give justificatory cover to deeply controverted laws and policies issuing from it, while still thin enough to be acceptable (for this purpose) to all or nearly all citizens in line with principles and ideals variously held by each. That is not a condition inconceivable of fulfillment in the world as we know it; we easily *conceive of* societies where it would obtain. If we hesitate to name one known to us today, that could be because the possibility of fulfillment hinges on supposition of a sociological milieu in which are combined a number of cognitive, motivational, and communicative elements (all perfectly conceivable) that are not found to hold in our societies as we find them today. The contemplation of possibility here will

[4] See Chapter 3, § 1.1.
[5] See Chapter 3, § 2.
[6] See Chapter 4, § 3.

have to be that of a "realistic utopia" (as Rawls would come to call it), which possibly can come about—or come close enough—"taking men as they are and laws as they might be."[7] Realistic, in that sense of achievable and maintainable by actual humankind under conducive institutions, the envisaged state of society believably must be, Rawls says, because only then could it be practically pursuable or arguably worth pursuit.[8] If the stipulation laid down by the LPL, for a sufficiently complete constitution, acceptable as such to all citizens as reasonable and rational, simply cannot be rendered as intelligible while also being credibly squared or fitted to other facts of society held to be practically fixed beyond possibility of repair, then the pursuit of that condition is not one that could be adopted by reasonable and rational citizens and the proposal contradicts itself on its face.[9]

Accordingly, our aim now will be to gather up all that the Rawlsian materials canvassed in chapters preceding have had to offer by way of explaining *how* Rawls thinks—about what is involved in his thinking—that (1) expectations classifiable as reasonable (2) of wide acceptability to citizens envisaged as reasonable (3) of some discrete and finite, justification-bearing set of constitutional essentials, can register as a realistic possibility in our world.

2. Elements

Rawls's thought in regard to possibility in this domain is, as I will now suggest, divisible into two steps. These are, first, a liberal-tinged ("political") conception of reasonability in politics, and then, second, an imputation to citizens in societies sufficiently liberal-tending of a moral motivation to civility in politics. Civility, I am by that division suggesting, is not already wholly contained in reasonability. It is not a matter of reason simply, but of passion as well. Reasonability alone does not carry the burden.[10]

[7] Compare John Rawls, *The Law of Peoples* (Harvard University Press 1999) 13 (following the lead of J.-J. Rousseau). In *PL* the same idea appears as "sufficient motivation of the appropriate kind acquired under just institutions." PL 142–43.

[8] See *PL* lx–lxii.

[9] See "Second Introduction" lx–lxii; John Rawls, "Justice as Fairness: Political Not Metaphysical" (1985) 14 *Philosophy and Public Affairs* 223, 231 ("Until we bring ourselves to conceive how this could happen, it can't happen.").

[10] For stimulation to setting up the case in this way, I owe much—as discussion later in this chapter can only partially disclose—to exchanges of ideas with Johan van der Walt. I have drawn some of that later discussion from Frank I. Michelman, "Civility to Graciousness: Van der Walt and Rawls" (2021) 23 *Ethics and Politics* 495 (commenting on Johan van der Walt, *The Concept of Liberal Democratic*

Let Rawlsian political reasonability be understood expansively (as will be our way) to encompass not only certain basic orientations toward the ends and corresponding forms of politics—"implicit," as Rawls writes, "in the public political culture of a democratic society"[11]—but a number of dispositional add-ons including (a) full appreciation by citizens of the fact and implications of burdens of judgment; (b) acceptance among them of the idea of the "at-least" reasonable," with a resulting liberal tolerance for political disagreement (within limits); (c) expectations of democratic openness to revision over time of applications of the constitutional essentials; and (d) acceptance and assumption of a constraint of public reason. Assuming all the corresponding dispositions to mutuality and toleration on the parts of citizens and officials, shortfalls realistically still must remain in the case for the possibility of full stability of the regime (as Rawls would say) "for the right reasons" (and not just as a modus vivendi).[12] As a bridge across the remaining gaps, I am going to suggest, Rawls offers his call to civility.

2.1. A Political Conception of the Reasonable

It is clear from the start that Rawls is not talking of a constitutional framework for which we are to expect spontaneous wholehearted endorsement from literally everyone in sight. Political reasonability is, for Rawls, already a distillation of "basic ideas implicit in the public political culture of a democratic society." Extracted as it claims to be from a historical-factual tradition, Rawlsian political reasonability is a substantive-morally preloaded idea. "[A] reasonable doctrine accepts a constitutional democratic regime and its companion idea of legitimate law."[13] Reasonability is, in that way, reasonability "for us."[14]

Law (Routledge 2020). See Johan van der Walt, "Liberal Democracy and the Event of Existence, Seen from a Not-So-Rickety Bridge Between Rawls and Merleau-Ponty. Reply to my Critics" (2021) 23 *Ethics and Politics* 521, 547–565.

[11] *PL* 43.

[12] Rawls draws a distinction between a sociological-factual stability anchored in a contingent convergence of calculations of self-interest, which he calls a "modus vivendi," and a society bound in convergence on a political-moral conception, which he calls "stability for the right reasons." See *PL* xlii–xliii, 143–48, and compare the Rawlsian condition of "publicity" for a well-ordered society, see Chapter 2, § 2.2.

[13] "PRR" 766.

[14] See *PL* 28 ("A conception of justice [that in reflective equilibrium articulates our more firm convictions of political justice] is the conception that, so far as we can now ascertain, is the one

Early in this book, I offered a starter version of the Rawlsian political conception of the reasonable.[15] Intervening chapters allow us now to expand and thicken that version with a mix of basic ideas "implicit" (to repeat the Rawlsian formula) "in the public political culture of a democratic society."[16]

As a first and most basic idea: liberal normative individualism.

In the tradition to which Rawls is appealing, the ultimate concern of political morality is respect and regard for each individual as a "self-authenticating source of valid claims."[17]

Let us pause there for a moment. That is an idea that I have in the past named as liberal individualism.[18] Now, Rawls has called it a mistake to speak of political liberalism as an "individualist" political conception, giving as his reason that this conception aims at "the protection of the various interests in liberty both associational and individual."[19] It becomes clear, though, that political liberalism's commitment to associational liberty counts *ultimately*—as in any liberalism—for the sake of the individuals for whom associations and relationships are indispensably supportive, even constitutive, of the self and its capacity for self-authentication. While no doubt the Rawlsian basic liberties encompass communicative and associational freedoms, it is *to each person* (not party, lineage, class, sect, chat room, or "view") that Rawls's first principle of justice as fairness assigns the equal right to a fully adequate scheme of liberties, including those.[20]

most reasonable for us."). See also John Rawls, "Kantian Constructivism in Moral Theory" (1980) 77 *Journal of Philosophy* 515, 519.

15 See Chapter 1, § 2.4. See also "PRR" 800–02.

16 *PL* 43.

17 *PL* 32.

18 See Frank I. Michelman, *Brennan and Democracy* (Princeton: Princeton University Press 1999) 366–67. I there put the thought at greater length as follows (leaving the pronouns as I wrote them then):

> An individualist in politics is . . . someone whose thought about politics is constantly alert to the dimensions of singularity and severalty in human existence and experience. He is someone who sees his social world as populated by persons regardful of themselves and others as singular beings, each having a mind and life of his or her own along with some ability, at least in a congenial social environment, to take some substantial charge of his or her own mind and life—to make and pursue (within limits) his or her own judgments about what to do, what to strive for, what is good, and what is right. Of course, the mere thought of a human *capacity* for self-direction of this kind cannot motivate any particular line of programmatic thought about politics. . . . What's required [for that] is the thought of a major human *interest* in the *exercise* of that capacity.

That accords pretty well, I think, with the Rawlsian political conception of the person. See Frank I. Michelman, "Review: The Subject of Liberalism" (1994) 46 *Stanford Law Review* 1807.

19 "PRR" 795.

20 See *PL* 291. It is, however, a mistake to call liberalism (as some have) an "atomistic" conception. We surely, for example, can and should affirm wholeheartedly that associations as such can have

The next three political-liberal basic ideas all descend from that first one.

As a second basic idea: political justification.

For any political formation endowed with coercive legislative and allied governmental powers, among a population of citizens free, equal, and divided by a plurality of comprehensive views, a question always impends of the justification by majorities to minorities of contested exertions of political power. From this precept of political reasonability comes, as explained in Chapter 1, the constitution-centered liberal principle of legitimacy.

As a third basic idea: deflection to framework.

Justification then takes the proceduralistic form of appeal to a "constitution," a framework law in a two-level legal system. This sort of deflection—of justificatory explanation from the ground level of policy choice to a more abstracted framework level—is our necessary recourse in response to the problem of democratic political justification, among free and equal citizens, in conditions of pluralism.

To put the point another way: When democratic citizens present to one another their justifications for support of controversial ground-level laws and policies, they state them necessarily (implicitly when not explicitly) in the proceduralistic form: *This action or policy has gained the duly expressed support of a current democratic majority, expressed through forms that some at-least reasonable constitution for a constitutional democracy at our time and place might prescribe, and falls within bounds of what some such constitution would anticipate or permit.*

As a fourth basic idea: extenuation of authorship of the laws by their addressees.

Required for a constituency of citizens free and equal is a lawmaking framework by which those who will be subject to force of the ground-level laws can sufficiently count themselves as authors of those laws.[21] Your and my sufficient links of authorship of the ground-level laws can be given by our convergence, actual or reasonably ascribable, on a constitutional-framework pact that constrains and directs the aims and outcomes of subordinate legislation, not anywhere nearly in full detail but still substantially enough so

interests and needs worth protecting, even at cost to some interests and concerns of some individual members. That is entirely consistent with liberal normative individualism, which "is neither a view about what gives value to the lives of individuals nor a view about the existential reality of groups. It is only the view that the lives of individuals are the ultimate moral concern for political arrangements." Michelman, *Brennan and Democracy* 67.

[21] See Chapter 3, § 3.

as (along with whatever further participation by us in daily politics our constitution may provide) to render us thereby sufficiently responsible for that legislation.[22]

Granting all the question-begging they contain, those four basic ideas in combination (the succeeding three all depending from the first) could fairly be said to take in a liberal-leaning fraction of the political opinion of humankind. Yes, true, that way of placing the ideas ideologically seems to leave them wanting as premises for a (liberal!) principle of legitimacy, in societies where not everyone shares a liberal outlook or its firm attachment to the first and generative basic idea ("individualism"). That is an issue to be taken up later in this chapter.

For now, though, our concern is with a different kind of possible deficiency. A combination of those four quite broad ideas extractable from the constitutional-democratic tradition (political reasonability "for us") does not yet suffice to generate, even among a company restricted to those holding them, a unique and finite scheme of constitutional essentials with well-defined central ranges. Attribution of those ideas to an existent such company of the reasonable does not yet suffice to explain (repeating my aforementioned formula) how (1) expectations classifiable as reasonable (2) of acceptability to citizens envisaged as reasonable (3) *of some discrete and finite, justification-bearing set of constitutional essentials* can register as a realistic possibility in our world. Such explanation, if available, will require some further thickening of the concept of the politically reasonable.

2.2. Burdens of Judgment (Including Raw Pluralism)

In the view of the Rawls of *PL* and succeeding works, restriction of the company of the politically reasonable to adherents to those four basic ideas of constitutional democracy does not yet support an expectation of a convergence of the reasonable on any *one discrete* scheme of justification-bearing constitutional essentials, as envisaged by the LPL. By the understanding of Rawls, there will still, within the circle of the politically reasonable, remain conflicts over the articulation, naming, and conception of central ranges of

[22] Agreement on "constitutional essentials and matters of basic justice" can suffice, Rawls suggests, for democratic political justification. "As long as there is rough agreement [there], fair social cooperation among citizens can, we hope, be maintained." *JAF* 41.

the component items in a scheme of essentials for a justificatory load-bearing constitution.[23]

That will be owing, in part, to the inconvenient social fact Rawls tables under the head of "burdens of judgment." As explained by Rawls (repeating, here, from Chapter 3), the burdens include (a) difficulties in assessing evidence, (b) disagreement over weights to be assigned to competing considerations, (c) ambiguities in political and moral concepts, (d) conflicts arising from different life experiences and perspectives, (e) incommensurability of relevant competing considerations, and (f) the difficulty of accommodating all recognized goods in a single political system.[24] Among these burdens, whether as a separate item or an overall aggravating factor, we can further include a raw social fact of a pluralism, in any modern free society, of comprehensive views.[25]

To begin to meet the sting from the social fact of the burdens of judgment, political reasonability must itself be understood to include an appreciation of that fact, as composing a part of the challenge posed by the moral and practical need, faced by all, for a fair and effective scheme of social cooperation (including the force of law) among citizens free and equal. "The reasonable" includes, as a "basic aspect," Rawls says, a willingness "to recognize the burdens of judgment and to accept their consequences for the use of public reason in directing the legitimate exercise of public power in a constitutional regime."[26] Reasonable persons, writes Rawls—those who stand ready to abide by fair terms of social cooperation between equals when others also do—

> recognize and accept the consequences of the burdens of judgment, which leads to the idea of reasonable toleration in a democratic society. . . . They know that in political life unanimity can rarely if ever be expected, so a reasonable democratic constitution must include majority or other plurality voting procedures in order to reach decisions.[27]

[23] See Chapter 3, § 2; Chapter 5, § 2.2.
[24] See *PL* 54–58.
[25] I am not here contradicting Rawls's own use of "burdens of judgment" (see *PL* 55) to designate causes of disagreement over the constitutional essentials even among those holding reasonable comprehensive views. Among the causes of disagreement across the general population will still be conflicts among the comprehensive views held by them, reasonable or not as the case may be.
[26] Ibid 54.
[27] "PRR" 805.

2.3. Liberal Political Toleration: The Idea of the At-Least Reasonable

And that, then, will open, in the judgments of the reasonable respecting a given constitution's moral supportability, the space for a finding of "at-least" reasonable ("close enough," as one might say)—that space being *not* preempted by what you or I judge "the most" reasonable constitution for us. Importantly, the idea here is not that you and I yield on our respective judgments of right and wrong, correct and mistaken, choices for the substantive-directive content for our country's constitution. It is rather that, retaining those judgments, we nevertheless find it right to join with expectations of compliance with the constitution in force (and so with its compliant, subordinate laws), which we judge to be (within limits) substantively faulty. Find it, I emphasize, not just expedient but *right* to do this—such insistence would be crucial for Rawls—given the place supposedly occupied, in your and my schemes of political-moral values, by values of social cooperation on fair terms among free and equal citizens, or what Rawls calls "the very great values of the political [which] are not easily overridden."[28] An appreciation of those values and their special weight is, from the start, included as a component of political reasonability. As Rawls has otherwise somewhat drily expressed the point: "I assume . . . that a reasonable comprehensive doctrine accepts some form of the political argument for toleration."[29]

2.4. The Idea of Democratic Openness

But it is not just that "*given*" of an appreciation of the very great values of the political that allows reasonable citizens to judge it right to support a short-of-most-reasonable constitution in force. Additionally serving to that end, in the Rawlsian view as I develop it here, is the openness of the constitution, through the democratic politics it prescribes, to ongoing processes of revision and correction, to which you and I as citizens have at all times full and equal access with others.[30]

[28] See *PL* 168–69, 218.
[29] "PRR" 804.
[30] See Chapter 5, § 3.4.

2.5. The Idea of a Constraint of Public Reason

Our realistic utopia thus envisages citizens whose political motivations imbibe from values both of the pursuit of social cooperation on fair terms among citizens free and equal and of democratic openness. Such citizens should further see why any judgment on which they act politically, exercising their shares of democratic, coercive political power pro or con a contested constitutional essential or application thereof, ought to be such as can be explained to disagreeing fellow citizens as supported by a balance of considerations which (the considerations) those others can accept as truly valid and applicable to the case. Acceptance for themselves of such a constraint of public reason, together with expectation of reciprocation from fellow citizens, thus becomes in its turn a component of political reasonability.

In summation, now, of everything we have before us up to here: We can understand Rawls to propose the following:

> **GIVEN** the exceptional moral weight (*the very great values of the political, not easily overridden*) of the quest for fair terms of political cooperation among free and equal citizens in conditions of reasonable pluralism (*the problem of political liberalism*)–
>
> **IF** there is now publicly in place a constitution that sufficiently corresponds to conceptions of justice that reasonable and rational citizens variously affirm, so as (the constitution) to be acceptable to them as *at-least* reasonable–
>
> **THEN** what is *most* reasonable for all of them is to accept *pro tempore* that constitution, even though it is not, in the view of all of them (or perhaps of any), the most reasonable constitution that could be devised for the country here and now.

Contained then also, as a part of the political-liberal ideal of democratic citizenship and its political conception of the reasonable, is a double-sided moral "duty," as Rawls calls it, of "civility": On the one side goes a restriction of one's political exertions affecting fundamental questions to those reasonably defensible before others in terms of political values only,[31] with on the other side "a willingness to listen to others and a fairmindedness in deciding when accommodation to their views should reasonably be made."[32] It is to

[31] See Chapter 1, § 1.1; Chapter 5, § 1.2.
[32] *PL* 216–17.

that second aspect of civility, the aspect of willingness to accommodate to political-moral error (as one honestly sees it), that our focus now will turn.

3. Remainders

Given the liberal-leaning slant of the political conception of the reasonable ("implicit in the culture of a democratic society"), there can be no prospect for a corresponding body of substantive constitutional law winning free acceptance from sections in our populations who are not in that way liberally disposed. Of course Rawls knows this. While he hopes and expects that the number of the unwillingly subjected and the severity of their subjection might be held down by an emergence over time of a widespread convergence, across subsisting comprehensive views, on a liberally acceptable set of constitutional essentials, he does not suggest that could ever bring to zero the number of the illiberal unreconciled. That fact cannot, however, obliterate, for the liberal-minded, the very great values of the political. It rather leaves us with "the importance of attempting to realize that ideal to the fullest extent possible"[33]—applying, as Rawls says, to the liberal "philosophy itself" its own principle of toleration.[34]

It obviously would help here a lot, if a spirit of willingness to accommodate could be said to flow from an idea of reason in politics by which the illiberally disposed in our midst find themselves feeling bound. What license have *we*, though, to suppose that is the case with others, or to respond to them as if it is? It seems there are always going to be an excluded remainder with whom any short-to-intermediate-term liberal peace—in Alessandro Ferrara's terms, "the best response to the tenuousness of consensus and ubiquity of dissent that political liberalism can offer"[35]—will have to be as modus vivendi, not "for the right reasons."[36] It seems no force of reason in itself or as such can answer, fully and finally, to this problem of political liberalism.

In more radical form, the question would be whether such a force can even take us very far along the way, without a boost from the start from impulses of toleration, civility, and reciprocity that work from outside, not inside, the

[33] "PRR" 806.

[34] See *PL* 9–10.

[35] See Alessandro Ferrara, *The Democratic Horizon: Hyperpluralism and the Renewal of Political Liberalism* (Cambridge University Press 2014) 108.

[36] See my exchange on this point with Ferrara. Frank I. Michelman, "A Constitutional Horizon?" (2016) 47 *Philosophy and Social Criticism* 641, 647–48.

force-field of reason and reasonability. John Rawls himself, it has been said, is "profoundly aware of the irreducible precariousness and fragility of any liberal-leaning consensus."[37] So writes Johan van der Walt, having in view, as we may suppose, Rawls's allowance of a "family" of all-of-them-reasonable but all-of-them-differing liberal political conceptions.[38] If you turn that thought around, then in the resort of Rawls to a "duty" of civility as part of liberal reasonability lies a recognition by Rawls that "the transformation of a *modus vivendi* into an overlapping consensus is never complete."[39] What we had just previously been treating as a nagging, residual problem of an outlying excluded few expands, on this reading, to a constant and general condition of liberal life. It is not, then, just an outlying few for whom we need to offer some reason beyond reason for complicity with a morally dubious regime. It is ourselves as liberal, all of us, all of the time.

The Rawlsian so-called duty of civility becomes, on this reading, his attribution, in any possible liberal society living up to liberal aspiration, of a widespread spirit of willingness to bear. To bear, that is, a liability to just that amount and degree of concession to injustice that must necessarily, at a minimum, result under any possible legal order designed for the maintenance of social cooperation. This willingness to bear goes beyond a reasonable person's acceptance of a space for reasonable disagreement; it operates in a gap of concession that this reasonability does not cover; it registers in a different key. It works by compounding your and my deductions of reason, in allowing for that space, with an additional motivational force for us of the very fact of our fellow citizens, having taken, by democratic processes, the measures they have. Impersonal reasonability slides to interpersonal civic fellowship. From the cerebral detachment of reasonability we pass to the committed act of "sacrifice,"[40] or, better (more recently says van der Walt), of "gift,"[41] or "graciousness."[42] Or try on, for a more acidulous take, that of Henry David Thoreau:

[37] Johan van der Walt, "The Gift of Time and the Hour of Sacrifice: A Philosophical-Anthropological Analysis of the Deep Difference between Political Liberal and Populist Politics" in Brian W. Nail and Jeffrey A. Ellsworth (eds.), *Law's Sacrifice: Approaching the Problem of Sacrifice in Law, Literature, and Philosophy* (Routledge 2019) 142 (hereafter Van der Walt, "Gift of Time").

[38] See Chapter 3, § 2.

[39] Van de Walt, "Gift of Time" (n 37) 142.

[40] See Johan van der Walt, *Law and Sacrifice: A Post Apartheid Theory of Law* (Birkbeck Law Press 2006); Johan van der Walt and Henk Botha, "Democracy and Rights in South Africa: Beyond a Culture of Justification" (2000) 7 *Constellations* 341, 352–53.

[41] See Van der Walt, "Gift of Time" (n 37) 115 (preferring gift to sacrifice as a hallmark of idealized liberal politics).

[42] See ibid, 142.

> Man recognizes laws little enforced, and he condescends to obey them. In the moment when he feels his superiority to them as compulsatory, he, as it were, courteously reënacts them but to obey them.[43]

Call it sacrifice, gift, graciousness: this motivation to collaboration in injustice-as-I-now-see-it must stand as a requisite final component in the Rawlsian realistic-utopian conception of political reasonability in a sufficiently liberal-tending political *milieu*. That Rawls himself so understood may possibly be signaled by a later-arriving change in formulation of the LPL to which we now turn our attention.

[43] Thus mused Thoreau, two years or so after publishing "Civil Disobedience." Henry David Thoreau, *The Journal 1837–1861*, ed. Damion Searls (New York Review of Books 2009) 91 (journal entry for Nov. 1, 1851).

Van der Walt traces the thought's inspiration to Saint Paul, not Thoreau. See Johan van der Walt, *The Concept of Liberal Democratic Law* (Routledge 2020) 236).

PART II

"THE CRITERION OF RECIPROCITY"

When *PL* appeared in paperback form in 1996, it came with its main original text from 1993 intact. Rawls did, however, see fit to include two new sections in the book. Following after the original "Introduction" of 1993, itself retained for the 1996 edition, now came a further "Introduction to the Paperback Edition" (the "Second Introduction," we have taken to calling it in this book). And following after the eight "Lectures" (chapters) of 1993 now came a ninth Lecture, reprinting Rawls's "Reply to Habermas" from a recently published exchange between the two philosophers.[1] The added materials offer clarifications or adjustments to some main ideas of the philosophy of political liberalism, as up to then presented by Rawls (and treated by us in Part I of this book).

Are the added materials, or some parts of them, perhaps better classed as new departures? They occur along three fronts. Two of these—allowances for intra-liberal conflicts among members of a plural family of all-of-them-reasonable liberal conceptions of justice, and for shifts over time in the topography of all-in-the-family debates over constitutional essentials—we have so far, in Chapters 3, 4, and 5, seen fit to treat as modifications, not displacements, of positions previously taken. I raise now a question about whether we should or can likewise treat the third: a seemingly new-minted proposition to hinge justification of our exercises of coercive political power to a combination of (1) a fact about our holding or not holding certain beliefs at the time, and (2) a belief we hold about the public reasonability of those

[1] See Jürgen Habermas, "Reconciliation through the Public Use of Reason" (1995) 92 *Journal of Philosophy* 109; John Rawls, "Reply to Habermas" (1995) 92 *Journal of Philosophy* 132.

beliefs. Comparing that with the LPL as previously set forth in the pages of *PL*, Rawls may seem to be replacing his former proposed justification condition with another of a different ilk: in place of a condition of publicly refereed compliance with a positive-legal constitution in force, a condition of action motivationally in line with an ethic of reciprocity.

The matter, however, is not so simple.

7

Legitimacy: Procedural Compliance or Ethical Attitude?

1. "The Idea of Legitimacy Based on the Criterion of Reciprocity"

Rawls's 1996 Second Introduction revisits the question of legitimacy—the same question as before, of the conditions on which exertions of democratic political power are justifiable among free and equal disagreeing fellow citizens.[1] The response comes this time, though, in terms ostensibly differing from those of the LPL of 1993—which still, however, is retained unchanged in the main text of the edition of 1996. The prior LPL (to recall it here) reads:

> Our exercise of political power is proper and hence justifiable only when *it is in accordance with a constitution* the essentials of which all citizens may reasonably be expected to endorse in the light of principles and ideals acceptable to them as reasonable and rational. This is the liberal principle of legitimacy.[2]

As offered in the Second Introduction, the new proposition reads:

> Our exercise of political power is proper only when *we sincerely believe that the reasons we offer for our political actions may reasonably be accepted* by other citizens as a justification of those actions. This criterion applies on two levels: one is to the constitutional structure itself, the other is to particular statutes and laws enacted in accordance with that structure. Political conceptions to be reasonable must justify only constitutions that satisfy this principle. This gives what may be called the liberal principle of legitimacy

[1] See Chapter 1, § 2.1.
[2] *PL* 137 (emphasis supplied).

Constitutional Essentials. Frank I. Michelman, Oxford University Press. © Frank I. Michelman 2022.
DOI: 10.1093/oso/9780197655832.003.0008

> [here citing to the unaltered LPL from the main text of *PL*] as it applies to constitutions and statutes enacted under them.[3]

A short time later, in a signal work of 1997, Rawls provided again a statement of what he there named as "the idea of political legitimacy based on the criterion of reciprocity."[4] We shall hereinafter sometimes call it, for short, Rawls's "ILBR" (for Idea of Legitimacy Based on Reciprocity). Here it is in its 1997 form:

> [T]he idea of political legitimacy based on the criterion of reciprocity says: Our exercise of political power is proper only when we sincerely believe that the reasons we would offer for our political actions—were we to state them as government officials—are sufficient, and we also reasonably think that other citizens might also reasonably accept those reasons. This criterion applies on two levels: one is to the constitutional structure itself, the other is to particular statutes and laws enacted in accordance with that structure. Political conceptions to be reasonable must justify only constitutions that satisfy this principle.[5]

Now, Rawls previously had posited, as part of his account of public reason, that citizens should "be able to explain their vote to one another in terms of a reasonable balance of public values"[6]—where "public" (or "political") values are values that all citizens conscientiously can accept as bearing properly on decisions of public policy.[7] The ILBR thus seemingly has taken what previously had appeared as an "ideal" of public reason for conscientious citizens to follow—explicitly *not* an obligation of law[8]—and made it into a requisite condition for political justification and legitimacy. We can make good sense of this, in line with our previous work, but only—as I now proceed to explain—by treating with due circumspection Rawls's first-person plural "Our" near the start of the ILBR.

[3] "Second Introduction" xliv (emphasis supplied).
[4] "PRR" 771.
[5] Ibid.
[6] Ibid, 241–43. "[T]he balance of political values a citizen holds must be reasonable and one that can be seen to be reasonable by other citizens. . . ." Ibid.
[7] See Chapter 1, § 1.1.
[8] See *PL* 253.

2. Objective Constitutionality Displaced?

Return with me to Chapter 1, section 2.3. There, I read the LPL of *PL* to cover both a "collective" and a "distributive" burden of political justification—a burden on the citizen body respecting governmental policies and acts, and another on you and me respecting our para-governmental stances and activities. Both burdens were to be met by claims of the compatibility of a questioned act, policy, or stance with a justification-worthy constitution-in-force. From that premise flowed all the implications in regard to positive legality, institutional settlement, differential constitutional fidelities of judges and citizens, and so on, that we developed and worked through in Part I. As also noted there, the constitution-in-force thus would serve as the society's manifest of fulfillment of the Rawlsian condition of publicity for a well-ordered society: that of standing under effective regulation by principles that "citizens accept and know that others likewise accept," and "this knowledge in turn is publicly recognized."[9] In a society adhering to the LPL of *PL*, publicity materializes in the social practice of political-justificatory appeal to the essentials of a publicly legible constitution in force.

A first textual comparison of the ILBR of 1996–97 with the LPL of 1993 might seem to show subjective reciprocity ("sincere belief," "reasonably think") displacing certifiable constitutional compliance ("in accordance with a constitution") as the crux of political justification. Say, the political act in question is support for a deeply controversial statutory enactment. *Per* the LPL of *PL* as expounded in Part I, the justificatory load would rest on an institutionally decidable claim of the reasonably sustainable compatibility of the statute with the terms of a certain constitution-in-force. Does the load now, *per* the ILBR, shift to your and my respective states of mind, our respective sincere beliefs in the statute's having sufficient support from reasons other citizens should reasonably accept as applicable to the case?

It seems that cannot be a correct reading of the ILBR. The reason lies in what I wrote in section 2.3 of Chapter 1. Here comes a newly conceived and contested political act or policy. You hold in all sincerity your reasons for support of it, and for belief in the reasonable sufficiency of those reasons for reasonable others. I hold in all sincerity mine. Each of us responsibly checks over our reasons. Yours and mine might or might not be exactly expressible in the same words. In no case, however, are they *the same* reasons; yours are

[9] *PL* 66.

yours, mine are *mine*. Nothing has occurred to meet the call on the citizen body to justify the coercion exerted by *its* ("*our*") statute. Nor has anything yet occurred to reconfirm, in the face of this new controversy, a public recognition of the society's effective regulation by principles that citizens accept and know that others accept, so as to meet the Rawlsian call to publicity.

With these concerns planted firmly in mind, and noting that the LPL and Lecture VI of *PL* remain in place without disturbance in the edition of 1996, we read the Second Introduction's reciprocity criterion not as a replacement for the constitutionality criterion of the LPL but rather as a supplement to it. Compliance with a justification-worthy constitution-in-force remains, as before (*per* the LPL), *the citizen body's* indispensable term of justification to dissenting citizens for its government's controversial policies and statutes. The ILBR's concern is with *your and my* justification to fellow citizens for our para-governmental stances and activities. Rawls thereby makes explicit a requirement for our respective sincere beliefs in a supported policy's or statute's wide compatibility with the constitution-in-force,[10] and then in that constitution's justification-worthiness as thus applied. Meanwhile, the collective justificatory obligation of the citizen body remains, and is fulfilled by (and only by) publicly certifiable constitutional compliance.

3. Reciprocity on the "Constitution" Level

We have seen that a body of constitutional-framework law currently in force (meeting the condition laid down by the LPL of acceptability as such to reasonable and rational citizens) marks out values to count as applicable public values for assessments of ground-level, day-to-day legislative policies.[11] From there, it follows easily that the ILBR's criterion of reciprocity demands of you and me, for justification of our para-political acts and stances, our sincere beliefs in the current constitutional compatibility of particular policies we thereby support and in the justification-worthiness of that standing constitutional law—its acceptability to fellow citizens in the light of principles and ideals reasonably held by them.[12] (And if—as already suggested by Chapter 5 and as further to be spelled out in Chapter 8—it is not always

[10] For convenience, I will use expressions such as "wide compatibility" and "widely compliant" as shorthand for compatibility under tolerant assessment. See Chapter 3, §§ 2 and 3, Chapter 11, § 3.3.
[11] See Chapter 1, § 1.2.
[12] See Chapter 1, § 2.2; compare Chapter 1, § 1.1.

easy to say where assertion of a favored policy's compatibility with currently standing constitutional law shades off into a call for change in that law, of course the reciprocity criterion applies in that case, too.)

4. On the Particular Statute Level, a Totalization of Public Reason?

We thus begin to explain how the criterion of reciprocity applies, as per the ILBR, on the levels both of "the constitutional structure" and of "particular statutes enacted" under it. By the same token, we see how this double-barreled application of reciprocity can be said—again as per the ILBR in its Second Introduction version—to "give" the liberal principle of legitimacy (from the main text of *PL*) "as it applies to constitutions and statutes enacted under them." But our expository work here is not yet nearly done.

Application of the criterion of reciprocity "on the level" of particular statutes no doubt does demand from each of us our sincere belief in the current constitutional compatibility of any statute whose enactment we support, and in the justification-worthiness of the constitution as thus applied. However, the apparent demand does not end there. Straightforwardly read, the demand is also for our sincere belief in the supportability of *the particular statute* by a balance of public reasons that all reasonable citizens could accept. That seems okay, until we notice that the effect of that would be to extend the call of the ideal of public reason—the call to limit one's political agitations to those one can defend by a balance of public or political reasons, not special to some comprehensive view—beyond agitations affecting "fundamental" matters ("the constitutional essentials and matters of basic justice"[13]) to take in all potentially coercive political stances.

That would not be a negligible extension. One might think to ask: If already required for justification, by the original LPL, is the law's compliance with a constitution that all citizens may reasonably be expected to find at-least reasonable in the light of principles they hold as reasonable and rational, isn't that all we need in order for the public-reason ideal to govern all political agitations? And the answer most decidedly is no, that does not follow. Remember, the "framework" or "background" status of constitutional law is

[13] *PL* 252–53.

designed ("not too thick") to leave wide spaces open for daily rule by democratic majorities.[14] Acceptance of the framework as reciprocity-satisfying *qua framework* thus leaves uncovered the reasons and motivations of citizens supporting or opposing particular concrete laws falling into the policy space the framework is meant to leave open.

We must try if at all possible *not* to read Rawls's introduction of the ILBR to close off that space to free democratic contention. He can't have meant to do so, unless he intended a flat-out repudiation of the proposition—the one we have worked at unfolding in Part I of this book—for justification *by constitution*. By that view as expounded there, an underlying political conception of justice, from which the essentials of a justification-bearing constitution are distilled, does not try and is not meant "to settle all legislative questions." That "is not desirable," Rawls maintained, there being "many questions legislatures must consider that can only be settled by voting that is properly influenced by nonpolitical values." Nor is it necessary for democratic political justification, for which reasonable agreement "on constitutional essentials and matters of basic justice" can suffice: "As long as there is rough agreement [there], fair social cooperation among citizens can, we hope, be maintained."[15]

That prior allowance, for influence by nonpolitical values of votes in the infra-framework policy space, will have seemed to many an attractive—for some, a crucially redemptive—feature of Rawls's view: a due and necessary embrace of democracy's liberatory side, its agonistic side, its receptiveness both to visionary insurgency and to the value for persons of fighting politically for what they deeply believe is right. To read Rawls now, by the ILBR, to revoke that allowance, subjecting democratic politics all the way through to curbing and trimming by public reason—in that way leveling "the crucial difference between the rules for political decisions and the decisions themselves"—will seem to many a not altogether attractive prospect.[16]

[14] See Chapter 3, § 1.1.

[15] *JAF* 41 (*Justice as Fairness*, remember, was published in 2001 but was substantially completed ten years or so before that. See Chapter 2, note 5.).

[16] The quotation comes from Paul Craig, remarking on complaints of "over-constitutionalization" in the treaties of the European Union. Paul Craig, "Written and Unwritten Constitutions: The Modality of Change" in Sam Bookman, Edward Willis, Hanna Wilberg, and Max Harris (eds.), *Pragmatism, Principle, and Power in Common Law Constitutional Systems: Essays in Honour of Bruce Harris* (Intersentia Ltd. forthcoming 2022). https://papers.ssrn.com/sol3/papers.cfm?abstract_id=3897906 [8].

Insofar as it is not, our question becomes one of how to read the ILBR in a way to evade it. We now take up for consideration some answers that may occur to you.

4.1. Reciprocity as Aspirational

Here again is the ILBR:

> [T]he idea of political legitimacy based on the criterion of reciprocity says: Our exercise of political power is proper only when we sincerely believe that the reasons we would offer for our political actions—were we to state them as government officials—are sufficient, and we also reasonably think that other citizens might also reasonably accept those reasons. This criterion applies on two levels: one is to the constitutional structure itself, the other is to particular statutes and laws enacted in accordance with that structure.[17]

Just as Rawls had taken care to say that public reason stands, for citizens at large, as an aspirational ideal of good citizenship and not as a civically binding obligation,[18] might he not mean the same (and on like grounds) for the public-reason ideal's close-companion criterion of reciprocity? That would leave room for voting sometimes on the basis of nonpolitical values (just as Rawls had previously said), by citizens who do in fact also rank reciprocity high (but not absolutely in all cases controlling) in their orders of civic aspiration.

That cannot succeed as a reading *of the ILBR*. The ILBR is offered as a criterion *of legitimacy*. As applied to citizens distributively, it says to you and to me, in no uncertain terms, that our exercises of our shares of democratic political power are illegitimate—unjustified, oppressive to disagreeing fellow citizens, wrong as to them[19]—absent certain accompanying sincere and reasonable beliefs on our part, and that this applies no less to our actions respecting ground-level laws and policies than to those respecting fundamental or framework matters. Reciprocity in politics, we must conclude, is no less civically obligatory for democratic citizens than is justification itself or the avoidance of oppression.

17 "PRR" 771.

18 See Chapter 5, § 2.4.

19 See Chapter 1, § 2.1.

4.2. "The Proviso"

Following some initial uncertainty on this point, Rawls came to specify, in his later accounts of the ideal of public reason, that nonpolitical values, drawn from comprehensive doctrines, could and indeed should properly figure in the genesis and explanation of a good and stably integrated citizen's political stances—"provided," Rawls said, that "in due course, we give properly public reasons to support the principles and policies our comprehensive doctrine is said to support."[20] That "proviso," as Rawls called it, would quite plausibly attach itself as well to the ILBR's reciprocity criterion for exercises of our shares of political power: Let our generative values be sourced where they are, as long as, once we have them in hand along with the political stances they have helped to generate, we are able honestly to see ourselves acting in line with reciprocity. My eventual sincere reliance on a reasonable balance of public reasons to support the political act in question might not be finally persuasive to the opposition. It would, however, satisfy reciprocity while still squaring with the prior work's allowance for votes on infra-framework laws that are "properly influenced" by nonpolitical values.

4.3. Borderline Uncertainty

The prior work drew its line on the reach of the public-reason ideal at "fundamental" or "framework" matters—"matters of basic justice" and "constitutional essentials"—thus exempting votes on other "legislative questions."[21] Actions regarding the former ideally are bound to balances of political values only, while those regarding only the latter are not. The location of that line of separation is not, however, always clear or fixed.[22] Where there is room for doubt and the question is divisive, "citizens have a duty of civility to try to articulate their claims on one another by reference to political values, if that is possible."[23] Thus Rawls in the prior work had already said, in effect, that the duty of civility—the constraint of public reason, the call to reciprocity—could crop up for you or for me *at any time* in the conduct of democratic politics, on any pending question, contingent on persuasion among the parties

[20] "PRR" 776; see ibid, 783–86.

[21] See *JAF* 41.

[22] "It is not always clear whether a question involves a constitutional essential. . . ." Ibid, 41 n 1.

[23] Ibid, 41.

of the reach of that question to fundamental concerns. But if the reciprocity criterion thus *could* apply to any matter coming up for legislation, and if citizens ideally are constrained to treat *that* question in line with reciprocity, then it is possible to say, as Rawls does, that the reciprocity criterion applies to particular laws enacted "under" the constitution, while still allowing an expanse for political contestation not bound to reciprocity. And that, then, does go some distance to ease, if it does not completely resolve, our sense of a rupture between the prior work and the ILBR.

4.4. Constitutional Proceduralism to Satisfy Reciprocity?

As we have seen, Rawls surely does not mean by the ILBR to bracket out from your or my considerations of support for a particular statute a due regard for subsisting constitutional law. Rather to the contrary, he appears to stipulate for something *beyond* a bare deflection by you or me to a judicial finding (actual or anticipated) of wide constitutional compatibility. He stipulates, to wit, for your or my own sincere belief in such compatibility. The question I now want to raise, though, is whether Rawls should or might be read count your or my sincere belief in constitutional compatibility as our full satisfaction of reciprocity at the particular-statute level.

The criterion of reciprocity calls for reasonability and sincerity of belief, by a law's supporters, in the sufficiency of reasons they offer in support of their support, and in the reasonable acceptability of those reasons to other citizens. But might not you or I always quite sincerely offer constitutional proceduralism *itself* as our reasonably acceptable reason for support of a disputed ground-level action or policy ("were we to state [our reasons] as government officials")? We sincerely believe that the policy in dispute falls within bounds of what the essentials of this country's reasonably acceptable constitution in force can reasonably be read to prescribe or permit. We furthermore sincerely believe that the policy therefore merits, on that sole and sufficient basis, every rational and reasonable citizen's support once it has gained (or since it has gained) the duly expressed approval of a constitutionally prescribed democratic majority, voting on the basis of whatever reasons occur to them as sufficient. That would leave the field wide open for uninhibited contestation over constitutionally compliant statutes not affecting fundamental matters (the constitution being, as we said, a "framework" law).

But, you ask, if the ILBR accepts *that* as satisfaction of reciprocity at the particular-statute level, are we not then back to exact redundancy with the proceduralistic LPL of *PL*? And doesn't that then disqualify such a reading of the ILBR from consideration? And the answers are, we aren't and it doesn't. At the very least, as we have seen, the ILBR makes explicit that citizens distributively owe justification for their para-governmental stances and activities, and furthermore specifies the criterion of reciprocity for fulfillment of that debt. It thus requires of you and me, in each case, our own sincere affirmation of a supported statute's wide compatibility with a justification-worthy constitution-in-force. No doubt we may take guidance on that point from actual or anticipated judgments of a supreme court, and the ILBR surely expects that we will. May we, though, go beyond guidance-taking to delegation? Do we fully satisfy reciprocity at the "particular statute" level by sincere affirmation of belief that the statute we support has gained or would gain the supreme court's stamp of good constitutional housekeeping? If not, and if enough of us judged frequently enough for guidance less than conclusive, that would affect the general tenor of a society's political debates in a direction away from the strictest procedural rigor one might have ascribed to the LPL pre-ILBR.

I will expand on those last remarks in Chapter 8. It would be helpful before going there to recapitulate some findings that have brought us to this point in our thought. First, we read the ILBR to leave standing the LPL's specification of the citizen body's collective burden of justification as one of justification-by-constitution. Second, for satisfaction of your and my distributive burdens, the ILBR specifies the criterion of reciprocity, to be applied by us at both the levels of the constitution and of particular statutes. Third, for the constitution, that calls for our respective sincere confirmations of the constitution's justification-worthiness when ruling particular statutes valid or not (according to whichever ruling for that statute matches our para-governmental stance). Fourth, at the particular-statute level of application, the criterion of reciprocity still envisages justification-by-constitution. Fifth, a question remains about whether that criterion allows for pure buck-passing by you and me to the supreme court, when a statute's constitutionality is in dispute. As a thesis to be picked up again in Chapter 8: The less permissive in that direction we find the ILBR to be, the greater the departure we will have from tightly proceduralistic justification-by-constitution.

8

Offsets to Proceduralism

Prototypically envisaged by Rawls's proposition for justification by constitution—the LPL of *PL*—is a country that has in place to govern its politics a ledger of higher directives, including substantive parts cast mainly at a framework level of generality, to which the country looks for a justificatory on top of a regulatory function. In Part I, we worked at drawing out some further implications regarding the mode of the requisite constitution's fixture in the public discursive space (custom/convention, codified positive law, "common" positive law?) and the institutional sites of its authoritative recognition and application (politically insulated court? channels of ordinary parliamentary or electoral politics?). The implications we drew were such as to echo our classification of the LPL as a distinctly proceduralistic response to the problem of political liberalism.

With Chapter 7, we launched a consideration of how or whether Rawls's later introduction of a proposition on legitimacy based on a criterion of reciprocity might herald some offset to the proceduralistic leaning of the LPL as developed in Part I. We left hanging there, awaiting a closer look, a question about how far a citizen's finding of constitutional-according-to-the-court would satisfy reciprocity with regard to para-political stances in support of particular statutes. If or insofar as the answer is that reciprocity always demands from you and me our own affirmation, on our own hook so to speak, of the constitutional compatibility of political acts we support, a second question then comes about expectations that citizens still will take guidance on such matters from the work of a supreme court. Note that these two variables, while related, are not the same. The first is a *stipulative* matter, about how far, if at all, reciprocity-according-to-Rawls demands from citizens supporting particular statutes some measure of personal commitment to constitutionality, beyond simply "I see that the supreme court says okay." The second is a *predictive* matter about how far citizens engaged in such own reflection will in fact find themselves taking guidance from the supreme court. (It doesn't seem that Rawls could impose a bar against guidance-taking, without erasing from Lecture VI of *PL* everything he has to say there

Constitutional Essentials. Frank I. Michelman, Oxford University Press. © Frank I. Michelman 2022.
DOI: 10.1093/oso/9780197655832.003.0009

about the supreme court's role as protector of the country's higher law and exemplar of its public reason.)

In this chapter, we pick up with consideration of these questions, the stipulative and the predictive, and ask how far the answers might go to offset to the proceduralism of the LPL of *PL*. "Not so much," will be our own bottom-line answer. No doubt readers may differ over how best to construe the Rawlsian position. As always, we work with the hope that our queries to the Rawlsian texts (and so to the thought behind them) might chime usefully with debates and puzzlements occurrent within our own practice and pursuit of constitutional democracy.[1]

1. Alternative Readings

As an aid to discussion, I now offer short names for each of two alternative readings of the Rawlsian "idea of legitimacy based on the criterion of reciprocity" (ILBR). Note that both these readings assume the case—which on my understanding remains always paradigmatic for Rawlsian thought on political justification—of a publicly recognized body of constitutional law in force, which all citizens can see as (approximately or nearly) justification-worthy (given this or that reasonably available application).

Reading A (guidance only)

The bottom-line requirement for your or my justification of our political stances to fellow citizens is the sincerity of your or my belief regarding what is or is not reasonably acceptable to the reasonable; no bare external fact about what an institutional authority may have said can by itself suffice. That is on the one hand. On the other hand, that demand on us is satisfied by our sincere belief in a political act's wide compliance with a justification-worthy constitution-in-force. Both of the affirmations contained therein—respecting constitutional compliance and respecting constitutional justification-worthiness—are ones for which we each have separately to sign in our own hand. That most surely does not prohibit consultation with others on the way to signing,

[1] For my own prior engagement, as US constitutional lawyer, with issues raised in this chapter, see Frank I. Michelman, "Living with Judicial Supremacy" (2003) 38 *Wake Forest Law Review* 579.

but no public official pronouncement can substitute in the end for our distributive justificatory obligations.

Reading B (full delegation)

Citizens claiming justification-by-constitution for political acts must do so holding a sincere and reasonable belief in the constitution's justification-worthiness under that claimed application of it. (That much is pretty plainly implicit in the LPL as originally stated.[2]) Under *Reading B*, "The statute has passed Congress, the supreme court says [or predictably will or would say] constitutionally okay, and I find the constitution to be justification-worthy under that application" fully satisfies reciprocity.

2. Whither Institutional Settlement?

In Chapters 2 and 3, our suggestion was that the project of justification-by-constitution, as proposed by Rawls in the LPL of *PL*, would finally have to fall back on a feature in positive legal orders now widely known as "institutional settlement."[3] The project thus would depend on the possibility of a social condition of widespread trust in a supreme court or other institutional body to resolve for the country *pro tempore* the reasonable disagreements that inevitably would arise over ground-level applications of the constitutional essentials. (Sure to arise, we said, such disagreements would be, given all of (1) the degree of abstraction in formulations of the constitutional essentials required to avoid the not-too-thick horn of the Goldilocks dilemma[4] and (2) the burdens of judgment under reasonable pluralism[5]—and then further underscored by (3) the idea of a plural family of sometimes-conflicting but all-of-them-reasonable liberal conceptions of justice.[6]) We look now to see whether or how far our resulting implication of institutional settlement into the LPL of *PL* might be offset by either of our readings *A* and *B* of the Rawlsian position post-ILBR.

[2] See Chapter 1, § 2.3.

[3] That name for the feature probably traces to Henry M. Hart, Jr., and Albert M. Sacks, *The Legal Process: Basic Problems in the Making and Application of Law*, ed. William N. Eskridge, Jr. and Philip P. Frickey (1995) 3–4.

[4] See Chapter 2, § 2.2; Chapter 3, §1.1.

[5] See Chapter 3, § 1.3.

[6] See ibid, § 2.

Under *A*, reciprocity requires your and my separate and sincere sign-offs on the justification-worthiness of the constitution-in-force as we would have it applied to the political act at hand. Beyond that point, reciprocity is fulfilled proceduralistically, by your or my sincere belief in the supreme court's actual or anticipated acceptance of the act in question as valid under the constitution-in-force. Institutional settlement remains firmly in place.

Under *B*, the case is obviously more complex. Barred, now, are your or my blank delegations to public authority of questions of the constitutional compatibility of questioned political acts. That runs us into a series of "maybes." *Maybe* in a given country at a given time some considerable fraction of the people are conducting their politics with reference to a higher-legal constitution and with measurable deference to a supreme court pronouncing on issues of compliance with its terms. And then *maybe* you and I as reasonable citizens owe, in all civility, some deference of our own to that court's pronouncements—*maybe* starting with our recognition ("reciprocity," remember) of how far our fellow citizens are finding it reasonable to defer. And *maybe*, even, the resulting political-practice scene could resemble what we'd expect to see under reading *A*. (Is that what Thoreau's "condescension to obey" and "courteous reënactment" were meaning to explain?[7]) Under reading *B*, however, none of those "maybes" will *necessarily* hold. They rather will hold in varying degrees as responsibly assessed by you or me in the here and now of our country. The grip of institutional settlement—"judicial supremacy"—will be correspondingly loosened, in some uncertain degree.

So it would seem so far. But is our analysis yet quite complete? By our proposed reading of the ILBR in Chapter 7, its topic is the distributive justificatory obligation, not the collective one. Add that the ILBR does not posit subjective reciprocity as a sufficient condition of satisfaction, only as a necessary condition ("only when"). An actual or expected *public* affirmation of wide constitutional compliance may then remain as a further necessary condition in Rawls's view. (Recall the Rawlsian principle of publicity for a well-ordered society.) With all that seemingly would come a need for institutional settlement.

When the dust has settled, Rawlsian justification-by-constitution may best be read to involve a conjunction of first-person-responsible sincere belief with a corresponding institutional settlement under a positive-legal constitution. If we now try to see how that could play out in an actual practice of

[7] See Chapter 6, § 3 & n 43.

constitutional-democratic politics, we may find the resulting scene not an utterly unfamiliar one.

3. Proceduralism Softened?

We recall from Chapters 4, 5, and 6 some features of the political scene in a Rawlsian realistic utopia. Suppose we have a controversial statute under challenge. Views reasonably differ over whether that law falls within the policy space left open under our not-too-thick constitutional law-in-force. (The US Supreme Court frequently divides by votes of 5–4 or 6–3.) That difference of views may in part be owing to all-in-the-family variations in the underlying political conceptions of justice to which citizens and judges respectively refer their understandings of the scriptural scheme of constitutional guarantees.[8] It may also in part be owing to burdens of judgment and the differing balances we strike among an agreed or overlapping set of values ensconced in the positive constitutional law as we respectively are reading it. The Rawlsian realistic utopia anticipates such disagreements over constitutional compatibility—while also, however, anticipating a resolution of them in the following way. Reasonable citizens, differing over their respective bottom-line "most reasonable" judgments regarding constitutional compatibility, are still able to converge on a subset of the judgments in actual circulation that they can accept as "at least" reasonable—as falling, so to speak, within the family—and they abide willingly by legislative outcomes they can place within the subset.[9]

Rawlsian citizens normally trust the supreme court for reasonable judgments regarding which statutes are and are not thus widely constitutionally compatible. A Rawlsian citizen thus normally follows along with a supreme court judgment confirming wide constitutional compatibility (even if privately doubting) and abides willingly by the statute. A like inference apparently follows if, to the contrary, the court decides the other way, placing the statute beyond the tolerance of any reasonable application of the constitution-in-force. The disagreeing Rawlsian citizen normally grins and bears it—while perhaps, Abraham Lincoln—like, continuing to agitate politically and legally for a change in rulings.[10] All of that is what we have

[8] See Chapter 3, § 2; Chapter 5, § 3.4.
[9] See ibid.
[10] For Lincoln, see Chapter 11, § 3.2.1 & n 27.

advanced in Chapters 4, 5, and 6 as packed into the proceduralistic LPL of *PL*. But still there has to be a limit to what the reasonable citizen can bear. As a general matter, that limit is reached when the citizen's perception is that judicial support of the statute—or, in the reverse case, judicial rejection of the statute as constitutionally recreant—can only have proceeded from a reading of the constitutional law-in-force that must have been inspired by an underlying political conception contrary to any that the citizen then finds can support a justification-worthy constitutional framework. The effect could then be to force the citizen to the conclusion that no support for or opposition to this or any coercive law can be justified in the country's current disordered state. This result could follow insomuch as the LPL would appear to lay down, as a necessary condition for anyone's justified support for any coercive political act, *there being in force* ("only when . . . in accordance with") a legitimation-worthy constitution (be it written or unwritten, legal or conventional).[11] As a less radical consequence, the citizen may conclude that the court in this instance has made a mistake still subject to rectification, in a dualist regime that (for the nonce, anyway) retains its putative legitimacy.

Here is what I think we have found. The ILBR does contemplate that where an approximately justification-worthy framework constitution is in fact in force in the country, reasonable citizens are duly heedful of it and reciprocity then will govern their judgments regarding a contested particular law's compatibility with that constitution. And then, too, a trusted court's judgment pro or con validity will often or normally—but not mandatorily or necessarily always—guide the reasonable citizen's own responsible judgments regarding whether this or that particular statute should be acceptable to other reasonable citizens. And then—still assuming an approximately justification-worthy constitution is in place in this country's affairs—the net effect of Rawls's turn to the ILBR may come down to loosening in some degree the reasonable citizen's beholdenness to the arbitral authority of the supreme court where constitutional justification of a law is in issue—in that way diluting to like degree the strictly proceduralistic efficacy of the LPL's resort to justification-by-constitution as a solution to the problem of political liberalism. (I find it hard to say how much more dilution that would be than what already flows from the Rawlsian differentiation of the constitutional fidelities respectively owed by judges and citizens, as traced by us in Chapter 5.)

[11] That inference will be up for re-examination soon, in section 4 of this chapter.

We can look a bit harder at various combinations of supreme court rulings pro or con validity of a statute with either confirmatory or contrary-tending judgments on the part of you or me. I will use the expression "satisfy reciprocity" (with respect to any judgment on your part or mine) to mean your or my sincere belief (1) in the truth or correctness of the judgment, (2) in its supportability by a reasonable balance of public reasons, and (3) in the sufficiency for other reasonable citizens of the public reasons (and balance thereof) that the you or I would offer in support of it.

We take up first the case of a citizen acting in support of a proposed or enacted coercive particular law. Given that a generally trusted supreme court is also on the scene, it seems a citizen normally satisfies reciprocity with a sincere belief in the court's actual or expected confirmation of the law's wide compatibility with the constitution in place, consistent with some understanding thereof that the citizen feels able to confirm as an at-least reasonable one. And then likewise for the converse case of the citizen seeking to justify, Lincoln-like, a persistence in public agitation for approval of a law previously found unconstitutional by the supreme court: reciprocity then is satisfied by sincere belief in the law's wide compatibility with the constitution in place under reasonable application.

We consider next the case of a citizen bent on ongoing opposition to a supreme court decision *sustaining* a particular law against constitutional challenge. The citizen could be contemplating either (1) a continuing political and legal agitation against the law on constitutional grounds, while meanwhile abiding by it, or (2) a refusal to abide by the law and agitation for resistance to it by others. Neither the LPL nor the ILBR is framed to address these cases.[12] Perhaps, though, we can draw some inferences from work we have accomplished up to here. It seems the citizen thus disposed should stand ready to satisfy reciprocity with respect to either (1) a claim that a law is noncompatible with the supreme court's own contemporaneously affirmed conception of the constitution-in-place or (2) a claim that no constitution receptive to that law can be tied to any reasonable underlying political conception—or, in other words, that the constitution then in place, if rightly construed by the supreme court as accepting of the questioned law, is not possibly a justification-worthy constitution.

[12] Rawls deals at length with the second under the headings of civil disobedience and conscientious refusal. See *TJ* 563–91.

4. Whence the Democratic-Monist Alternative?

We have been proceeding on the premise that *public* justification-by-constitution remains, post-ILBR, still firmly in place at the base of Rawlsian thought on democratic political legitimacy. The thought there is that your and my respective fulfillments of the reciprocity criterion, in regard to any particular political activity or stance of ours, would leave as yet unmet the citizen body's collective justificatory obligation, and furthermore would leave as yet empty the communicative space of political-moral publicity on which Rawlsian societal well-ordering depends. Indeed, we have gone so far as to say that the absence of a justification-worthy constitution-in-force would, *per* the LPL, leave citizens collectively and severally unable to justify either support or opposition for any particular law or policy in question.

Here's a lingering problem with those readings. They seem to run squarely against Rawls's clear allowance of the possible superiority, for some countries at some times, of a democratic monist regime ("parliamentary supremacy") over one of dualist democracy.[13] Rawls thus must be allowing for the possibility of justification of a citizen body's political acts in the absence of a higher-normative constitution-in-force. We have puzzled over how to explain that allowance as compatible with the LPL's prescription for justification-by-constitution. One might momentarily have thought that introduction of the ILBR would radically explain it, by putting satisfaction of subjective reciprocity at the core of liberal political justification, *in place of* publicly certifiable constitutionality. Our readings against such an erasure of justification-by-constitution close the door against such thoughts. And yet I think those readings must be right, for the reasons I have given. We seem to be at an impasse. Where do we go from here?

In search of refuge, I offer the following. In a country where a defensibly justification-worthy constitution is in force, justification for a ground-level governmental or para-governmental act will always run through a claim of that act's wide compatibility with *it*. Where not, justification is rather by claim of wide compatibility with some or other *hypothetical* constitution that *could* qualify as reasonable for that country at that time. When democratic citizens present to one another their justifications for support of

[13] See *PL* 234–35; Chapter 2, § 2.1.

controversial ground-level laws and policies, they state them necessarily (implicitly when not explicitly) in the proceduralistic form (I take it verbatim from Chapter 6): *This action or policy has gained the duly expressed support of a current democratic majority, expressed through forms that some at-least reasonable constitution for a constitutional democracy at our time and place might prescribe, and falls within bounds of what some such constitution would anticipate or permit.*[14] Justification-by-constitution (the LPL) is in that way still available in institutionally monist democracies, only the constitution in play will be a constitution *in mente* (as we may call it) and not a constitution-in-force. Rawls's acceptance of the possibility of political justification in monist democracies thus stands explained without departure from justification-by-constitution.

You will object that this solution must fall to our nemesis of publicity, as shown by my own critique in Chapter 7.[15] "You have your constitution *in mente*, I have mine, they may look and sound similar, but they are not the same," and then so on through the rest of that passage. That objection is correct, but we have now come to a point of some desperation to see if there is some way to turn it back. And we can see a way. First, the ILBR's criterion of reciprocity undoubtedly requires adherence by you and me to an ideal of public reason as we chart and explain our para-governmental stances and activities.[16] Second, we recall from Chapter 6 how a Rawlsian liberal realistic utopia relies on a political conception of the reasonable, meaning a conception containing from the start some very basic liberal or proto-liberal ingredients.[17] If we make that political conception of the reasonable thick enough with such ingredients, and if that conception effectively underlies and shapes each one of the respective constitutions *in mente* to which we severally appeal (in fulfillment of reciprocity) in our daily courses of political conduct, the aggregate result could be a palpable web of communication—a background political culture—capable of sustaining a condition of political-moral publicity for our society, and thereby also a platform for proceduralistic justification of political acts of kind envisaged by the LPL.

"If," I said, "we make that political conception of the reasonable thick enough." A question that hangs is whether we can stipulate for a political

[14] See Chapter 6, § 2.1.
[15] See Chapter 7, § 2.
[16] See Chapter 7, § 4.
[17] See Chapter 6, § 6.2.1.

public reason thick enough to sustain publicity and procedural justification, but still thin enough to satisfy the liberal commitment to toleration, evinced by Rawls insisting on embrace of a family of conflicting but all-of-them-reasonable liberal political conceptions. It is Goldilocks all over again: thick enough but not too thick.

PART III

SOME CHRONIC DEBATES

Parts I and II together compose my main work of exposition of the political-liberal conception of a procedural response to the problem of political liberalism, with a legal constitution serving in the place of a procedural platform ("justification-by-constitution") and a supreme court serving in the place of a trusted arbiter of constitutional compliance. The exposition includes my probe (Chapter 6) into some sociological contingencies on which the project's possibility of fulfillment seemingly depends. Also included are some wide-angle impressions of a constitutional democracy thus envisaged in action over time (Chapters 5, 7, and 8).

Part III now takes us into some more focused debates, within and among the world's constitutional democracies, regarding the authority of a supreme court and the contours of its assignment as constitutional arbiter. We look into these chronic debates having two aims in view. One is further specification of the Rawlsian conception of the justificatory service of constitutional law; we ask whether and how that conception might point toward a preferred resolution of the debate at hand. But we also want to see how pursuit of that question might help to clarify for us *why* these issues have stayed so resistant to settled resolution (and I mean among lawyers and legal thinkers whose shared connection to the broad tradition of constitutional democracy is not in question).

9

Constitutional Application: Between Will and Reason

Anyone familiar with American debates about judicial applications of positive legislative enactments will know how they move between poles (I describe them extremely roughly) of (1) sticking to the scripted enactment and oppositely (2) looking behind or beyond the script to broader considerations of purpose or motivating values.[1] At the constitutional-legislative level, where the age of the script may quite dramatically open possibilities of differing significations of the words to those who wrote them then and those who read them now,[2] the more text-bound approaches tend to keep company with what we call "originalism." Interpreters are to apply the Constitution's verbiage according to the best historical recovery they can make of the public meanings carried by that verbiage at the time it was submitted to ratification by popular votes or assemblies. We can leave open here the much-mooted question of the level of abstraction to which we should ascend in our constructions of those historical public meanings, because our point is going to be that even the most generously permissive answers to that question must stand, in principle, opposed to a "philosophical" approach (sometimes called a "constitutional-constructivist" or "moral reading" approach) that calls upon judicial interpreters to apply the verbiage so as to make its applications conform as closely as possible to some ideal conception of the (liberally) best

[1] This chapter draws from Frank I. Michelman, "Israel's 'Constitutional Revolution': A Thought from Political Liberalism" (2018) 19 *Theoretical Inquiries in Law* 745 (hereafter Michelman, "Israel's Constitutional Revolution"), and Frank I. Michelman, "Political Liberalism's Constitutional Horizon: Some Further Thoughts" (2017) 4 *Rivista Internazionale di Filosofia del Diritto* 599.

[2] For example, Americans of subsequent generations have debated over the central range of application, as originally understood, of the phrase "the freedom of speech, or of the press" in the First Amendment. Does that phrase apply solely or primarily to advance prevention of publication, or does it apply with equal force to post hoc penalties for publications of prohibited content? See, e.g., Paul McCosby, "In Search of a Solution: The Centrality of History to Constitutional Interpretation as Illustrated by the 19th Century First Amendment Controversy" [2019] *Liberty Lawyer* 20; Christopher Wolfe, "Originalist Reflections on Constitutional Freedom of Speech" (2019) 72 *Southern Methodist University Law Review* 535.

Constitutional Essentials. Frank I. Michelman, Oxford University Press. © Frank I. Michelman 2022.
DOI: 10.1093/oso/9780197655832.003.0010

constitution—no doubt always within some outer bound of contemporaneous verbal plausibility but without controlling reference to past historical facts either of public usage or of authorial intention or expectation.[3]

1. A Contradiction of Aims

That crude rendition of an opposition of textualist-originalist and purposive-philosophical constitutional-interpretive approaches may possibly draw howls of protest, maybe first of all from those who've worked at bridging the apparent gap between them.[4] The crude opposition though is what we want for present purposes, just because it appears to correlate quite nicely with a sorting of constitutional functions between regulation and justification. Where constitutional law is to serve, and serve only, as a medium of fixation by the authors—"the people," as we like to say—of certain general aims regarding future political outcomes, the corresponding assignment to judicial appliers must be exactly, as John Rawls has written, to "protect" the people's enacted higher law.[5] We must then expect from these appliers their best effort at extracting from the words and surrounding facts the historically enacted will of the authors. Suppose constitutional authors write a text protecting rights of "life," "property," and "liberty of the person." They deliberately, for politically calculative reasons that everyone knows, exclude from their text any mention of rights of "equality" or "non-discrimination," or of "speech" or "expression," or of religious pluralism. Courts cannot then, in the people's name, intervene on behalf of the deliberately non-mentioned rights.[6] "Well," you say, "except as those non-mentioned rights might be found covered by some other included clause." And then what if the authors did also speak of a

[3] See, e.g., James E. Fleming, *Fidelity to Our Imperfect Constitution: For Moral Readings and Against Originalism* (Oxford University Press 2015) 20–21 (noting connection to John Rawls's work of a favored "constitutional-constructivist" approach to constitutional interpretation); ibid, 80–81 ("philosophic" approach); Ronald Dworkin, *Freedom's Law: The Moral Reading of the American Constitution* (Harvard University Press 1996) 1–3 ("moral reading") (hereafter Dworkin, *Freedom's Law*).

[4] See, e.g., Jack M. Balkin, *Living Originalism* (Harvard University Press 2014); Alessandro Ferrara, "Judicial Review and Its Discontents: A Reply to Frank Michelman" (2017) 4 *Rivista Internazionale di Filosofia del Diritto* 615.

[5] *PL* 233 ("A supreme court . . . fits into . . . dualist constitutional democracy as [an] institutional device[] to protect the higher law.").

[6] I have in view here the case of Israel and its Basic Laws on Human Liberty and Dignity and Freedom of Occupation. See, e.g., Daniel Friedmann, *The Purse and the Sword: The Trials of Israel's Legal Revolution* (Oxford University Press 2016) 193–95.

right to "the dignity of a person"? And what if it is argued that the dignity of a person entails some kind and measure of a regard to civic equality, freedom of expression, and religious pluralism?[7]

Granted, constitutional-authorial will in regard to such matters must typically move on a moderately abstract plane of principle.[8] But a will to condition the validity of any later-arriving law on its due deference to a principle named by the authors as "the dignity of a person" still calls for the later law's deference to whatever *that principle*, the principle to which *those authors* adverted while attaching that name to it, may turn out to encompass in future applications. The authors' principle may well turn out to cover applications not expressly considered by them, in social conditions not foreseen by them, and perhaps coming then into arguable collision with other abstractly named constitutional principles. The task must still remain one of historical-factual inquiry into what *the authors* envisaged as the gist and content—the DNA, so to speak—of the named principles in play. If inquiries of that kind fail to turn up clear and decisive answers either way to current controversies over the political-moral merits of various legal acts, then judges in a democracy simply lack, in those cases, a foothold for ruling against the choices of the state's executive and legislative authorities.

Or rather, they lack a foothold in a judicial duty of protection of a regulatory will of constitutional authors.[9] The judges might still, though, find a foothold elsewhere—to wit, in a political society's reliance on its constitutional law to supply sufficient justification *now* for freely willing submission by dissenters to the coercions of ordinary law. For then the corresponding assignment to judicial appliers must seemingly be (well, yes, within some outer limit of semantic defensibility) to enforce a set of constitutional essentials that *really does* supply the needed justification. Judges so understanding might see reason to seize on "the dignity of a person" to guarantee some measure of freedom of expression or civic equality across divisions of sex, religion, ethnicity, and national origin, where the written constitution is otherwise silent on those matters.

[7] See Michelman, "Israel's Constitutional Revolution" (n 1).

[8] See Chapter 3, § 1.1.

[9] See, e.g., Robert H. Bork, "Neutral Principles and Some First Amendment Problems" (1971) 47 *Indiana Law Journal* 1.

2. Not a Digression: Rawls to Dworkin and Back

The judges, then, proceed on the premise of the society's reliance on them for trustworthy judgments of the requisite essentials for a justification-worthy constitution *now*. That will indeed be a substantial trust, because the judges will always have to look inside themselves, beyond anything that public evidence can show, for the seeds of those judgments.

For explanation, we may now bring onstage another prominent liberal political philosopher, Ronald Dworkin by name. Dworkin saw his political philosophy as in some ways divergent from that of Rawls,[10] but not plausibly so (as I am about to maintain) in the respect of concern to us now. For it was a key claim of Dworkin's that responsible judicial resolution of constitutional-interpretive disputes first of all requires from judges a conscious conception of purpose or aim in a society's observance of a body of constitutional law, and Dworkin's development of that point turns out to hinge on an attribution of a justificatory function to that observance.

As maintained by Dworkin, any truly respectful applier of a constitutional text will read the words against a backdrop of the textual authors' own supposed conception of the political-moral "upshot or point" of writing a basic-law constitution in the first place. A historically concrete political community's commitment to such a writing with its particular provisions, writes Dworkin, necessarily reflects their "prior commitment to certain principles of political justice which, if we are to act responsibly, must therefore be reflected" in the way we now read their constitution. A reader, Dworkin says, cannot truly show regard for either the text or the authorship of those who made it without ascribing to those authors certain "principles of political morality which in some way represent [for them] the upshot or point of constitutional practice more broadly conceived."[11]

[10] See Ronald Dworkin, *Justice for Hedgehogs* (Harvard University Press 2011) 63–66; Alessandro Ferrara and Frank I. Michelman, *Legitimation By Constitution: A Dialogue on Political Liberalism* (Oxford University Press 2021) 6–7.

[11] Ronald Dworkin, *A Matter of Principle* (Harvard University Press 1985) 35–36. Dworkin soon thereafter would generalize the thought beyond its application to "constitutional practice" to the larger social practice known as "law." See Ronald Dworkin, *Law's Empire* (Harvard University Press 1986) ("Law is an interpretive concept. . . . Judges normally recognize a duty to continue . . . the practice they have joined."); ibid, 66 ("[T]here must be an interpretive stage at which the interpreter settles on some general justification for the practice. . . . This will consist of an argument about why a practice of that general shape is worth pursuing.").

It seems, furthermore, that any conception of "upshot or point" ascribed to authors by a respectful interpreter will have to be one that makes good sense to the interpreter. The interpreter "proposes value for the practice by ascribing some scheme of interests or goals or principles the practice can be said to serve or exemplify." But plausibly defensible ascriptions will differ among interpreters, so any interpreter's choice will have to reflect that interpreter's own view of which ascription "proposes the most value for the practice—which one shows it in the better light, all things considered."[12]

Suppose now a political-liberal-minded judge, who finds that the historically embedded "upshot or point" of a given country's constitutional-legal project is to ensure justification—not just on the day the text is written but over some future course of political time, while that constitution remains in place—for calls among fellow citizens for willing submission to laws with which some of them may disagree profoundly. Such a judge might be a follower of Rawls. They might equally be a follower of Dworkin. Dworkin quite explicitly proposed, as the point of substantive constitutional law, the establishment of conditions, in what Rawls would have called the legal "background" or "framework" component of the society's basic structure, for imbuing all citizens with a warranted sense of full (now Dworkin again) "moral membership" in the collectively self-governing political community, by which each can "treat himself as bound together with others in a joint effort to resolve [political] questions, even when his views lose."[13] Dworkin thus pointed straight at what we have been calling here a justificatory function for substantive constitutional law.

Passing back now from Dworkin to Rawls: Today's judicial appliers must read and apply the scripted constitutional essentials in the light of "political values . . . that they [the judges] believe, in good faith . . . all citizens as reasonable and rational might reasonably be expected to endorse."[14] The legal text will not be set aside. It rather will be read against the backdrop of a political-moral purpose—Dworkin's lesson—that the judicial reader cannot simply find already in the text (because it indispensably informs the reading of the text) and so must of necessity bring to it.

[12] Ibid at 52–53.
[13] Dworkin, *Freedom's Law* (n 3) 24–26.
[14] *PL* 236 (emphasis supplied).

3. A Gap That Cannot Be Closed?

Between calls for originalist and for philosophical approaches to judicial constitutional interpretation there stands an unbridgeable gap of concept and principle. Samuel Freeman saw and urged this point thirty years ago, even in advance of the publication of *Political Liberalism*.[15] It is one thing to search out a historical legislative will from recorded words and other facts. It is quite a different thing to ask which among reasonably supportable assignments of meanings to the recorded words will best comport with some non-past-fixated normative standard (e.g., the standard of acceptability to any and all free and equal citizens hypothetically conceived as reasonable and rational in the here and now). The principle of bending and applying the scripted constitutional essentials as required in reason to sustain a liberal justification for the force of law stands in contradiction to the principle of reading and applying the scripted essentials to match the will or understanding of any historical author. It is the difference, as Alessandro Ferrara neatly puts it, between saying what the sovereign people "*did* will" and saying what they "*should* will."[16] But can't we, you ask, suppose a people willing that the words they write down now are to be read by judges in future to make those words mean what they ought in all reason to mean *then*, to free and equal, reasonable and rational citizens of that country at that stage of its history? Answer: Yes, and the difference still would remain between a judge doing so because of that supposed instruction and one doing so regardless of it.

There is no middle ground; no hermeneutic theory can dissolve the difference. Granting that any judge's sincere and honest reading of what the people did will must bear the marks of filtration though that judge's priors regarding what they must in all reason have willed, judges still will be *doing* one thing when they conscientiously read as historians and a different thing when they conscientiously read as political-liberal moral philosophers. True, the judges might get lucky with the historical contingencies. If their findings of what the people did will match their views of what the people should will, then the gap between those two inquiries will not matter in practice: Apply the constitution, then, for the sake of regulation in accordance with the authors' directions, and you will also ipso facto apply it with regime-justifying effect.

[15] See Samuel Freeman, "Original Meaning, Democratic Interpretation, and the Constitution" (1992) 21 *Philosophy and Public Affairs* 15–17.

[16] Alessandro Ferrara, "Political Liberalism Revisited: A Paradigm for Liberal Democracy in the 21st Century" (2016) 24 *Philosophy and Social Criticism* 681, 686.

But alas that happy ending can be guaranteed to follow only where the constitutional authors happen to have constitutionalized all the rights whose observance is required to make a democratically and liberally justifiable regime—and none that would defeat it. And what if (in the judge's liberal-tinted estimation) they have not? What then would follow for responsible conduct by this judge imbued with the political-liberal idea of the justificatory burden of constitutional law? At least this, it would seem: that between judgments of what the people did will and what they should will remains a gap in concepts that cannot be closed, and judges sometimes must navigate a course across that gap.

4. Originalism Either Way?

Does that, then, cement a case against originalism for all who admit to reliance on constitutional law as their country's procedural platform of justification of the force of majoritarian laws in conditions of reasonable pluralism? Not so clearly, it seems, in the view of John Rawls. Rawls, here following Bruce Ackerman, expressly endorses engagement of a supreme court as an institutional device of protection of the people's constitutional higher legislation against subsequent betrayal by ordinary-course majoritarian law-making. "Constitutional democracy," Rawls writes, "distinguishes . . . the higher law of the people from the ordinary law of legislative bodies," and a supreme court then fits into this idea as an "institutional device to protect" the people's higher law. "By applying public reason," Rawls continues, "the court is to prevent that law from being eroded by the legislation of transient majorities or . . . by . . . narrow interests skilled at getting their way."[17]

Save for a detail soon to be noticed, that reads like a sign-up by Rawls with a primarily regulatory function, pro tanto overriding any justificatory function, for a country's higher-law constitution. It would be as if, in the end, the point of it all (Dworkin's "upshot") would be to entrench in the country's ongoing politics a set of instructions from the historical authors of the constitution. Yet, from everything I have written in the preceding chapters of this book, it seems that cannot be right. And indeed, it would be a misreading. And the further sign of *that* (along with the bare fact of the salience in Rawls's work of the LPL) is the express stipulation from Rawls that it is "by applying

[17] *PL* 233 (emphasis supplied).

public reason" that the supreme court is to protect the higher law against majoritarian betrayal. *For what has the public reason of the here and now got to do, after all, with recovery of a past generation's attributions of meanings to words?*

From this exegetical contretemps in which we have managed to land ourselves, I see a plausible escape. The perception by Rawls of need for an institutional device of protection of a laid-down higher law, against despoilment by heedless or faithless transient majoritarian action arises (I think we must conclude) not solely and simply from ascription of a regulatory function to constitutional law (to carry out a legislative will laid down in that law), but also as a requisite part of the justificatory function ascribed by the LPL of *PL*.

There are two ways in which that could be so. One way, which I have already introduced in Chapter 3 and developed further in Chapters 4 and 5, would be by holding in mind that the credible democratic authorship of the regime is itself a condition of the regime's acceptability in the present to any and all reasonable and rational citizens. The other, which I take up now (continuing with a point I hope to have nailed down in Chapter 2), is that the justificatory aim cannot itself get off the ground without an observable fixture in place already, at the moment when citizens point them out to each other by way of justification, of a commonly legible set of constitutional essentials. In a slogan I have used, justificatory ambition presupposes regulatory effect. Justification says: "*Given that* the legal system in force requires and assures that legislative majorities will uphold *these* norms"—pointing by "these" to the scripted constitution, the basic law—"the system should in all reason be found acceptable among free and equal citizens, and so we may all justifiably look forward to each other's compliance with the laws that duly issue from the system."

But that "*given that*" sends us right back to the regulatory conception of substantive constitutional law. It returns us to the link between semantic confidence and predictive hope that comprises, as I suggested near the start of this book,[18] the very core and essence of the regulatory conception. And so just there do we catch our glimpse of the spark of originalism that I now want to say must always already be firing in any Rawls-style setup of the higher-law constitution as our procedural platform for the justification of the force of law to free and equal dissenters from majoritarian legislation. That "given that" sets an originalistic inner bound to any practice of constitutional

[18] See Introduction, § 3.

interpretation that would come within the idealizing pull of the Rawlsian principle of legitimacy.

Here, then, is where I leave the argument. A non-resolvable tension between "did will" and "should will" exists, not just between the regulatory and justificatory functions of constitutional law but within the justificatory function itself. Justificatory ambition presupposes regulatory effect.

10

Justification-by-Constitution, Economic Guarantees, and the Rise of Weak-Form Review

The possibility, in our times, of a society just and stable among persons free and equal rests on the hope of constitutional faith, of public confidence sustained in a justification-worthy constitution. So argues political liberalism. That still leaves judicial constitutional review as an open question. Constitutional fidelity does not conceptually or logically entail or require this particular institutional feature,[1] and in fact it will be a part of this chapter's business to show how the political-liberal idea of justification-by-constitution may sometimes fight against it. That turnabout will occur when guarantees deemed essential for a justification-worthy constitution include some whose application would seem to stretch beyond the breaking point the capacities of courts of law as dominantly conceived in the surrounding legal culture. We can see there one plain reason why the question of inclusion of socioeconomic guarantees in constitutional law has been a topic of chronic debate among the world's constitutional democracies. The same cause will also help explain a push in recent times toward receptivity to forms of judicial engagement in constitutional review that do not leave the ultimate decision to the courts.[2]

[1] See Chapter 3, § 1.4.

[2] What follows, from here to the end of this chapter, draws substantially from Frank I. Michelman, "Legitimacy, the Social Turn, and Constitutional Review: What Political Liberalism Suggests" (2015) 3 *Critical Quarterly for Legislation and Law* 183. This material includes a recapitulation of some political-liberal basics covered in earlier chapter of this book, which I have thought it best to retain.

Constitutional Essentials. Frank I. Michelman, Oxford University Press. © Frank I. Michelman 2022.
DOI: 10.1093/oso/9780197655832.003.0011

1. Socioeconomic Rights in a Liberal Constitutional Conception

1.1. "SER" and "Social Minimum" as Constitutional Matters

As it occurs in constitution-talk, the expression "economic rights" can carry a quite broad signification, extending to matters of labor policy, competition and concentration policy, tax policy, inheritance policy, spatial-planning policy, occupational freedom of choice, and rights respecting private property. Here I use the term "socioeconomic rights" (in the form "SER") in a narrower sense to cover, in the first instance, what John Rawls calls a "social minimum" guarantee, leaving open questions of further assurances respecting material conditions and distributions of access to social goods and opportunities.

The idea of a social minimum is that of assurance of social outcomes in which no one ever lacks the means of access to the fulfillment of certain material needs deemed basic. As used in constitution-talk, the idea envisages corresponding obligations falling on the state. We can postpone for now how further to define or delimit the state's obligations, except to say this: Because, in free societies, social outcomes of the targeted kinds will always depend heavily on patterns of conduct by actors in society, the expected state exertions would plausibly cover not only the state's own directly distributive fiscal and budgetary actions but also its settings of the bodies of regulatory and general background law that guide, sanction, and incentivize economically consequential conduct in markets, families, and so on.[3]

A country's constitutional law might or might not contain a commitment regarding SER or a social minimum. In a political-liberal view, that suggestion sets going a series of questions, possibly up to the number of four. We start with (1) a question of ideal political justice or morality. Political liberalism makes space for a bounded "family" of political conceptions for regimes aspiring to justice in modern pluralist conditions. Is that family ideal receptive or not to the idea of SER? Will family-member regimes encompass that idea as a requisite of justice, or will they not? If not (or if not necessarily), then *justice* would not be a cause in political-liberal thought to pursue further the matter of SER commitments in constitutional law. But

[3] See, e.g., Dennis Davis and Karl Klare, "Transformative Constitutionalism and the Common and Customary Law" (2010) 26 *South African Journal on Human Rights* 403.

if so necessarily, still the next question would be (2) whether such a commitment is required not only for the ideal justice of the regime but also for its minimal-moral legitimacy; and then, if so, whether (3) that necessarily would provide a reason to write that commitment into the country's constitutional law. And then if, but only if, we find that it would will we reach the fourth and final question—about how, if at all, our writing the commitment into constitutional law would involve the country's courts of law in policing over the state's management of society's economic affairs.

I shall call these four questions respectively the questions, in regard to SER, of *justice*, *legitimacy*, *constitutionalization*, and *judicialization*.

1.2. A Standard Worry

I have set up the questions as a conditional series, so that the first "no" could put a stop to going further. We must notice, though, that it may not be possible to work fully through the second query (regarding legitimacy) without having already in mind the fourth one (regarding judicialization). For suppose you thought that engagement of the country's judiciary in the state's SER performance-assessments would be flatly unacceptable—say, because it would so drastically encroach on the authority of current political majorities as to put into question the overall democratic legitimacy of the regime. That might lead you to tip the dominoes backward: An insuperable objection against putting questions of the state's SER compliance into the juridical arena becomes a reason to keep SER out of the constitution, which then becomes a reason to deny that a commitment to SER can be required for the legitimacy of the regime—and all of that regardless of whether such a commitment is demanded by your or my conception of ideal justice.

I recall here what I have in the past named an American "standard worry" about a constitutionalized commitment to SER. By constitutionalizing SER, I wrote (describing the standard worry),

> you would force the American judiciary, and especially the Supreme Court, into a hapless choice between usurpation and abdication, from which there would be no escape without either embarrassment or discreditation. Down one path [would lie] the judicial choice to issue concrete, positive enforcement orders in a pretentious, inexpert, probably vain but nevertheless resented attempt to reshuffle the most basic resource-management

> priorities of the public household against the prevailing political will. Down the other [would lie] the judicial choice to debase dangerously the entire currency of rights and the rule of law—the spectacle of courts openly ceding to executive and legislative bodies a nonreviewable privilege of indefinite postponement of a declared constitutional right. In sum, a formal act of writing or reading socioeconomic assurances into constitutional law would pose grave risks of serious damage to the integrity (and to public confidence therein) of the country's practices of constitutionalism, of law and legality, and of democracy, upon which political legitimacy depends.[4]

So goes the standard worry. It speaks from what I have been calling a regulatory mission for constitutional law. This chapter takes note of a pushback against it from the justificatory mission. A recent burgeoning interest in "weak-form" judicial constitutional review has been (so I argue) an upshot from that pushback.

2. Four Questions: From Justice to Justiciability

2.1. Social Minimum and Justice in the Basic Structure

Locating itself within the social-contract tradition in the history of political ideas,[5] political liberalism starts out from a conception of a political society as a large-scale practice of cooperation across a diversely inspired and motivated population of citizens. "Co-operation" is germinal. Already ensconced within that notion is a conception of the citizens—the cooperators—as individualized agents: each one distinctly a "self-authenticating source of valid claims,"[6] each endowed with an own life to live for the better or for the worse, each possessed of certain agency powers and a higher-order interest in their development and exercise. (In the conception of Rawls, these encompass "moral" powers not only to "have, to revise, and rationally to pursue" a conception of the good or of one's aims in life but also to "understand and . . . act from principles" of due regard for others likewise endowed and situated).[7]

[4] Frank I. Michelman, "Socioeconomic Rights: Explaining America Away" (2008) 6 *International Journal of Constitutional Law* 663, 683.
[5] See *PL* 285–88.
[6] Ibid, 32.
[7] Ibid, 74; *JAF* 18–19.

We come then to the notion of "basic terms" for social cooperation. The basic terms are those made manifest in the society's major political, social, and economic institutions—its "basic structure"—which combine to produce the array of positions, conditions, and prospects of life that various persons will occupy from time to time.[8] Consider, then, a population of would-be social cooperators, reciprocally bound in recognition of each others' motivation by the moral powers and corresponding higher-order interests. It seems there would arise within this population a common concern for *fairness* in the basic terms of social cooperation amongst them. Social justice, then, would correspond to the satisfaction of the presumed desire of free and equal persons, within a company of likewise free and equal persons so recognized, for fair basic terms of social cooperation.

Some notion of economic assurance or safety net seems a likely implication. Modern liberalism can hardly help but presuppose a largely market-based economy within a mainly majoritarian lawmaking system. These, for us, are prime basic-structural corollaries to political and economic freedom. But then—so runs the line of thought—we cannot fairly and reasonably expect our primordially free and equal cooperators to submit their fates to the operations of these freedom-serving structures, without also committing our society, from the start, to run itself in ways aimed at securing to everyone the conditions anyone would require to be or become a competent participant in them, a respected and self-respecting contributor to political exchange and contestation and furthermore to social and economic life at large. Fairness—justice—in the basic structure may thus quite defensibly be held to necessitate some principle of socioeconomic assurance.

Straightforwardly, it would be a principle looking to provision for the "basic needs" of all citizens,[9] a "social minimum," defined as a package of material goods and services up to the levels required for a person's capability to "take part in society as [a] citizen[],"[10]and "to understand and to fruitfully exercise" his or her capacities as a self-actuating person.[11] Rawls in fact went further, to find that justice ideally requires a broader-reaching economic-distributional commitment, to what he called "fair" (in pronounced contradistinction

[8] A society's basic structure consists in its "main political and social institutions [and the way] they fit together into one system of social cooperation [and] assign basic rights and duties and regulate the division of advantages that arises from social cooperation over time." Ibid, 10.
[9] *JAF* 47–48.
[10] *PL* 166.
[11] Ibid, 7.

to merely "formal") equality of opportunity.[12] Such a principle might, for example—depending on how we assess the relevant social and economic facts—point toward any or all of a quite muscular antidiscrimination policy, jobs policy, industrial policy, family policy, fiscal-redistributive policy, and educational adequacy going beyond the most basic level.

But let us focus, for now, on the narrower idea that justice for the basic structure requires a safety net of assured provision for everyone's basic needs. And note, please, that the claim here is relatively modest: not that a principle of commitment to the social minimum is the only possible or even the most reasonable deduction from the economic-distributional requirements of liberal social-systemic justice, but only that there is nothing like an antipathy—rather, there is a strong, natural sympathy—between the deeper inspirations of liberal political thought and embrace of a basic-structural principle of assured fulfillment of everyone's basic needs. Such a principle is one that liberals can affirm, not just as a happenstance political preference but as part of a more encompassing conception of political morality to which, *as liberal*, they feel committed.

2.2. Social Minimum and Legitimacy in the Political Order

So much, then, for SER, social minimums, and justice. *Legitimacy*, however, is something else. Political liberalism takes for granted that the basic structure will saliently include a practice of positive legal ordering. It joins with liberalisms of all stripes in the belief that stable, effective, social ordering by law is an indispensable requirement for decent forms of human social coexistence. It shares with them, furthermore, the belief that the efficacy and stability of any legal order depend on a general expectation of regular compliance with the order's duly issued laws by everyone within range, regardless of inevitable, sincerely held, reasonable disagreements about the wisdom or rightness of those laws.[13] And yet it remains the case, in the sight of political liberalism, that every concrete instance of a liberal rule-of-law regime presents unremittingly a question of moral justification. That is because persons living within a liberal order inevitably—this is what John Rawls calls

[12] Ibid, 6; see *JAF* 42–43.

[13] See *TJ* 240 (discussing "Hobbes's thesis"), 269–70 (on the sovereign solution to "the problem of assurance"); Frank I. Michelman, "Ida's Way: Constructing the Respect-Worthy Governmental System" (2003) 72 *Fordham Law Review* 345, 345–47 (elaborating on this view).

"the fact of reasonable pluralism"[14]—will find themselves sincerely, within the bounds of reason, divided over not just the wisdom or prudence of various laws and policies but about their compatibility with morality and justice. And then how—liberals must ask—can a demand for general compliance with duly issued laws be justified morally, consistent with a view of citizens as individually free, equal, and responsible moral agents?

"Legitimacy" is an idea that presents itself in answer to that question. This will be legitimacy in what is often called a moral or normative sense of that term, as opposed to a purely sociological or empirical use of it.[15] Legitimacy in the normative sense sets a minimum standard for the operation of a state regime, a floor of decency required to authorize morally a civic demand for a regularity of compliance by citizens with the laws and policies that issue from that regime.[16] A denial of legitimacy to a state's practice of legal ordering thus casts into doubt any claim of that state's citizens to a moral permission to collaborate in support of the system's demands for a regularity of compliance with its laws by everyone. Liberals will be careful, then, about setting the legitimacy bar too high. One might think, for example, that a state could be, in the minimal-moral sense, legitimate as long as its political structures were ostensibly democratic in design and its operations displayed, in practice, a due regard for a small core of nonnegotiable, so-called "basic liberties" of persons—even though (let's say) that state was plainly delinquent, by our standards, in the field of economic-distributive justice.[17]

Why introduce such a gap between justice and legitimacy? It seems we do so in order to allow for human imperfection and for honest political disagreement.[18] In any possible human practice, not only must we expect shortfalls from justice, but so must we expect serious disagreements about what counts as a shortfall. If full and perfect justice were to set the standard for legitimacy, no modern real-world, concrete legal order could ever be deemed truly deserving of support by any fraction of the citizens remotely

[14] *PL* at 36–37.

[15] Richard Fallon, for example, differentiates between legitimacy in a "sociological" sense referring to current facts of acceptance by the populace of the regime's claim to merited political authority, and legitimacy in a "moral" sense referring to the regime's "worthiness to be recognized," according to some measure that we as external evaluators bring to the table. See Richard H. Fallon, Jr., "Legitimacy and the Constitution" (2005) 118 *Harvard Law Review* 1787,1795–96 & n. 25.

[16] See ibid, 1799.

[17] Compare *PL* 227–29.

[18] Rawls, for example, wrote that unjust institutions can sometimes be tolerable because "a certain degree of injustice . . . cannot be avoided, [or] social necessity requires it, [or] there would be greater injustice otherwise." John Rawls, "Legal Obligation and the Duty of Fair Play" in Sidney Hook (ed.), *Law and Philosophy: A Symposium* (New York University Press 1964) 3.

approaching a totality. A legitimacy standard, it appears, in order to do its assigned work—to provide a public justification for the regime's projection of pressure and force to induce a prevailing regularity of compliance with its duly issued laws—must be more accommodating of real-world political imperfection and disagreement than any corresponding ideal standard of justice conceivably could be.

Let us, for the moment, accept without further question the political-liberal proposal for a somewhat forgiving standard for the moral legitimacy of a state regime—forgiving, that is, by comparison with your or my ideal standards of justice. Shall or shall not the legitimacy standard include the state's commitment to SER? John Rawls answered "yes" to that question. He did so by including, as one of the liberal "constitutional essentials," a guaranteed "social minimum" covering the "basic needs" of all citizens.[19] A state, Rawls evidently thought, would gravely weaken its claim to the presumptive compliance with its laws of all who live their lives within its domain if—having within its grasp the means to do so at no more than a moderate cost to anyone's enjoyment of the system's goods, and without violation of anyone's basic liberties—it failed of commitment to eliminate the traps of structural poverty that it seems must inevitably otherwise arise and persist within a liberal market-based economy.

Again, I pause to state in modest terms a point I hope to have established, at least sufficiently to go on with the argument: *Not* that the retreat from justice to legitimacy provides a sure-fire solution to the quandary of bottomless, reasonable disagreement; and *not*, either, that a commitment to SER is, beyond all possibility of counterargument, a condition of minimal-moral legitimacy for a liberal state. Only, rather, that neither of those propositions is alien to liberalism; only, that both are claims for which compelling motivations can be found in the deepest layers of liberal thought.

2.3. Social Minimum as Constitutional Essential

Rawls saw fit to class a commitment to a social minimum as an essential component in any liberally justification-worthy constitution as envisaged by the liberal principle of legitimacy. A constitution lacking such a commitment, Rawls evidently concluded, fails to meet the LPL's requirement—acceptability

[19] See *JAF* 47–48.

to all free and equal, reasonable and rational citizens—for justification-worthiness. So he must also have concluded (we'll see soon more exactly how he did so) that a constitution that *does* include a social-minimum commitment does not thereby fail to satisfy other constitutionally essential basic liberties regarding (say) property rights or political-participation rights of democratic citizens; the commitment can be met, Rawls must have judged, without trenching on the central ranges of those or other basic liberties.[20] So now we have moved three steps along the way toward a highly credible endorsement, from well within the bastions of liberal consciousness, of a constitutional right to a social minimum: from a demand of justice, to a key support for state legitimacy, to incorporation in constitutional law.

2.4. Social Minimum and Judicialization

That then brings us to our fourth question, regarding judicialization. Perhaps this one seems trivial—already, in effect, decided by admission of a social-minimum guarantee as fitting to a liberally justification-worthy constitution. But there we run into a contretemps, in the form of the standard worry and the reverse domino effect of which I spoke previously in section 1.2. Take it that the country's settled practice relies on a law court to serve as the trusted referee of constitutional compliance required by the second procedural turn in justification-by-constitution.[21] Take it also that judicialization of economic policy is deemed intolerable to democratic political liberty. The apparent logical consequence is that a sweeping constraint on economic policy (and that would cover SER in the form of a social minimum) cannot be allowed to be requisite in a democratically justification-bearing constitution. But then neither, by the political-liberal doctrine of justification-by-constitution ("only when"), can any such constraint be deemed a condition for the minimal-moral legitimacy of the state's regime of legal ordering. And all of this would follow regardless of any conviction we might hold that some principle of SER or social minimum is a requirement for a just basic structure.

We see, then, that in order finally to defend its assignment of a social-minimum commitment as a constitutional essential, political-liberal constitutional thought must find a way to disarm or evade the standard worry.

[20] See Chapter 3, § 1.2.
[21] See Chapter 2, § 2.2; Chapter 3, § 1.4.

Only thus can it carry through in full its promotion of constitutionalized SER: from demand of justice, to condition of legitimacy, to incorporation in constitutional law. Under the conditions described, that third step depends on a deflection of concern about excessive judicialization of economic policy.

3. Constitutional Essentials and Transparency

John Rawls did not himself pause long over that concern or its deflection. He apparently took for granted that law courts can make socially credible determinations of shortfalls from fulfillment of a social-minimum commitment, without undue strain on either normal adjudicative methods and skills or general confidence in the judiciary as authoritative referee of constitutional compliance.[22] My inference to that effect has a back story of interest to our investigations here.

Remember: Justificatory force presupposes regulatory effect. *Per* the LPL of *PL*, political justification lies in assurance to all that a certain set of scripted constitutional essentials is effectively in control of coercive state action. If, then, judicial constitutional review is to stand as our prime institutional fallback for such assurance, and if (as posited by the standard worry) observance of strict justiciability standards undergirds public confidence in judicial determinations of compliance with constitutional essentials,[23] the LPL can succeed at its proceduralizing mission only if we rigorously exclude from constitutional-essential status any guarantee that will not fit credibly under prevailing justiciability standards.

Such, apparently, was John Rawls's own view of the case. Among the basic principles of justice Rawls would uphold for a society's basic structure is one that he called "fair equality of opportunity."[24] That principle demands from state policy a good deal more than provision for basic material needs. It demands the set of policies currently required to demolish structural barriers and handicaps posed by poverty in the full social sense: family socioeconomic status, ghetto conditions and cultures, educational neglect, and other social impediments to movement and mobility. Rawlsian fair equality of opportunity—a component of justice conceived as fair terms of social cooperation—might entail any or all of antidiscrimination policies,

[22] See *PL* 228–29.
[23] Chapter 11 takes up this premise for closer examination.
[24] See *JAF* 43–44.

jobs policies, monetary policies, spatial-planning policies, family policies, educational adequacy going beyond the most basic level. It means all of those policies not only declared in legislation but effectively and thoroughly implemented—but subject, however, to a condition of non-encroachment on the basic liberties equally guaranteed to all.[25]

That is a complicated prescription. In Rawls's view, it adds up to exclusion from the essentials of a justification-supportive constitution of a guarantee respecting fair equality of opportunity—despite that it is a basic principle of justice. The question of a state's current compliance with such a guarantee is too opaque to demonstration to let it be an essential component of a justification-supportive constitution—by contrast, Rawls thought, with that of compliance with a guarantee of fulfillment of basic needs, a social minimum.[26] But a constitution limited to conventionally justiciable guarantees, including a social minimum, can still suffice, Rawls thought, as a reasonably acceptable starting framework for government. The right collection of such guarantees, Rawls urges, can provide assurance enough for reasonable citizens to accept the resulting political framework as the one through which they thenceforward will work to satisfy the more complex and debatable demands of economic and social justice.[27]

That suggestion has run into substantial resistance—as represented, say, by political philosopher Tommie Shelby. Shelby maintains that a political regime's lack of an anchoring commitment to the constant and vigorous pursuit of fair equality of opportunity for all can render that regime more than barely or marginally unjust—can render it, indeed, "intolerably" unjust—to some fraction of its citizens.[28] That is a failure, in Shelby's view, that cannot be cured by the regime's faithful observance of any more narrowly drawn set of constitutional essentials. By Shelby's reckoning, a regime that fails of an essential commitment to deliver on fair equality of opportunity thereby forfeits its claim to be a regime reasonably acceptable to all reasonable and rational citizens, and thus (by force of the LPL) its claim to the loyalties of all who live their lives within its domain. A fair-equality guarantee would thus become a constitutional essential for a justification-bearing constitution.

[25] See ibid, 42.
[26] See *PL* 228–29; *JAF* 162.
[27] See ibid, 227–30; Frank I. Michelman, "Poverty in Liberalism: A Comment on the Constitutional Essentials" (2012) 60 *Drake Law Review* 1001, 1016–17.
[28] Tommie Shelby, "Justice, Deviance, and the Dark Ghetto" (2007) 35 *Philosophy and Public Affairs* 126, 145–47.

4. "The Bind"

4.1. A "Best Efforts" Commitment

John Rawls thought that a social-minimum guarantee could evade the standard worry. That has not, however, been—nor does it show signs of becoming—the prevailing view among American professionals in the field of constitutional law. Those professionals who are nevertheless drawn to agree that SER—whether as a social minimum or in some broader form—is indispensable from a legitimation-worthy constitution thus find themselves in a bind.

Recall our initial, somewhat cursory definition:[29] A social minimum targets a set of social outcomes—roughly, that no one at any time lacks the means of access to the fulfillment of certain basic material needs. "Corresponding" obligations, we vaguely added, would fall upon the state. But then what obligations correspond? Obligations how strict, for exertions how strong? No doubt the idea of a "right" to the state's exertions (in a justification-worthy constitution) presupposes some standard for a sufficiency of effort in the indicated direction. But need that standard necessarily be whatever it takes to make it be the case that everyone has by tomorrow a decent house to live in (and so on)? Won't it much more reasonably and plausibly be a standard qualified and guarded to leave room for democratic lawmakers to take account of other principles—liberty, dignity, responsibility, security, general economic prosperity—that might also have traction in that society's ordering of political values? Take, as a rough example, something like this: "The state shall, in all its fields of operation, formulate its policies and direct its conduct with a view to fulfillment of SER targets as soon, as widely, and as dependably as possible, paying due regard to other constitutional values and availability of resources."

4.2. Discursive Cogency

Such a standard quite glaringly lacks the property of "ruleness" or Weberian strong formality.[30] Granted, strict ruleness is seldom deemed a requirement

[29] See *supra* § 1.1.

[30] See Max Weber, 2 *Economy and Society: An Outline of Interpretive Sociology*, ed. Guenther Roth and Claus Wittich (University of California Press 1968) 56–57 ("Law is . . . formal to the extent that . . . only unambiguous general characteristic of the facts of the case are taken into account.").

for a norm-statement's inclusion as a requirement of constitutional law. Consider, however, a weaker property that I will name as *cogency* in public discourse. A norm-statement is discursively cogent insofar as it connects with its relevant audience—fits into its cultural context—in such a way that debates about its correct or preferred application will be, for that audience, more or less persuasively examinable and decidable by appeals to publicly available reasons, or a balance of them. Discursive cogency is an obviously necessary property for any supposedly binding constitutional guarantee, even if strict ruleness is not.

Our discussion to follow assumes that a constitutional commitment to SER can be and will be cast in terms that satisfy discursive cogency. That assumption, however, will not by itself suffice to meet the standard worry. The political-liberal project of justification-by-constitution hangs on an expectation of a more-or-less dependable public satisfaction with fulfillment in practice of the constitutional essentials, not just in the word but in the act, and discursive cogency does not cancel reasonable disagreement at the point of application of those principles and standards to ground-level legislative policies and agendas. We can concur on what we are arguing about (the most reasonable balance of agreed constitutional values) and still disagree about the outcome. That is why, as we have seen, John Rawls comes to think we need a trusted arbiter of disagreements at that applicative stage of the constitutional-justificatory procedure.[31]

But then, you see, when the constitutional essential in play is one of economic policy, and the trusted arbiter is to be a court of law, we have before us the prospect of the law court pronouncing on the reasonability of government economic policy, and the standard worry gets in the way of the entrustment. Consider, then, how the stage is set when these three conditions simultaneously hold in a single mind: (1) a regard for the legal constitution's service as a platform for justification of coercive exercises of political power (justification-by-constitution); (2) a conviction that SER assurances belong among the essential components of any possible justification-bearing constitution; and (3) a perception that proposals for constitutionalized SER fall foul of currently prevailing idealizations of the province and operations of law courts in political democracies. One possible outcome is a deeply troubled rejection of SER from constitutional-essential status. Another, though, might be receptivity to some kind of modification of currently prevailing

[31] See Chapter 2, § 2.2.

idealizations of justiciability. Those dominoes we spoke of (in section 1.2) can, after all, tip in either direction.

5. Enter Weak-Form Judicial Review

That is all, of course, a speculation. Now here is an observation to lay beside it. Legal scholars working detectably within the gravitational field of the broadly speaking liberal-constitutional tradition are these days turning out a profusion of theories and conceptions of so-called "weak-form"[32]—"dialogical,"[33] "experimentalist,"[34] "catalytic"[35]—judicial review. We can take as illustrative a "democratic experimentalist" version.[36] The court acts in the first instance as instigator and non-dictatorial overseer of engagements among stakeholders very broadly defined—governments of course included—in an ongoing process of interpretative clarification of what a constitutionally declared right of (say) "access to health care services" consists of in substance. The court engages the parties over what sorts of steps by what classes of actors are concretely (in the current conditions of society, economy, and so on) now in order toward the achievement of due and adequate service to everyone's core interest—a process of successively clarified "benchmarking" as it is sometimes called. As the discursive benchmarking moves along and the emerging answers gain public recognition and authorization, the court turns up the heat on deployment of its powers of review. At a relatively early stage, what the court presumes to dictate will be agendas of questions to be addressed and answered by one or another stakeholder group or class. At later stages, the court starts calling for substantive compliance with an emergent best-practice consensus, in the name of the constitutional right. The screws tighten on what can count as a reasonable, sincere governmental response. The court serves as arbiter but it never has or claims a door-closing last word.

[32] See Mark Tushnet, *Weak Courts, Strong Rights: Judicial Review and Social Welfare Rights in Comparative Constitutional Law* (Princeton University Press 2008) 18–42.

[33] See Rosalind Dixon, "Creating Dialog About Socioeconomic Rights" (2007) 5 *International Journal of Constitutional Law* 391.

[34] See, e.g., Oliver Gerstenberg, "Negative/Positive Constitutionalism, 'Fair Balance,' and the Problem of Justiciability" (2012) 10 *International Journal of Constitutional Law* 904.

[35] See Katherine G. Young, *Constituting Economic and Social Rights* (Oxford University Press 2012) 167–91.

[36] See, e.g., Gerstenberg, "Negative/Positive Constitutionalism"; Young, *Constituting Rights* 150–55.

My introduction of the experimentalist model is meant to suggest how the question of state compliance with a constitutionalized antipoverty commitment might be credibly proceduralized, while evading a standard worry of liberal constitutionalism. The model might thus open a path of lessened resistance to treating antipoverty as a liberal constitutional essential. The case might perhaps be generalized to a thesis on modern constitutional thought, preoccupied as that thought is with mappings of institutional situses—legislatures, administrations, courts of law (and we might add an institutional press, a political public sphere, a space for social-movement activity)—along with assignments to each of capacities and limitations, competencies and functions. In any given instance of a mapping, the idea of justification-by-constitution might or might not have purchase. Where that idea *has* in fact taken hold, constitutional actors responding to it—and I include, for this purpose, speculative constitutional theorists among constitutional actors—will be subject to a constant pull toward finding an acceptable fit between their current sense of the requirements for the moral legitimacy of a political regime and the institutional mappings they affirm or accept as settled. Movement on one side of that function must always portend the possibility, at least, of a compensating movement on the other. In a cultural setting of reliance on courts as institutional guardians of justification-bearing constitutional law, conviction of the dependence of political legitimacy on constitutionalized SER begets ideas of weak-form review. And conversely, a rise and spread of those ideas across a community of comparative constitutional scholars might signal an inhabitation of their thought by the idea of justification-by-constitution.

11
Judicial Restraint (and Judicial Supremacy)

In most constitutional democracies today, courts of law—one or more of them—pronounce from time to time on the constitutional compatibility of acts and pursuits of established political agencies. In what ways and degrees (if any) should we wish courts in such matters to proceed with restraint?[1]

But then what do we mean by restraint? As envisaged by John Rawls in *Political Liberalism*, a supreme court serves as protector of a democratic people's standing instruction for the conduct of their politics and government over trans-generational time. Simultaneously, that court serves as arbiter of a justification-worthy constitutional procedural pact in the here and now. In Chapter 9, we asked whether those two assignments might launch conflicting demands on the court when faced with contesting concretizations of abstractly worded constitutional guarantees. Now we ask whether the two assignments point toward the same or differing measures of restraint in their execution. Can there be a unified Rawlsian doctrine of judicial restraint? What would it look like? Would it stand in contradiction to ideas of "judicial supremacy" as those crop up in current debates?[2] Does pursuit of these questions help explain the durability of judicial restraint as a bone of contention in constitutional democracies?

[1] This chapter follows in general outline my "Political-Liberal Legitimacy and the Question of Judicial Restraint" (2019) 1 *Jus Cogens* 59, while incorporating a number of shifts in my thought since publication of that article.

[2] Compare, e.g., Richard H. Fallon, Jr., "Judicial Supremacy, Departmentalism, and the Rule of Law in a Populist Age" (2018) 96 *Texas Law Review* 487, 491 (hereafter Fallon, "Judicial Supremacy") ("[O]ur system is not, never has been, and probably never could be one of pure judicial supremacy.") with Larry Alexander and Frederick Schauer, "Defending Judicial Supremacy: A Reply" (2000) 17 *Constitutional Commentary* 455.

Constitutional Essentials. Frank I. Michelman, Oxford University Press. © Frank I. Michelman 2022.
DOI: 10.1093/oso/9780197655832.003.0012

1. Three Axes of Judicial Restraint

Constitutional-legal talk may use "judicial restraint" to refer to various postures of reviewing courts. Here I will distinguish among three, which I will name as "reserved," "tolerant," and "weak-form." Each term designates a relative location along an axis of possible positions.

Axis	"ACTIVIST"	"RESTRAINED"
COURT'S CONTITUTIONAL-EXPLICATIVE SERVICE TREATED AS	A primary function of the court ("free-spoken" pole)	Incidental to concrete dispute resolution ("reserved" pole)
TO WHAT QUESTION THE COURT SPEAKS	singular right or best answer ("dogmatist" pole)	outer bound of reasonability ("tolerant" pole)
WITH WHAT SYSTEMIC EFFECT THE COURT SPEAKS	Conclusive ("strong-form" pole)	Interlocutory ("weak-form" pole)

1.1. Restrained as Reserved (Opposite: Free-Spoken)

I have in view here a range of views regarding a possible special functional assignment to a country's "supreme" or "constitutional" court. At one pole, the view is that the so-named tribunal serves simply as the court of final review for some class or classes of litigated cases. It is in other respects an ordinary court, holding its powers strictly and only in pursuit of orderly resolution, by law and judicial process, of concretely live and active social conflicts. At the other pole, the supreme or constitutional court in particular has been set up to serve as arbiter to society of its divisions over correct understandings of the society's basic laws—in the words of one noted opinion from the US Supreme Court, "to call the contending sides of a national controversy to end their national division by accepting a common mandate rooted in the Constitution." I posit these as polar positions on an axis of possible stances, understanding that various mixtures and blends will turn up in practice.[3]

[3] Planned Parenthood of South-Eastern Pennsylvania. v. Casey, 505 U.S. 833, 867 (1992) (plurality opinion).

(The *Casey* plurality, for example, took care to confine occasions for the Court's exercise of its arbitral powers over constitutional meanings to those that would arise "in the performance of its judicial duties."[4])

Suppose a fairly extreme version of the reticent, case-bound view of its assignment to be the one professed by a given supreme court and its professional entourage. Judicial pronouncements on constitutional-applicative questions then will still occasionally come forth, but only when—as famously explained by Marshall, C.J., in *Marbury v. Madison*—the court finds them required for the resolution according to law of some live controversy properly brought before it, to which the constitution arguably has application as higher positive law in the county's legal order.[5] But of course not every supreme court everywhere (and perhaps not any supreme court always) will stick in purist form to the case-bound view of its assignment. Some courts will act more openly and regularly in response to a sense of the country's dependence on them for a constitutional-arbitral service that the country (or so it may be widely believed) cannot well do without.

Among supreme and constitutional courts around the world, we can observe differing dispositions to widen or to narrow the range of disputes over legal applications on which these courts stand ready to pronounce in the constitution's name. The differences may show up as relatively strict or loose applications of gateway doctrines of "standing" and "ripeness," of rules or norms against merely "advisory" judgments, of doctrines of nonjusticiability of "political questions," and so on. They may also appear as relatively broadened or narrowed readings of the substantive reach of constitutional guarantees.[6] In a given court's relative inclination toward open doors, we can perhaps detect its relatively heightened sense of society's reliance upon it for service as arbiter of political divisions over matters constitutional. A court thus inclined will be relatively *free-spoken*, in my classification here. A *reserved* court is opposite to that, inclined toward tightened notions of justiciability and narrowed readings of the scope of constitutional guarantees.

[4] Ibid.

[5] Marbury v. Madison, 5 U.S. (1 Cranch) 137 (1803).

[6] See Daniel Friedmann, *The Purse and the Sword: The Trials of Israel's Legal Revolution* (Oxford University Press 2016) 54–56 (summarizing aspects of a perceived political activism on the part of Israel's supreme court in the latter part of the twentieth century).

1.2. Restrained as Tolerant (Opposite: Dogmatist)

A court's posture is *tolerant*, I shall say, when the following conditions hold: (1) The court works within a political community which accepts that questions of a law's compatibility with constitutional requirements can sometimes be open to answers pro and con that are honestly and competently defensible on both sides, so that those on the losing side of a constitutional case in court need not always see the loss as a rupture of a regnant constitutional pact; and (2) the court turns aside challenges to laws that it, for its own part, would judge to be constitutionally noncompatible, as long as it finds an opposite conclusion to fall within bounds of what is competently defensible.[7] I will call dogmatist a court that takes the opposite position.

Well, you say, one can see how a court could exercise tolerance of that kind by declining to take up a presented case for consideration at all, assuming the laws governing the court's operation allow for such refusal. But if the court's designed service to the country is that of trusted resolution *pro tempore* of potentially destabilizing political disputes over constitutional commitments, is that service not then in some measure forgone if the court declines to answer—to give its own true judgment—when called?

Well, yes, of course, but there's nothing there to rule out judicial tolerance of reasonable disagreement. Presented with a duly mounted challenge to a statute's validity in the country's legal system, a court responds in accordance with the system's norms (its "rules of recognition") for the legal validation of statutes. Those norms, in the country concerned, may after all cast a statute as valid with reference to the country's constitution as long as its constitutional compatibility is supportable by arguments that reasonable citizens can count as reasonable. If so, then when the court upholds a statute as valid in the face of constitutional-legal challenge, a claim of the reasonable supportability of that statute's constitutional compatibility is what and all we will understand the court thus to be confirming.

[7] Does a tolerant court thus, paradoxically as it may seem, proceed to give effect to some number of laws whose enactment its members would have felt obliged to oppose as sitting parliamentarians sworn to support and defend the constitution? See Chapter 4, § 3.

1.3. Restrained as "Weak-Form" (Opposite: "Strong-Form")

A weak-form court accepts (and comports itself accordingly) that its pronouncements on matters constitutional are in normal course rejectable by other constituted political agencies, perhaps up to and including whole electorates—the court's voice to that extent becoming one more or less respected voice among others.[8] A court's posture is oppositely "strong-form" insofar as the court counts on the country to treat its pronouncements on constitutionality as fixtures thenceforward in the country's constitutional law-in-force, binding as such on other political agents and revisable only by formal constitutional amendment or subsequent reversal by that court.[9] (And by "pronouncements," there, we mean not just a court's punctual thumbs-up or thumbs-down on this or that law's constitutionality but the court's full *ratio decidendi*—say, the steps in its reasoning (or "doctrine") that would be taken as binding on lower courts in the system.)

Mark Tushnet, to whom we owe the "strong-form"/"weak-form" terminology, writes that the mark of a weak-form court is that its constitutional-legal pronouncements will be "expressly open to legislative revision in the short run."[10] "Short run" is important here. In Chapter 5, we took up the liability of judge-declared constitutional-legal doctrine to modulate over historical time in response to cultural shifts reflected in extrajudicial political movements and events.[11] As long and as far, however, as the understanding prevails that only the court itself can displace its latest doctrinal pronouncements from their operative position as law binding throughout the system, the practice is strong-form, not weak-form, in the classification I have in view.[12] Judicial supremacy is in that respect a limited institutional, not a broadly epistemic or a credal proposition. It poses no bar against public and political agitation for reversal of currently prevailing constitutional-legal

[8] See Mark Tushnet, *Weak Courts, Strong Rights: Judicial Review and Social Welfare Rights in Comparative Constitutional Law* (Princeton University Press, 2008) 2, 10 (hereafter Tushnet, *Weak Courts*). Tushnet takes as one leading example courts under the UK Human Rights Act 1998, which authorizes judicial declarations of a statute's noncompatibility with stated human rights norms while also authorizing parliamentary declination to abide by such declarations. See ibid, 7.

[9] See ibid, 1 (equating strong-form review with "judicial supremacy . . . in which the courts have the final and unrevisable word on what the Constitution means").

[10] Tushnet, *Weak Courts* (n 8) 2.

[11] See Chapter 5, § 3.

[12] Here I may depart a bit from Tushnet, who has classed such long-term developments as a variation on weak-form review. See Tushnet, *Weak Courts* (n 8) 16–20.

doctrine, including by means such as filling vacant court seats with sharers of one's own constitutional-interpretive inclinations.[13]

Note that our three polarities of judicial restraint are notionally discrete. A weak-form court, whose pronouncements on constitutionality may be more or less influential on other authorities but will not be conclusive upon them, might still—or might even all the more—be disposed toward expansionary views of its calling to speak at all; and it might still hew to the dogmatist idea that constitutional-compliance questions have singular right answers ("yes" or "no"), which each authority stands duty-bound to pronounce to the best of its ability. And conversely, a court that tolerantly allows for a possible range of reasonable, differing but all of them valid answers may still call upon the country to accept, as operationally conclusive on the system as a whole, the outer boundaries *it* would set on that space of reasonability;[14] and it may still treat more or less expansively the range of occasions on which it will speak to that question; and so on around the circle.

2. Grounds for Judicial Restraint: Democracy and Legitimacy

American legal pundits have been prone to frame the question of judicial restraint as one about democracy—or, more precisely, as one about choice among various conceptions of democracy. Judicial postures of reticence to speak, tolerance for differing opinions, and acceptance of a colloquy of constitutional-legal authorities all present themselves as counters to excessive juridical blockage of rule by current political majorities. Such blockage is deemed problematic in the first place—a "difficulty," as it has been called[15]—just insofar as we count it ipso facto deviant from democracy rightly understood.[16] But then not everyone does so count it. Some would locate democracy rather in submission by transient political majorities to the people's constitutional law laid down in moments of exceptional political arousal.[17] Some contend for liberal conceptions of democracy in which

[13] Compare Fallon, "Judicial Supremacy" (n 2) 528–29 ("The principle of institutional settlement . . . poses no impediment to . . . decisions and votes on confirmation based on independent judgments concerning how the Constitution is best interpreted."); ibid, 498.

[14] Here we may think again of the *Casey* plurality opinion. See *supra* § 1.1.

[15] Alexander Bickel, *The Least Dangerous Branch: The Supreme Court at the Bar of Politics* (Bobbs-Merrill 1962) 16–23 (on "the counter-majoritarian difficulty").

[16] Ibid, 18.

[17] See Bruce Ackerman, *We the People: Foundations* (Harvard University Press 1991) 6–7.

substantive rights are essential components from the ground up.[18] Debates over judicial restraint in matters constitutional thus have tended, with us, to end up as contentions over the best understanding of a bedrock political value of democracy.[19]

A different bedrock political value is also, though, observably at work in these debates. The value, I mean, of political legitimacy, in its Rawlsian sense of justification, among supposedly free and equal co-citizens, for collaboration in the force of laws enacted over strong opposition and dissent. An adequate grasp of the judicial-restraint debates requires a bifocal view of them, simultaneously through the lenses of democracy and legitimacy. That is because the pull to justification-by-constitution is not a mere speculative lucubration from the brain of John Rawls but a political-cultural fact alive and at work in the constitutional-democratic thought and practice of our times. That the philosophical work of Rawls might bear implications, then, for our judicial-restraint debates should come as no surprise.

3. Restraint for the Rawlsian Supreme Court

How does the Rawlsian supreme court locate itself along our three axes of reserved/free-spoken, tolerant/dogmatist, and weak-form/strong-form?

Prior chapters set the stage for answering this question. We start by reminding ourselves of the reason why—in terms of the Rawlsian program—we are, in the first place, setting up a supreme court with powers of constitutional review. Given reasonable pluralism and burdens of judgment, operation of a constitutional-justificatory procedural pact apparently requires at least one trusted agent to nail down decisive applications of its terms in disputed cases, and the supreme court is to serve as such an agent.[20] Accordingly, we ask: What is there in that assignment of judicial role and responsibility to impel us in one or the other direction along any of our three axes of judicial restraint? The answers, we anticipate, will not necessarily accord with those we would draw from purely democracy-based concerns.

[18] See Ronald Dworkin, *Freedom's Law: The Moral Reading of the American Constitution* (Harvard University Press 1886) 17–18, 23–26 (on the "constitutional conception" of democracy).

[19] See, for a critically distanced recapitulation of the debates, Nimer Sultany, "The State of Progressive Constitutional Theory: The Paradox of Constitutional Democracy and the Project of Political Justification" (2012) 47 *Harvard Civil Rights–Civil Liberties Law Review* 371.

[20] See Chapter 2, § 2.2; Chapter 3, § 1.4.

To pose the question most sharply, we can begin by supposing the system before us to be one that expressly sets up the supreme court—assisted, as it may be, by lower courts—as its one-and-only trusted final decider of applications of the constitutional essentials, on a certifiable compliance with which (in a Rawlsian well-ordered constitutional democracy) political justification can be claimed among all reasonable and rational, free and equal citizens. We will want before finishing to relax this assumption, but it gives us a good place to start.

3.1. Reserved Court? ("Justiciability")

Consequences quite arguably might follow that would strain acceptability in some constitutional democracies today. The oversight of the supreme court should seemingly then extend to all potentially divisive, currently salient issues of compliance, by statute law or government administration, of the guarantees of the constitutional-justificatory pact. That logic entails an expansionary push on the range of occasions on which the court will pronounce in the constitution's name, perhaps colliding with restrictive norms of justiciability currently regnant in some (not all) of the world's constitutional democracies.

I have here in mind the cluster of norms restricting law courts to decision of presently live (not past, not imminent, not imaginable) controversies, between parties having immediate concrete stakes in the outcomes, for which the law presents to the more-or-less naked eye what US jurists call judicially manageable standards.[21] The motivation for these restrictions is always, in part—and especially so in the constitutional field—the protection of majoritarian democracy against overreach by headstrong courts. The restrictions do not fit so neatly with the constitution's justificatory function. Insofar as they would block the supreme court—on our starting assumption, the country's uniquely trusted institutional arbiter of constitutional meanings—from addressing disputes over application of constitutional essentials on which legitimacy might well be thought to depend, they do to that extent undermine the settlement envisioned by the Rawlsian LPL.

[21] See Richard H. Fallon, Jr., "Judicially Manageable Standards and Constitutional Meaning" (2006) 19 *Harvard Law Review* 1275.

For a recent American case in point, take *Rucho*.[22] Our Supreme Court there issued a ban against response by our national judiciary to Constitution-based claims against partisan-political gerrymander.[23] Without denying the fact of the problem or its constitutional gravity, the Court concluded that any chance of correction must be left to nonjudicial political agencies. The Court cited as its reason a perceived impossibility of drawing from the Constitution, or from any applicable legislation, a measure of excessive partisanship in districting choices, sufficiently well-defined to place a court applying it above suspicion of its own partisanship. In support of that stance, one might reasonably summon a need for public confidence in the Supreme Court's nonpartisanship in its role as arbiter of constitutional meaning—a consideration to which the Rawlsian proposition for justification-by-constitution must certainly attend. If trust in the Court's nonpartisanship should fail, then so, too, in a society rent by partisan divisions, must fail any proposition for justification-by-constitution that depends on confidence in the courts.

From the standpoint of a Rawlsian conception of constitutional guarantees as our platform of justification for the force of majoritarian laws among free and equal citizens of divided political, ideological, and moral outlooks, what results is thus a standing dilemma, internal to the political-liberal project of justification-by-constitution. But this, we now must notice, is a consequence of our *arguendo* assumption of the society's installation of a law court as its sole trusted final decider of applications of the constitutional essentials. Granting that some form of institutional settlement is needed here,[24] the dilemma would abate with entrustment of that function or some share of it to some more openly political process, one whose perceived nonpartisanship would rest not (or not exclusively) on attribution of special skills of decryption of legal texts and precedents but rather (or also) on breadth, quality, and vigor of participatory input.[25] We might accordingly think of entrustment of the needed institutional-settlement function to a colloquy of official and popular political agencies, in which the supreme court takes part but in

[22] Rucho v. Common Cause, 139 S. Ct. 2484 (2019).

[23] This expression designates a calculated shaping by state legislatures of electoral districts for local, state, and federal legislative representation, so as to give advantage to a favored political party, allowing that party, although overall outvoted, nevertheless to gain and keep control of the legislative body in question.

[24] See Chapter 2, § 2.2.

[25] See Martha Minow, "Not in the Room Where It Happens: Adversariness, Politicization, and *Little Sisters of the Poor*" [2020] *The Supreme Court Review* 1 (hereafter Minow, "Room Where It Happens").

course of which it recedes when its credibility credentials (relative to those of others involved) are weak.

3.2. Weak(er) Court?

Is a Rawlsian comfort zone then to be sought in retreat from a conception of the court-of-law as sole trusted final arbiter *pro tempore* of disputed questions of constitutionality, to one of trust in a colloquy of institutions, in which the supreme court's relative influence would wax and wane with the kind of question at hand? With that thought, Americans (just to stick with our case for illustration) would be contemplating a shift away from a stronger-form toward a weaker-form (or mixed-form) conception of our supreme court's role in the field of institutional settlement of constitutional-legal applications.

Such a shift, if accomplishable, would ease concerns about judicial overreach in a democracy—a weak-form (or mixed-form) court being defined as one whose pronouncements on constitutional compliance are not (or are not always) conclusively binding on the country but rather invite response from other constituted political agencies. But then the question comes about the baby in the bath water—the baby being the proceduralizing ambition of the Rawlsian program for justification-by-constitution. If the constitutional-procedural pact requires designation of some specified agency or process to serve as its finally trusted institutional protector, and if in some country that role has landed historically on a supreme court, it seems an open allowance to other agencies to override that court's pronouncements must undermine the pact. Can that court's authority *now* safely be allowed to recede from strong-form to weaker-form, from the last and final word on constitutional applications to just one voice in the mix?

3.2.1. Short-Term Legislative Consultation

Before plunging further into that question, we should take note of a well-known variation on strong-form judicial review that we can name as short-term legislative consultation. Strong-form review, we have said, means the court's constitutional-legal pronouncements remain binding on the country until such time as the court itself may revise them.[26] That does not mean, though, that determinations of constitutional meanings and applications

[26] See *supra* § 1.3.

from an otherwise strong-form court need take full and final legal control from the instant of their first utterance.[27] The LPL's proceduralizing strategy requires that a trusted arbiter's determinations of constitutional meaning, once finalized, be treated as controlling system-wide unless and until revised by a trusted arbiter. Within that constraint, system and practice can cater in various ways for a court's further short-term exchange with a legislature, following upon the court's initial finding of constitutional violation. A system can, for example, allow for judicial suspension of remedial orders pending remand to the legislature for its further consideration, following upon a court's initial finding of a constitutional violation but still pending finalization of a judicial order to implement that finding. Such allowances plainly are designed to leave some wiggle room for negotiation between regard for majority rule and a specially trusted judicial oversight of compliance with the essential terms of a justificatory load-bearing constitution.

3.2.2. Strong-Form Interagency Constitutional Colloquy

Back now to the possibility of retention in the legal system of an ultimate strong-form decisive authority on constitutionality, while taking that authority (in Mark Tushnet's phrase) partly or wholly "away from the courts."[28] The Rawlsian proposition for justification-by-constitution does undoubtedly require a trusted institutional authority or process for the short-term resolution of disputed matters of constitutional law. There is, however, no abstract necessity—nor is there any final insistence by Rawls—that the entrustment go to a supreme court or any court or courts of law.[29] It could be rested in a committee of the parliament, or in some other, specially constituted body. Or it could reside in a process of communicative exchange among constituted political agencies up to and including whole electorates, *as long as* the process could dependably operate to deliver resolutions, with acceptable dispatch, in a manner transparent to citizens and acceptable by them.

[27] Abraham Lincoln famously took this view. See *The Collected Works of Abraham Lincoln*, vol. 2, ed. Roy P. Basler (Rutgers University Press 1953) 494–96 (Speech at Chicago, Ill., July 10, 1858) (discussing the proper attitude of political actors toward the Supreme Court's ruling, in Dred Scott v. Sandford, 60 U.S. (19 How.) 393 (1857), that the Constitution bars both Congress and territorial legislatures from enacting laws barring slavery from any part of the territorial holdings of the United States prior to statehood); ibid, vol. 3, 543–45 (Address at Cooper Institute, New York City, February 27, 1860) (same).

[28] See Mark Tushnet, *Taking the Constitution Away from the Courts* (Princeton University Press 1999).

[29] See Chapter 3, § 1.4.

A Rawls-compatible process of interagency colloquy on the demands of constitutional law would not be all-out "departmentalist," if that term signifies an invitation to each major agency or department to go on indefinitely applying its own considered views on constitutional meanings to matters claimed to fall within its particular keeping.[30] For the constitution-centered liberal principle of legitimacy, it just won't do to have a supreme court confirming a constitutional guarantee of marriage equality while officials in some places persist in refusal, on grounds of a differing constitutional interpretation, to issue marriage licenses in contravention of standing statute law or what they take to be established common law. Whether or not such a state of affairs could ever be compatible with your or my abstract ideas of the rule of law, it plainly is not compatible with the LPL's proposition for justification-by-constitution, by which (as I described it in Chapter 1)

> the constitution's content [supposedly] is such that any citizen can look any other in the eye and say: Accepting the need for some system of social ordering by law, and given the special challenge of justification of the force of law among free and equal citizens in pluralist conditions, a system constituted by *just these* basic-level commitments and expectations (here pointing to the constitution) is sufficiently worth upholding to give each of us prevailing moral reason to accept presumptively as binding law whatever issues duly from the system.[31]

Any Rawls-compatible practice of resolution of constitutional issues outside the courts would thus have to be designed, whether by legislated script or reliable constitutional convention, to issue in sufficiently timely, sufficiently definite resolutions of constitutional- essential applications. If a supreme court should happen to be there ruling on constitutional questions in cases coming before it, that court will have a place in any such practice. And then if, within that practice, the court happened to be granted or to gain a leading or influential voice, that could be just an accident of how matters historically have turned out. Or it might be because the culturally embedded modes of legal discourse have been found after all—despite doubts expressed by some

[30] See Fallon, "Judicial Supremacy" (n 2) 495 ("The basic idea of departmentalism is [that] each branch interprets the Constitution for itself."); ibid, 497.
[31] Chapter 1, § 3.1.

contemporary observers of US-style judicial supremacy[32]—to hold some genuine advantages for a process of continued development, over time, of the cluster of constitutional meanings on which stability and legitimacy are believed to depend.[33]

Parts of Chapters 5, 7, and 8 will have suggested how such a view might reasonably come be held in one or another country. A further condition no doubt would be that the country's courts over time have met the culture halfway by refraining from judgments that too large a fraction of the public would find not reasonably entertainable.[34] The sum of it is that a given country's historical experience and current situation may be such as to warrant a reasonable hesitation to entrust institutional settlement of constitutional meanings to a process of politics *not* under judicial leadership. We turn now to see whether our second axis of judicial restraint, that of judicial tolerance for public political disagreement, might offer the possibility for capturing, under judicial leadership, some pro-democratic advantages of the colloquy model without sacrifice of the institutional settlements required by the Rawlsian proposition for legitimation-by-constitution.

3.3. Tolerant Court?

Rawlsian procedural justification-by-constitution, I have argued, requires entrustment to some institutional setup of conclusive (strong-form) authority to decide for the short-term some (I do not say all) pending questions of the validity of legislation under constitutional challenge. Does that setup then have to decide dogmatically, according to its purported finding of a singular best or right answer, or might it tolerantly read the constitution to allow space for differing answers to questions of application? We take from prior chapters that the Rawlsian supreme court adopts the latter view of the constitution for which it serves as arbiter and protector, but perhaps that does not entirely answer our current query. We still have to ask whether there might be a difference worth noticing between a dogmatic and a tolerant approach

[32] See, e.g., Minow, "Room Where It Happens" (n 25) 45–47; Frank I. Michelman, "Why Not Just Say No? An Essay on the Obduracy of Constitution Fixation" (2014) 94 *Boston University Law Review* 1141, 1148–50 (gathering examples of the doubts without endorsing or rejecting them).

[33] Compare Fallon, "Judicial Supremacy" (n 2), 528 ("The nature of judicial decision-making . . . renders it peculiarly well suited to achieve clarity, settlement, and stability in constitutional law.").

[34] See ibid, 508 (explaining why courts concerned to preserve the trust are unlikely to issue decisions that could plausibly be "regarded as *ultra vires* or as imminently dangerous").

to the trusted authority's work of pronouncing on the outer bounds of constitution-applicative reasonability.

Recall the general Rawlsian program for judicial constitutional appraisals. In the face of plausible conflicting claims for protection from one or another of the constitution's essential guarantees, restrict the set of admissible solutions to those that can credibly claim to be aimed at maintaining the overall scheme of liberties in shape conducive to each person's full and adequate development and exercise of his or her moral powers.[35] Assuming its adherence to that guideline, a dogmatist court applies it by imposing on the country its view of the uniquely superior balance of applicable constitutional principles and values, condemning any legislative choice not squaring with that. The dogmatist court is not concerned with any differentiation between judgments of the singularly best balance and (say) an "at-least reasonable" balance. By contrast, owing in part to what he has come to see as a plurality of liberally reasonable underlying conceptions of justice, I have read Rawls to allow that the set of liberally reasonable solutions under any given justification-bearing constitution will not always be restricted to a single member.[36] He expects that sometimes there will be multiple solutions credibly claiming support from a reasonable balance of constitutionally sanctioned public reasons.

And then Rawls would be further bound, I think, to say that the strong-form, dogmatist court, by imposing on the country its own "most reasonable" balance of the applicable public reasons, would be writing into the constitutional pact a foreclosure of the contest of reasonable balances, thus running straight against his argument for keeping thin and sparse that pact's substantive guarantees.[37] By that argument, it rather seems, a law supportable by any at-least reasonable balance must be held within a democratic legislature's power to enact or not as it sees fit. Accordingly, Rawls's citizens—each expected to exercise political voice on behalf of what they respectively judge to be the most reasonable orderings of political values—are still expected all to abide willingly by legislative outcomes they all can find at least reasonable.[38] A Rawlsian supreme court—but let us now, instructed by this chapter's section 3.2, speak instead of a Rawlsian entrusted constitutional

[35] See Chapter 3, § 1.2.

[36] See Chapter 3, § 2.

[37] See Chapter 2, § 2.2; Chapter 3, § 1.1.

[38] See "PRR" 798 ("[T]he outcome of the vote . . . is to be seen as legitimate provided all government officials, supported by other reasonable citizens, of a reasonably just constitutional regime sincerely vote in accordance with the idea of public reason."); see ibid, 765, 770, 773, 797–99.

authority—accordingly must be one that allows for possibilities of differing resolutions consistent with good-faith adherence to the constitutional-justificatory pact—"not all reasonable balances are the same."[39]

We could use here an illustrative case. Say the state has recently extended its antidiscrimination statutes to prohibit commercial refusals to deal on the basis of a customer's perceived LGBQT status or identity, and the country's constitution, written well in the past, contains guarantees respecting liberties of conscience, association, expression, and religion, and also of the equal protection of the laws. Does the combination of those guarantees prohibit—or does it require—application of the new statute to purveyors of wedding-related goods and services engaged in faith-based refusals to serve or supply same-sex lawful weddings? Democratic citizens in our times, all adhering conscientiously to the listed set of constitutional guarantees, are fated to disagree about the singularly true or best answers to these questions, or about the details of one or another proposed legislative design for mediation of the conflict. The Rawlsian supreme constitutional authority accepts that two or more differing balance-judgments can sometimes all be seen to be at-least reasonable by citizens, and so be seen by them as consistent with a credible commitment to the extant constitutional deal on justification. The Rawlsian authority, so far, is a tolerant court.

To say so is not to contradict either of our deductions that a supreme court serving as Rawlsian entrusted constitutional authority is not excessively reserved or that the Rawlsian proceduralist principle of legitimacy requires *pro tempore* institutional settlement of controversies over constitutional applications. A court or other authority that speaks widely to questions of constitutional compliance can still, when it speaks, confine judgments of disqualification to legislative choices falling outside the range of tolerably reasonable balances of the relevant public values. The authority's pronouncements upholding or rejecting the reasonability of one or another legislative choice must still contain their statements of major and intermediate supporting premises, and those can then still stand, in strong-form style, as the country's settled resolutions of constitutional law, unless and until revised by the authority. Thus, even for an authority that leans toward expansionist (free-spoken) in its outreach and strong-form in its expectations of submission to its doctrinal pronouncements when finalized, a tolerance for reasonable disagreement can open some space for negotiation

[39] *PL* 253.

between ongoing popular infusion to constitutional law and the legal-positivist tilt to the LPL.

4. Summation: Rawls and Judicial Supremacy

> "In constitutional government, the ultimate power cannot be left to the legislature or even a supreme court, which is only the highest judicial interpreter of the constitution. Ultimate power is held by the three branches in a duly specified relation with one another with each responsible to the people."[40]

It is one thing to set up a supreme court to serve as the country's highest judicial interpreter of its constitution; a constitutional democracy may require no less. It would be, however, a quite other thing—a wrong one, Rawls says, a betrayal of constitutional democracy—to concede to that court an "ultimate power" in the country. But exactly how, then, does Rawls mean for us to be drawing the line that stops the highest judicial interpreter of the constitution from holding ultimate power? Does the crucial emphasis there go on "the constitution," or rather on "judicial?"

On the first option, we read this Rawlsian manifesto as a reminder of the restriction to "framework" level of any constitution suited to a democracy. The proposition is that the constitution in a democracy is not a total *corpus juris* but rather is a framework law setting certain forms, limits, and demands on the democratic production of the great mass of the laws. It follows that a judicial body set up to rule over applications of that framework law lacks any further power to set the laws governing matters of social concern. In constitutional government, then, ultimate power (in *that* sense of the term) is not left to a court serving only as highest *constitutional* interpreter.

But Rawls did not write "is not left." He wrote "cannot be left," and by doing so pointed us straight at an emphasis on "judicial." A country's highest *judicial* constitutional interpreter does not ipso facto become its *sole or final* constitutional interpreter. A sole final power to construe at discretion the country's law of limits and demands on the aims and contents of ordinary lawmaking would properly count as "ultimate" in the hands of any body that held it, and Rawls plainly is to be read here as entering a denial that investment of

[40] *PL* 232.

a supreme court with such a power could be consonant with constitutional-democratic government. The issue Rawls addresses here is precisely that of "judicial supremacy" *in the constitutional-legal field*—in Richard Fallon's words, concession to the supreme court of "ultimate authority in matters of constitutional interpretation."[41] And then we can see Rawls, in his response, casting a sympathetic eye in directions we might label as departmentalist (talk of "the three branches") and popular constitutionalist ("responsible to the people"). My claim, however, is that we cannot read Rawls as meaning to land us in either of those camps of outright contradiction (if so we construe them) or flat-out opposition to judicial supremacy. Rather we are landed in a field of compromise.

Political philosophy, by Rawlsian lights, encompasses obligation for a model, at least, for a realistically possible institutional instantiation of its ideal political conceptions.[42] Of course that holds for the proceduralistic proposition for justification-by-constitution (the liberal principle of legitimacy), proffered in response to the problem of political liberalism. Throughout *Political Liberalism* and "The Idea of Public Reason Revisited," Rawls's model of a realistically possible institutional instantiation is that of a practice, reliably entrenched in political culture, of ordinary deference to judicial leadership in constitutional interpretation. I do not think we can or should sharply differentiate the sort of ordinary-deference practice thus envisaged by Rawls from ideas of judicial supremacy as those actually circulate in constitutional-democratic societies today. It falls comfortably, for example, within Richard Fallon's approving description of our own country's evolved historical practice as one of judicial review "within politically constructed bounds."[43]

We have noticed, in the course of this chapter, various avenues for a sharing of constitutional interpretation among the court, other branches, and the people, all of which I think Rawls could endorse and none of which contradict a strong-form understanding of the supreme court's doctrinal pronouncements on the limits of wide constitutional compatibility—that is, that these pronouncements remain in place as constitutional law for the country, subject only to revision or restatement by the supreme court or by a recognized political process of constitutional revision. The combination of

[41] Fallon, "Judicial Supremacy" (n 2), 488.

[42] See Chapter 1, § 4.1

[43] See Fallon, "Judicial Supremacy" (n 2) 492. Fallon differentiates the practice thus described from strict-sense (or "pure" or "robust") judicial supremacy, see ibid, 491, 508, but he also suggests it's what Americans normally envisage as judicial supremacy within reason, see ibid, 491 & nn 26, 27 (compiling modified conceptions of judicial supremacy in recent US scholarship).

those avenues with that understanding adds up to the practice of ordinary deference to judicial leadership that I want to say is the Rawlsian response to the question of judicial supremacy.

Sharing of constitutional interpretation among the branches and the people occurs over both the short run and the long run. In the long run, as Rawls writes, "a strong majority of the electorate can eventually make the constitution conform to its political will."[44] Rawls treats that as "a fact about political power as such," which no institutional setup can alter.[45] That's not to say, though, that he holds the fact to be regrettable. To the contrary, as we have seen, Rawls relies on that ultimate popular power as the medium of reconciliation, over the long run, of the demand for rule by the people in a democracy with the need at all times for an institutionally settled body of justification-supportive constitutional essentials.[46] The stipulated condition is that the inevitable long-run conformity of constitutional law to political will normally occurs *through*—not in place of—modification of judicial pronouncements on constitutional-legal doctrine. If that condition is maintained, then over the long run the people rule even as the proceduralistic requirements of justification-by-constitution are upheld.

But there is more to political life than the long run; the present time, the time of our lives, counts, too, and what about that? Shorter-run sharing of constitutional-interpretive authority can occur through remedial devices such as judicial remands to political branches; through judicial abstentions from rulings on matters or in causes classed as nonjusticiable; and through a judicial and a general public posture of (widely) bounded tolerance for constitutional-interpretive disagreement—all without unacceptable deviation from a liberal idea of the rule of law, on a reasonable and realistic understanding thereof, as the actual experience of constitutional democracies around the world will attest.

That's not a stunningly new or original take on questions of judicial restraint and judicial supremacy in a constitutional democracy. As Richard Fallon demonstrates, a pure practice of judicial supremacy could not possibly pass as a normatively reasonable or a rationally attributable aim for any constitutional democracy, and reasonable defenders of judicial supremacy can be championing at most "a regime of presumptive, [not] absolute, judicial finality."[47] Classification of a judicial-review practice as strong-form

[44] *PL* 233.
[45] Ibid.
[46] See Chapter 5, § 3.
[47] Fallon, "Judicial Supremacy" (n 2) 507.

can accordingly only ever be relative, never absolute. What Rawls distinctively contributes to the debate, I think, is a strength of determination not to recede entirely from a strong-form conception of judicial constitutional review, rooted in the idea of constitutional law as a procedural platform of justification for political power, among free and equal citizens in conditions of reasonable pluralism, in answer to the problem of political liberalism.

12

Legal Formalism and the Rule of Law

1. Fixing Ideas

1.1. "The Rule of Law"

Metaphysically speaking, "the rule of law" names an idea—you might hold it yourself or attribute it to others—of a kind of cosmic ideal force called "law," or maybe better "legality," to which human affairs are at all times and everywhere beholden, like it or not. Politically speaking, by contrast, the formula "rule of law" names a category of preferred or desired governmental practices, comprising elements of authority and obligation, transparency and accountability, regularity and fairness in the extension and administration of state power. On the metaphysical notion, the rule of law is a condition of Being (as it were), the way things are. Whatever we do or say, lawness—legality—holds sway. Scramble as we may to evade the mandate, delete it from the world we cannot. On the political notion, the rule of law is a contingency of society, a condition we sustain (or not) by the choice and practice of humans in positions to decide; we choose for it or we do not, you have to look and see. It is in that sense, the political sense, that a Rawlsian account treats "the rights and protections of the rule of law" as falling among the essential substantial guarantees in a liberally justification-worthy constitution.[1]

These two notions of the rule of law, the political and the metaphysical, are conceptually discrete. You can embrace some version of the political notion while having no truck with the metaphysical. And indeed the converse is equally true if you think about it. We may at any moment see ourselves standing under a cosmic liability that we are materially free to disregard (if at peril of some sort), but not metaphysically so.

[1] See *PL* 227 ("protections of the rule of law"); ibid, 291 ("rights and liberties covered by the rule of law").

Constitutional Essentials. Frank I. Michelman, Oxford University Press. © Frank I. Michelman 2022.
DOI: 10.1093/oso/9780197655832.003.0013

1.2. "Legal Formalism"

As a political notion (it, too, has a metaphysical variant), "legal formalism" refers to preference respecting modes of expression of legal norms. Formalist-minded lawyers and judges want to find in the law books the verbal wherewithal for decision of cases coming before the courts without fresh injection from the judges of considerations of policy or value.[2] They accordingly seek rendition of applicable legal norms wherever possible in the grammatical mode of "rule" rather than "principle" or "standard."[3] Concurring with Rawls on the indispensability from any just or legitimate political regime of the protections of the rule of law, they find these protections best served by a law of rules. They furthermore see ruleness in the law books as required for a due subordination of the adjudicative to the legislative power in a democracy.[4] By no means, however, are such views universally held among the liberal-minded. Virtues and vices of formalistic leanings in legal administration have been and remain an enduring topic of controversy in broadly speaking liberal legal intellectual circles. The judges in our societies obviously differ, and by a lot, in the extents of their attachments to a formalist style.[5]

1.3. A Question: "Liberal Legalism" Applied to Rawls?

Politically conceived, the rule of law takes shape as of a set of strictures or guidelines for the administration of the coercive force of the state, which may or may not be observably in force at a given time and place. The guidelines

[2] *Wex*, an online legal dictionary maintained by the Cornell Law School's Legal Information Institute, offers this as its definition of "legal formalism": *a theory that legal rules stand separate from other social and political institutions. According to this theory, once lawmakers produce rules, judges apply them to the facts of a case without regard to social interests and public policy.*

As the *Wex* definition shows, legal formalism can come in metaphysical dress, as a claim about what law properly just *is*.

[3] In the jurisprudential common usage we follow here, "ruleness" in a legal directive has the sense of application rigidly determined by "the presence together of each of a list of easily distinguishable factual aspects of a situation"—such as, for example, the state of residence, prior criminal record, and chronological age of an applicant for a driver's license. A legal directive speaks rather as a "standard" or "principle" insofar as it calls on the applier not just "to discover the facts of a particular situation [but further] to assess them in terms of . . . purposes or social values embodied in the standard"—say, a directive to apply a test of competency to drive. Duncan Kennedy, "Form and Substance in Private Law Adjudication" (1976) 89 *Harvard Law Review* 1685, 1687–88.

[4] See, e.g., Antonin Scalia, "The Rule of Law as a Law of Rules" (1989) 56 *University Chicago Law Review* 1175–88.

[5] See, e.g., Kathleen M. Sullivan, "The Supreme Court, 1991 Term—Foreword: The Justices of Rules and Standards" (1992) 106 *Harvard Law Review* 22.

come mixed and matched in a variety of dresses. One might think here of Lon Fuller's eight precepts for King Rex[6] and also of the comparative constitutional lawyer's doctrinal grab bag of "due process," "administrative justice," "principle of legality," "law of general application," and so on. Dyed-in-the-wool liberals and deep democrats may not all easily converge on a final listing, but they will agree on a lot of it. The main point for now is that as long as they are contesting over choices to be made by whoever in society is thought to be in control of such determinations, our liberals and democrats will be engaged with what I am calling a political notion of the rule of law.

No one I aim to converse with here has any quarrel with the idea of the rule of law as political. Metaphysical intimations meet, by contrast, with strenuous objection from democracy-minded critics. They quite plausibly see there two bad tendencies. One is an excessive attraction to legal formalism. The other is a tendency toward popular political passivity inimical to democracy—an attitude of acceptance of the laws as they stand as an expression of the way things simply are—sometimes named by critics as "reification" and explained by them as an accompaniment to liberal legalist metaphysics.

In the critiques, the two bad tendencies travel together. An idea of legality as an impersonal force—an idea (or a wish) that true government proceeds from "laws" and not from "men"—entails that lawness should take the form of a rule that leaves no space for politics from the judge.[7] A recent fine essay from Steven Winter calls "quintessentially liberal" a resulting unfortunate conjunction of reification and formalization in the constitutional-legal field.[8] How accurate, I want ask, would that characterization be as applied to the political-liberal constitutional thought of John Rawls?

"Not at all," one might hastily reply, for the simple reason that when Rawls speaks expressly of "the rule law," it is always in what I have been at pains to distinguish as a political-not-metaphysical sense of that expression. When the Rawlsian texts make reference to a constitutional-democratic ideal named as "rule of law," it is never to any idea of the subordination of

[6] See Lon L. Fuller, *The Morality of Law* (Yale University Press, rev. ed. 1969) 33–151 (on "the morality that makes law possible").

[7] See Steven Winter, "'Who' or 'What' Is the Rule of Law?" (2021) *Philosophy and Social Criticism* <https://journals.sagepub.com/doi/abs/10.1177/01914537211021148#> accessed 17 April 2022_ (hereafter Winter, "Rule of Law"). ("So understood, the rule-of-law ideal is closely entwined with [a] tendency toward formalism. . . . On this view, the logical compulsion of a rule is what gives law its impersonal force.").

[8] Ibid

democratic rule to a higher-order normative conception detached from democratic politics, but always to practices of regularity, fairness, generality (and so on) in impositions of governmental force on the lives and activities of individuals and groups in society. That response, however, may move too fast. True as I believe it to be, it does not foreclose a detection in Rawlsian constitutional thought of a dose of Winter's liberal reified rule-of-law quintessence, under some heading other than "rule of law." I will be suggesting we can see a trace of it there in plain sight under the head of "legitimacy" and the constitution-centered "liberal principle" thereof. It will be a part of my business in this chapter to ask how great a separation thus results between liberal political thought and opposing democracy-based models. The difference is not nil, I will conclude, but it may not lie exactly where the democracy-minded sometimes seem to suppose.

2. What the Rawlsian Liberal "Rule of Law" Principle Is Not

2.1. Higher Law in a Dualist System

Before proceeding to that argument, I want first to acquit Rawls of a certain kind of rule-of-law metaphysic that indeed has had its place in the history of liberal constitutionalism. I put myself in the witness chair. "In Frank Michelman's words"—thus recalls Steven Winter—"law becomes [in the liberal understanding] 'an autonomous force' that provides 'an external untouchable rule of the game.'"[9] Well, yes, those are my words. I want now to recall them in the context in which they appeared, by way of fuller explanation both of what Winter has in his critical sights and what a Rawlsian constitution-related notion of the rule of law is not. The source is a paper of mine from 1988.

The American constitutional framers of 1787–88—such was my postulate for that paper—had in contemplation a certain sort of common good for the American republic, centered on expectations of respect for property, performance of contracts, and regularity and predictability in the law and the modes of its administration. Good republican government accordingly

[9] Winter, "Rule of Law" (n 7) __, quoting from Frank I. Michelman, "Political Truth and the Rule of Law" (1988) 8 *Tel Aviv Studies in Law* 281, 287 (hereafter Michelman, "Political Truth").

would encompass a continuing deliberation toward the right and best means to securing those expectations. A corresponding American civic virtue would be a person's motivation and ability to join that sort of deliberation. To the American framers' observations, such motivations and abilities were not to be expected at all times from all citizens. The challenge was to constitute a form of government in which the governors, at least, would reliably be among the civically virtuous or at any rate would be led so to act in their exercise of governing powers.

Historians and theorists have long been drawn to explaining how the framers sought to do that through institutional devices such as federalism, departmental checks and balances, the "extended republic" of large constituencies, indirect elections, and so forth. Their inventions, as I wrote in 1988, confronted a dilemma: on the one horn a republican commitment against class rule, on the other a distrust of popular politics. In their predicament, my account continued, the framers found their way to a conception of a people both constituting themselves as sovereign and, by that same self-constitutive act, fixing limits and constraints on the powers of the governmental agent they set up to act on their collective behalf. They produced, as I wrote, "the remarkable idea of a sovereignty both popular and self-limited, a people's collective self-government limited by a collectively self-imposed rule of law—thus a rule that, while it originates in the people, also stands imperiously above them."[10] But in order (now to come to it) to serve the idea of a self-limiting sovereign will, that law, once laid down,

> must become, vis-a-vis ordinary politics, an autonomous force, elaborated through its own nonpolitical modes of reason by its own nonpolitical organ. It must stand forth as . . . an external untouchable rule of the political game.[11]

So there you have it, an epitome of a metaphysical idea of the rule of law at a historical wellspring of democratic-liberal constitutionalism, at least on my account as of 1988.

That account has its distant echo in this book. It comes with my repeated insistence on the necessary implication, in Rawlsian justification-by-constitution, of an always already prior fixation of constitutional law to govern

[10] Ibid, 286–87.
[11] Ibid, 287.

current political choice. I will have more about that soon , but I want first to nail down that this idea of a necessary antecedence of a prior-to-politics law to govern everyday politics is not—it cannot be—any part or attribute of *"the rule of law"* as used by Rawls to name a guarantee internal to—contained in—a liberally justification-worthy constitution.

2.2. "The Rule of Law" as Constitutional Essential

In the Rawlsian proposition for justification-by-constitution, the essentials for a liberally justification-worthy constitution include guarantees respecting "equal basic rights and liberties that legislative majorities are to respect." Among those liberties Rawls includes (as a bundled item) "the protections of the rule of law"[12]—or, a bit more expansively, "the rights and liberties covered by the rule of law."[13] In the written constitutions envisaged by Rawls,[14] those protections take verbal shape as clauses on "due process of law," "equality before the law," "administrative justice," and so on. As propositions for qualitatively approvable governmental conduct (good, right, permissible, legitimate, valid), they stand on a footing quite distinct from ideas about a systemic hiving-off of constitutional law from the daily run of democratic politics. You do not have to accept the latter in order to affirm the former.

Consider the views of Democrat, as we'll call this person. Democrat says a political regime is deplorable insofar as it does not commit to certain policies of regularity, prospectivity, predictability, generality, fairness, and so on—"legality," in a word?—in the administration of state force. Democrat simultaneously says a regime is deplorable insofar as it removes decision and control over those same aspects of state practice (and indeed any aspects of state practice) from the keeping of sufficiently determined current political majorities. The first of those claims from Democrat is one about substantively good or right outcomes from a political structure: Does the structure or does it not instigate the common substance of a rule-of-law regime? The second

[12] *PL* 227.

[13] Ibid, 291. To be precise: "The protections of the rule of law" in Rawls's itemization of rights-based constitutional essentials is a carryover to the stage of the constitutional convention of "the rights and liberties covered by the rule of law" adopted at the stage of the original position. (On Rawls's notional "four-stage sequence" in the specification of the laws of a liberally just or legitimate regime, see *TJ* 196–97; Chapter 5 § 3.2.).

[14] On Rawls's supposition of a written constitution as the normal case for a liberal constitutional democracy, see Chapter 2, §§ 2.2, 3.2.

is about a good or a right sort of political structure. Democrat might see the two claims as fused together in a certain conception of democratic equality for which he advocates. (So it is with the conception of Steven Winter on which I have been drawing for this chapter.) He is at any rate not caught in any contradiction. His democratic majorities either will or they won't make it their business to have their government live up to those rule-of-law ideals of regularity, generality, and so on. If Democrat thinks it right or best to rely on unrestricted majority rule for the better outcome, then presumably he harbors some hope of that coming to pass (a realistic utopia). Democrat's hope could turn out misplaced. His strong-democratic criterion of rightness in politics could turn out ill-starred. But a misplaced hope is not a contradiction, and neither is an ill-starred criterion of rightness. *Fiat justitia, ruat caelum* could be some kind of mistake, but a contradiction it is not.

John Rawls takes a somewhat different view from Democrat's of the political-structural issue. I view that difference in relation to Rawls's placement of *his* hopes (for a realistic utopian answer to the problem of political liberalism) on a proceduralistic idea of justification-by-constitution. That idea presupposes—it depends on—a commonly legible fixture at a given time and place of a set of constitutional essentials that all citizens then and there classifiable as reasonable-for-citizens should accept as reasonable-for-constitutions. Democrat might or might not agree to that way of defining the challenge. (He might or might not see Rawls's "problem of political liberalism" as one to be taken to heart.) If he did, we could say his disagreement with Rawls then lies exactly in their differing thoughts about where reasonability comes out on the question of a bill of rights in an otherwise democratic constitution: require it, exclude it, or leave it to depend on the country's historical situation?

3. Formalist Remainders in Rawlsian Constitutional Rights

A Rawlsian proposition for justification-by-constitution in a modern liberal democracy results, as I have argued in this book, in a particular structure of argument to attend upon rights-based judicial constitutional review of ordinary-level legislative activity. The test for intra-systemic validation for a questioned legislative policy or directive then takes a particular shape. It consists of a comparison of the questioned policy with a scheme of guarantees set out in a constitution-in-force, to see whether the policy complies with the guarantees. But the judgment regarding compliance will sometimes have to occur in a field of competing conceptions of the reaches of some of the guarantees in the scheme and competing proposed balances among their respective demands on the policy in question. The standard of judicial assessment then is one of the reasonability of the conceptions and balances required to validate the contested law as compliant with the constitution-in-force.

On that account of it, the Rawlsian view may seem—with its implication of a normal plurality of reasonable conceptions and balances—immediately to fall on the anti-formalist side of intra-liberal contention over legal formalism in the constitutional-interpretive field. So it mainly does, but not without qualification or complication. Justification-by-constitution still depends on the court for strong-form *pro tempore* pronouncements on the outer bounds of reasonability for legislated policies and directives.[15] That means reasonability as a reading of something "out there" in the public view, a commonly legible constitution-in-force. Required by the Rawlsian proposition (the LPL) for political justification in a modern-pluralist constitutional democracy is a reading of the constitutional law-in-force, detached on the one hand from political currents of the day and on the other hand from free-floating political-philosophical speculation. There you see the element of *positivism* (as jurisprudence would name it) in the Rawlsian constitutionalist program.

That doesn't yet make it into a program for *reification* in Winter's sense of alienation of the higher positive law from human or social or democratic sources (or "formalist" in that sense of the term). To sustain the latter charge, you would have to look beyond the positivism in the Rawlsian conception to Rawls's expectation—also packed in, as we have argued, to his conception for a justification-sustaining constitution—that judicial determinations of the outer bounds of reasonability in constitutional-interpretive controversy are to be charted with reference to what is common across a family of differing *but still all-of-them liberal* underlying political conceptions. No doubt that does introduce a moment of the subjection of the exercise of democratic political authority to "an external untouchable rule of the game." A question that remains is about how liberal-leery democrats like Winter then escape the same charge. They do escape it, no quarrel there. What is interesting is to see exactly how they do.

[15] See Chapter 11, §§ 3.3, 4.

4. How Does Strong Democracy Finally Differ?

It is not by refusing to treat a commitment to what we may call a common policy ideal of "the rule of law" as antecedently regulative for a morally approvable political regime. No doubt liberalism, including that of John Rawls, does do that. But doing so is no more to set that ideal in opposition to democracy than (say) Jeremy Waldron would do in counting such a commitment among his prior stipulations for "a democracy in good working order," on which he premises his case against judicial review;[16] or than British followers of A.V. Dicey and John Griffith do in counting such a commitment—as they always do—as a key part of Britain's "political constitution";[17] or than Steven Winter does in his article I have been citing. In none of their conceptions is democracy normatively or conceptually free to trash or set aside the common policy ideal of the rule of law (and still be a "democracy" worth contending for, a regime of collective self-government among equals). Nor can we believe that any of those authors thinks—any more than liberalism thinks—that that ideal is normative for a democracy only because and insofar as current democratic majorities contingently say so. Wherever our two companies, the liberal and the democratic, part ways, it won't be at the point of affirmation that a commitment to the common idea of the rule of law is definitional for a commendable political regime *regardless of anything that regime might say or do to the contrary*. The call to such a commitment is to that extent, for both companies, " 'an autonomous force' that provides 'an external untouchable rule of the game.' "

Where the two companies do part ways is at the point of saying whether some of the norms they take as regulative for a democracy worth fighting for have to be, or ought to be norms *of law*, meaning within the keeping of some institutional setup outside the daily operations of democratic politics to decide and impose upon those operations. On that question, Rawls inclines to yes where strong democrats like Winter say no.

I see three ways in which possibly to define and explain that disagreement. *First way*: Rawls takes to heart, in a way that some strong democrats

[16] See Jeremy Waldron, "The Core of the Case Against Judicial Review" (2006) 115 *Yale Law Journal* 1346, 1360.

[17] See John Griffith, "The Political Constitution" (1979) 42 *Modern Law Review* 1, 15 ("If the Rule of Law means that there should be proper and adequate machinery for dealing with criminal offences and for ensuring that public authorities do not exceed their legal powers, and for insisting that official penalties may not be inflicted save on those who have broken the law, then only an outlaw could dispute its desirability.").

do not, the problem of the justification of the force of controversial laws among free and equal citizens of divided conviction over public policy. That is what drives him, but not them, to the proceduralistic proposition for justification-by-constitution, including guarantees respecting basic liberties. Rawls envisages a supreme court as a publicly trusted arbiter of compliance with a justification-worthy constitution in force. But take away judicial constitutional review, leave compliance inspection entirely to parliamentary or popular venues, and some strong democrats will still feel resistance against the very idea of fidelity owed by current democratic majorities to constitutional mandates not immediately made or agreed to by them.[18] *Second way*: Some strong democrats may share with Rawls the concern about justification. Along with him, they will see the risk that majoritarian government may act in ways that defeat justification. But they further see suppression of majoritarian government by constitutional-legal bills of rights as posing its own threat to justification, and they weigh the latter risk as dominating the former. *Third way*: Some strong democrats may share with Rawls the concern about justification but think that political majorities (under astute organizational arrangements) are likelier than extra-majoritarian institutions to settle on policies that are truly justification-sustaining.

[18] See, e.g., Louis M. Seidman, *On Constitutional Disobedience* (Oxford University Press 2012); Michael J. Klarman, "Antifidelity" (1997) 70 *Southern California Law Review* 381.

13

Constitutional Rights and "Private" Legal Relations

1. The "Horizontal Application" Question, Addressed to Rawls

Reading along in some country's written constitution, you come to a ledger of clauses on basic rights or liberties—a "bill" or "charter" of rights.[1] These clauses, we'll assume, are received not as mere exhortation or advice but as an operative part of the country's positive law. They figure there as grounds for claims and defenses in civil and criminal proceedings in the country's courts—taking precedence, where applicable, over other, infra-constitutional legal sources in cases of conflict with them.

But then where are they applicable? Surely in so-called "vertical" cases, where rights and liberties claimed by persons and groups on the social street level stand exposed to force or threat from a government pictured as "above."[2] But whether the guarantees are to have any bearing on the law applicable to "horizontal" controversies not involving the state or its agents as parties, and if so in what manner or form, has been and remains a contentious issue within and among the world's constitutional democracies. Debates take shape under legal-doctrinal rubrics of "state action," "color of law," "third-party" or "radiating" effects, "protective function," "indirect application," and so on, as those crop up in various countries in line with their various constitutional-legal histories and traditions. We do not here enter that space of cross-system doctrinal comparison.[3] Our interest rather goes to the liberal political philosophy of John Rawls.

[1] This chapter draws from my "Constitutional Rights and 'Private' Legal Relations: A Note on a Rawlsian View" (2021) 23 *Ethics and Politics* 133.

[2] For explanation of how this account can apply to constitutional guarantees cast in terms of obligation to provide, as rights (for example) respect in education or health care, see Frank I. Michelman, "Legitimacy, The Social Turn, and Constitutional Review: What Political Liberalism Suggests" [2015] *Critical Q for Legislation and Law* 183, 188–92.

[3] The literature is large and fine surveys can be found. See, e.g., Stephen Gardbaum, "The 'Horizontal' Effect of Constitutional Rights" (2003) 102 *Michigan Law Review* 387; Stephen Gardbaum, "Where

Constitutional Essentials. Frank I. Michelman, Oxford University Press. © Frank I. Michelman 2022.
DOI: 10.1093/oso/9780197655832.003.0014

That philosophy, as liberal, has sometimes come in for charges of a tilt against full-bore extension of constitutional basic-liberty guarantees to the field of private law. Implicated in that charge is the philosophy's supposed support (again, as liberal) for the idea of a range personal and associational liberties to be kept mainly off limits to intrusion from society or subjection to society's wishes. For example, a recent essay invokes a claim from liberal feminism that

> by insisting that certain social structures, actions, and ideologies are part of an inviolable private sphere within which almost no state involvement should be tolerated, liberals have often been too quick to free themselves from the obligation to critique unjust and discriminatory aspects of [social] structures, actions, or ideologies, and to allow their unhindered existence and growth.[4]

So there we have a question for this chapter. Does the constitutional conception of Rawls lean one way or the other, pro or con applications of constitutional bill-of-rights guarantees to private legal controversies, through whatever doctrinal categories may be in play?

"But what do you mean by 'private'?," one might ask. Rawls, after all, is on record with the view that "the principles defining the equal basic liberties and opportunities of citizens always hold in and through all so-called domains"; and so if, he says, we *define* the private as a space beyond reach of those principles, then there is "no such thing" to be found.[5] Plainly needed here is a noncircular definition of a "private" (= "horizontal") legal relation or controversy, one that does not already answer the question I want to put to Rawls. Accordingly, I use "private" here simply to mean "not involving the government as a party plaintiff or defendant."

But then (your next question), why *doesn't* that remark from Rawls I've just reported quite plainly settle the Rawlsian stance as calling for full horizontal application of constitutional guarantees? Because, I answer, for

the (State) Action Is" (2006) 4 *International Journal of Constitutional Law* 4 760 (responding to a book-length collection of essays, András Sajó and Renáta Uitz (eds.), *The Constitution in Private Relations: Expanding Constitutionalism* (Eleven International Publishing 2005).

[4] Gila Stopler, "The Personal Is Political: The Feminist Critique of Liberalism and the Challenge of Right-Wing Populism" (2021) 19 *International Journal of Constitutional Law* 393, 395; see ibid, 394 n 3 (attributing this error to Rawls).

[5] "PRR" 791.

him to say that certain principles of equal basic liberty extend everywhere throughout society is not yet for him to answer the question of turning those principles into positive constitutional law for horizontal as for vertical cases. As we shall see, one might reasonably support a hesitation to do so, even while affirming that liberal commitments to equal basic liberty apply in full to social encounters and relations typically classed as private or personal. It will take some further work to see why Rawls could not adopt that anti-horizontalist view of constitutional-legal application—drawing that conclusion as an inference from four chief notions in Rawlsian constitutional thought that by now should carry a familiar ring for readers of this book: *basic structure, justificatory function, scheme of liberties, "at-least" reasonability*.

2. Main Liberal Arguments Pro and Con Horizontal Application

2.1. On the Side of Horizontality

I find it helpful, before delving more specifically into the Rawlsian stance on bill-of-rights horizontality, to sketch out what I take to be the main lines of liberally cogent argument around that question. The general case favoring horizontality starts out from a claim about a normal fact of experience in liberal societies. That fact consists in the appearance in such societies of concentrations in private hands of social and economic powers that (if left unregulated) can be as substantially threatening to the basic liberties of those exposed to them as are the powers of government itself. That may not be a fact about our world that anyone in liberalism necessarily cheers. We can assume it counts for most of the liberal-minded as regrettable, but maybe a price that comes unavoidably with liberal freedom.

Wide agreement among the liberal-minded may then go one step further—that is, to acceptance that the emergence of private (nongovernment) power centers threatening to basic liberties is not ex ante preventable in liberalism. A good comparison here would be to the Rawlsian response to the fact of reasonable pluralism. That fact—the emergence in a free society of a plurality of differing moral, metaphysical, and religious orientations—poses a major obstacle, Rawls thinks, to the liberal pursuit of government by consent. He sees it also, though, as an evitable outcome from the exercise of human intelligence in a social setting of free institutions,[6] for which the remedy cannot lie in ex ante prevention through policies of suppression of conflicts among views. The upshot is a liberal contretemps for which we have urgent need of a workaround (for Rawls, it turns out, in the form of a constitution-centered process of justification with inputs from civility, sacrifice, gift, what have you[7]). Likewise may we see the emergence of oppression-capable power-concentrations in society, as predictable from the exercise of human energies and pursuits in a setting of general freedom of action, presupposed and cherished in the culture of a liberal society. We can put into place laws and policies (say anti-monopoly or other market-structuring laws) to mitigate in advance the threats to liberty from any such potentially oppressive power-concentrations, but any attempt at an ex ante regulatory blanket sufficiently thick for advance complete foreclosure of such threats could only come—or so it reasonably might be thought—at too great a cost to the liberally cherished idea of a general regime of freedom to act and to strive.[8]

Where that is the judgment that prevails, the search for devices of correction must turn to what we may call ex post regulation of potentially dangerous powers whose emergence into society has not been prevented by regulation ex ante, and possibly could not have been by liberally tolerable forms of restriction. The pro-horizontalist argument is that the constitutional guarantees respecting basic liberties, essential to any liberal justification of the force of majoritarian laws, must then, in all liberal logic, come into play wherever potentially oppressive powers are found, not excluding in private/horizontal relations.

2.2. Against Horizontality

That argument meets intra-liberal opposition. At its subtlest and best, the opposition takes the form, not of denial of threat to basic liberties from

[6] See *PL* xviii, 36–37 (on "the fact of reasonable pluralism").

[7] See Chapter 6, § 3.

[8] On the valuation of general freedom of action in the Rawlsian liberal philosophy, see Frank I. Michelman, "The Priority of Liberty: Rawls and 'Tiers of Scrutiny'" in Thom Brooks and Martha Nussbaum (eds.), *Rawls's Political Liberalism* (Columbia University Press 2012) 175, 189–90. A statement from Rawls, that "no priority as assigned to liberty as such, as if the exercise of something called 'liberty' has a preeminent value" (*PL* 292), should not be read as disparagement of a general liberal leaning toward background freedom of action. See Michelman, "Priority of Liberty" 197–99.

nongovernmental powers on a plane with threat from the state, but of objection to resort to constitutional law as the regulatory engine for meeting the former source of threat. Constitutional law, the argument runs, is an instrument too blunt to be fit for the work. It may, alas, have to be our last resort in response to threat from the state. Not so, however, for threat from society. For that, we have available the medium of ordinary regulatory law, superior both technically as tool and morally as democratic. That states the anti-horizontalist case in brief.

Here now comes that case in modestly expanded form. Restrictions on the exercise of powers lawfully assembled by actors in society, imposed for the sake of the basic liberties of those exposed to those powers, can immediately implicate not only the general freedom but quite arguably the basic liberties of those upon whom the restrictions fall. At-least plausible claims to constitutional-essential protection will then be in play on both sides of a controversy brought to court. The situation calls for balancing, adjustment, accommodation of some kind across these claims. There won't be just one line of accommodation open for reasonable consideration but possibly quite a few of them. Assignment of this decision-space to jurists—so runs this anti-horizontalist argument—amounts to bypass of democratic legislative competence, popular knowledge and wisdom, and political freedom. It hands over to a judiciary not chosen either for regulatory acumen or sensitivity to public opinion the translation into concrete regulatory policy of the abstractly formulated clauses of guarantee native (for reasons Rawls supplies[9]) to liberal constitutions.

The argument continues: When the question is one of regulation *of the government* as a threat to basic liberties, two considerations may tilt the case toward acceptance of constitutional law as a last-resort vehicle of offset to power. First, in this case, it can sometimes be constitutional law or nothing; if constitutional law does not supply a legal-institutional brake against betrayal of basic liberties by state lawmakers and officials under their control, then nothing is left to supply it. Second, in this case a due regard for basic liberties requires no balancing of conflicting claims from opposing parties in court; liberalism weighs at nil any claims from governments or their minions to unhindered freedom in their deployments of powers entrusted to them. The case is opposite for conflicts between and among actors in ordinary society. Conflicting, prima facie plausible claims to protections for liberties can then

[9] See Chapter 2, § 2.2; Chapter 3, §1.1.

easily come in from both or all parties to a controversy, and no such claim is disqualified from consideration by the claimant's status as a state official wielding an entrusted power. The correct answer, then, in a democracy—so runs the argument—is to apply the constitutional bills of rights only to the government while leaving the rest to the ordinary processes for legislation. (Those processes, of course, would take in whatever share of a country's law-making we may consider to lie within the keeping of a common-law judiciary, a point to which we soon return.)

But here is the question still left blinking before us by that anti-horizontalist answer: *What if those processes fail?* If we are going to say it is the state with its unique powers to which constitutional guarantees are particularly directed, then do not our ordinary lawmakers constitute the very core of that state whose unique powers we have in view? If our reliance goes to those lawmakers for due protection by law against threat to guaranteed liberties from powers in society, is not their failure to supply it a manifestation of the very betrayal, from the very source, that the guarantees are meant to save us from? And does not that failure then bring the guarantees into play as constitutional law, with the court then filling the place of the defaulted legislators, *faute de mieux?* In other words, "horizontal" application?

To that question, our anti-horizontalists of course have their response. We have to choose, they can say, between risks: on the one side that of heavy-handed, ill-informed, doctrine-befuddled dictation from headstrong courts, on the other that of failure to exercise capability, as promised, on the part of politicians answerable to voters. In a democracy, they can conclude, the presumption finally must lie in favor of the latter option, risky as doubtless that always will be.

That does not seem a crazy stance to take. It is, however, as I now will maintain, a stance that is precluded to John Rawls by his attribution of a primary justificatory function to constitutional law.

3. The Rawlsian Case for Horizontality

3.1. "Basic Structure" as Subject

A Rawlsian justification-supporting constitution is derived conformably to an underlying conception of political justice. It could be the conception favored and named by Rawls as "justice as fairness," or else some fellow member of the family of liberal conceptions, worked out from a few basic ideas about politics as a site of cooperation among a severalty of free and equal persons. As liberal, these conceptions all have in common that they pick out certain rights, liberties, and opportunities to which they assign a special priority.[10] As conceptions of justice, they all take as their primary topic of concern a society's basic structure.[11]

The rights and liberties presumably then go wherever the basic structure goes. The basic structure comprises the society's "main political and social institutions [and the way] they fit together into one system of social cooperation [and] assign basic rights and duties and regulate the division of advantages that arises from social cooperation over time."[12] Law governing private relations (at least above a certain level of detail) must surely count as part of that.[13] Principles of liberty that go where the basic structure goes should accordingly have application there.

On the level, then, of a liberal *conception of justice* as envisaged by John Rawls, principles of liberty extend to much of so-called private law. Presumptively, it seems the same would hold for rights-guarantees in a positive-legal constitution cast in the mold of a liberal conception of justice. But that can only be a presumption, pending considerations to arise in the move from normative conception to institutional design—from an "original position" to a "constitutional stage."[14] We have just been seeing how a case against horizontal application of the rights principles, by judicial officers as constitutional positive law, may arise in just that interval of institutional design. The case then would doubt not at all that basic-liberty guarantees do in principle cover the field of private legal relations. To the contrary, its doubt would go to whether those principles are best served by a program of implementation as positive law for horizontal cases.

3.2. Justificatory Function

We already know that Rawls will not, as political philosopher, turn aside as ipso facto meritless or out of place this kind of practical concern. A regime

[10] *PL* xlviii. See Chapter 3, § 2.

[11] *PL* 257, and see generally *PL* 257–88 ("Lecture VII. The Basic Structure as Subject").

[12] *JAF* 10. See *PL* 257.

[13] See *PL* 258 ("[T]he political constitution, the legally recognized forms of property, and the organization of the economy, and the nature of the family, all belong to the basic structure.").

[14] See Chapter 1, § 4; Chapter 5, § 3.2.

of parliamentary supremacy "with no bill of rights at all" could after all sometimes do better by liberal principles of liberty than "a dualist regime in which these [matters] are settled by the higher law." Thus has Rawls expressly allowed.[15] What I think he could not allow is a regime that does rely on justiciable constitutional guarantees, but reserves them for application to "vertical" cases only. I do not see how he could allow that in line with the proceduralizing, justificatory function he assigns to constitutional law, in response to the problem of political liberalism.

Rawls's proposition (the liberal principle of legitimacy) is that dissenters from majoritarian exertions of legal force can find reason for willing submission in an assurance of the compliance of those exertions with a publicly legible set of constitutional essentials. That proposition necessarily envisages—so I have maintained—a trusted public arbiter to referee compliance.[16] That arbiter need not necessarily be a constitutional or supreme court, but often, in practice it is. Where that is the case, law-setting dispositions by an authority *not that trusted institution* are presumptively reviewable *by it* for constitutional compliance. Now, the essential guarantees of a liberally justification-worthy constitution apply to the field of private legal relations as part of the society's basic structure. It follows that private-law dispositions by tribunals not the trusted one are subject to review by the latter for constitutional compliance. The result will approximate closely to a horizontal application of constitutional bills of rights. The case is between nongovernmental parties, and the law applicable to it undergoes, at the behest of a party aggrieved, an inspection for bill-of-rights compliance.[17]

But wait just a minute, you say. Surely a Rawlsian system could set up as its trusted institutional arbiter of constitutional compliance, in the field of horizontal legal relations, the traditional array of private-law tribunals themselves, and in particular their appellate branch? Indeed so, I reply, and if it did expressly do that you would have not a denial of the application to private legal relations of the essential-to-justification constitutional law of basic rights and liberties, but the exact opposite of that: a supposition of an institutionally automated perfect fusion of private with constitutional law.

[15] See *PL* 234–35; Chapter 2, § 2.1.

[16] See Chapter 2, § 2.2.

[17] Some call what I am describing here an "indirect" horizontal application of constitutional guarantees because the inspection runs to the law applied to the acts of the parties, not directly to the acts of the parties. In practice it hardly makes a difference. See Frank I. Michelman, "The Bill of Rights, the Common Law, and the Freedom-Friendly State" (2003) 58 University of Miami Law Review 401, 408–11.

3.3. Scheme of Liberties, "At-Least" Reasonability

Rawls takes as typical for constitutional democracies the case of a supreme court installed in the trusted arbitral role. That does not blind his conception to the risk that jurists will bungle the job when it comes to effectuation of basic-liberties guarantees across the horizontal encounters of daily social life. Rawls is certainly alert to the complexity of that work as policy-setting. He sees and insists that constitutionally essential basic-liberties guarantees can none of them be taken as "absolute" but all of them rather as always subject to adjustment as required to maintain them as a scheme of equal liberties.[18] (Does not "scheme of equal liberties" already clearly sound in horizontal application?) He stipulates for a kind of reasonability, on the part of citizens supposedly alert to facts of pluralism and burdens of judgment, which must widen their tolerance for "at-least" reasonable governmental resolutions of conflicts of liberties. He takes citizens to be moved by a shared understanding that only in that tolerationist way can they hope to find mutually acceptable justification for democratic political power and hence an available path to government by consent in conditions of reasonable pluralism. And he must correspondingly then advocate—thus have I argued—for a style of judicial constitutional review that I have called tolerant.[19] Self-styled "classical" liberals won't like that; "faint-hearted liberalism," they might call it. We don't necessarily have to read John Rawls as loving it, either, from a partisan-political standpoint. We move here, remember, on the turf of institutional design, inevitably imperfect, not that of a cheap and easy affirmation of normative ideals. But I do not think that self-excusing response is the one that Rawls would give. Rather he will say we are facing up, here, to a hard fact of liberal life, that of reasonable disagreement in politics, and to the resulting problem of political liberalism—and in consequence applying the liberal philosophy's own principle of toleration to "philosophy itself."

18 See Chapter 3, § 1.
19 See Chapter 11, § 3.3.

14

Liberal Tolerance to Liberal Collapse?

Virtually definitional, it would seem, for liberalisms of all stripes and varieties is dedication to the pursuit of an equal basic right of everyone to freedoms of conscience, thought, association, and expression. Accordingly, it seems that the liberal political program of equal basic liberties must always be living in the shadow of crisis. That is because, when enmity to that program is astir, resort to what in fact may be the indispensable means to defeat it already counts as setback to the program. That is the Achilles heel of liberalism, its paradox of tolerance. It did not arrive just yesterday at our doorstep with the tolerationist "political" liberalism of John Rawls. It is a concern of ancient standing, and to it there has arisen a standard liberal make-do response: to tolerate on principle as we must, but not beyond the point of endangerment of the regime itself of toleration of everyone's enjoyment and exercise of basic liberties. "In the name of tolerance," wrote Karl Popper, as one of many examples, we claim the right "not to tolerate the intolerant."[1] Exactly similarly spoke John Rawls in 1971 in *A Theory of Justice*. Citizens under a just constitution, Rawls then wrote, when they "sincerely and with reason believe that their own security and that of the institutions of liberty are in danger," may then, in emergency, "properly force the intolerant" to toe the liberal line.[2]

But that was *A Theory of Justice*. Emergency is a slippery seesaw. The move of *Political Liberalism* is to application of the principle of toleration "to philosophy itself."[3] Might one then find in Rawls's later work on political liberalism an invitation to backslide on readiness to confront, if need be to a point of suppressing, the illiberal? Is that what comes along with a shift in the strategy of Rawls's philosophical defense of a liberal political regime,[4] to allow for the existence in any modern free society of outlooks toward life, world, and society that are not what we'd classify as comprehensively liberal

[1] Karl R. Popper, *The Open Society and Its Enemies, Vol. 1: The Spell of Plato* (Princeton University Press, 5th ed. rev. 1962) 265.
[2] *TJ* 219–20.
[3] *PL* 10; see Chapter 4, § 3.1.
[4] See Chapter 1, § 4.2.

Constitutional Essentials. Frank I. Michelman, Oxford University Press. © Frank I. Michelman 2022.
DOI: 10.1093/oso/9780197655832.003.0015

but might nevertheless still count as reasonable? Does allowance of reasonability for some non-quintessentially-liberal views come along with an excessively or dangerously accomodationist stance toward such doctrines, and with that an aggravation of hesitancy in liberal states and minds about lowering the boom on illiberal preachings and incitements?

Here are two quotes from *Political Liberalism*:

> [T]here are always many unreasonable views. That there are doctrines that reject one or more democratic freedoms is itself a permanent fact of life, or seems so. That gives us the practical task of containing them—like war or disease—so that they do not overturn political justice.[5]

> Political liberalism . . . supposes that a reasonable comprehensive doctrine does not reject the essentials of a democratic regime. Of course, a society may also contain unreasonable and irrational, and even mad, comprehensive doctrines. In their case the problem is to contain them so that they do not undermine the unity and justice of society.[6]

Those texts easily come across as a continuation of the defend-when-necessary stance of Rawls in *Theory*. Reading between the lines, though, there might still be a backsliding of readiness to take arms because, as we said, emergency is a slippery seesaw, and toleration is more heavily thematized in the later work than in the prior. That is a suggestion I read from recent concerned observers.[7] Along with *Political Liberalism*'s newfound sensitivity to the fact of reasonable pluralism might also have come—so run the suggestions—a reboot for thoughts of an insulated "private" haven for nurturance of off-mainstream social ideas (tolerationist liberalism figuring now as mainstream): the feminist critique of liberalism come round for another turn.[8]

[5] *PL* 64 & n. 19.

[6] Ibid at 18–19. Rawls speaks there of "the essentials of a democratic regime." I take him to mean what he repeatedly calls elsewhere in the book "the constitutional essentials." These include the basic liberties of the first principle of justice as fairness, equally for all: "freedom of thought and liberty of conscience; the political liberties and freedom of association, as well as the freedoms specified by the liberty and integrity of the person; and . . . the rights and liberties covered by the rule of law." Ibid at 290; see ibid at 227 (on constitutional essentials).

[7] See, e.g., Gila Stopler, "The Personal Is Political: The Feminist Critique of Liberalism and the Challenge of Right-Wing Populism" (2021) 19 *International Journal of Constitutional Law* 393 (hereafter Stopler, "Feminist Critique"); Gila Stopler, "Patriarchal Populism: A Rejoinder" (2021 19 *International Journal of Constitutional Law* 423 (hereafter Stopler, "Rejoinder").

[8] See Stopler, "Feminist Critique" (n 7) 395 ("The feminist claim holds that, by insisting that certain social structures, actions, and ideologies are part of an inviolable private sphere within which

Rawls does indeed write in places of inclusion of some nonliberal comprehensive views within an ambit of reasonable pluralism. When he does so, however, it is never, so far as I can see, with any signification of concession to such views of exemption from the constitutionally compliant, democratically enacted laws of a state justly organized under liberal principles. The signification rather is of a potential in any included view for willing acceptance of a political framework of sufficient tolerance for liberals also to embrace it, given recognition all around of the social facts of pluralism and burdens of judgment and the distinct, great values "of the political."[9] No retrenchment from Rawls's express rejection of any idea of a private sphere placed beyond the full reach of liberally essential equal basic liberties is afoot, at least not expressly.

It is surely right to be on guard against any such retrenchment. Ideas of an exempt private sphere have no doubt been a past and are still a lingering cause of trouble needing correction in liberal thought and practice. Longstanding in liberal constitutional-legal debates has been contestation over deployments of some legal categories—property and contract, family and market—to sustain oppressive exercises of power in matters and spaces coded as "private," in seeming compromise (or worse) of liberal professions of commitment to the equal basic liberties of everyone. Feminist-inspired works of recent decades have sharpened, broadened, and deepened the terms of debate from forms they took earlier in American Legal Realism.[10] But one problem for which we should not be casting blame on a private-sphere reflex in liberalism is the beleaguered state of liberal democracies beset by (say) "right-wing populism."

What hobbles an all-out liberal-state quarantine of the propagation and spread of right-wing populist ideas and passions is not some assignment of a "private" classification to the disfavored activity. It is purely and simply

almost no state involvement should be tolerated, liberals have often been too quick to free themselves from the obligation to critique unjust and discriminatory aspects of such structures, actions, or ideologies, and to allow their unhindered existence and growth").

[9] See Chapter 6, §§ 2.2, 2.3, 3. Rawls writes accordingly of his "suppos[ition], perhaps too optimistic[]," that the comprehensive views mainly to be met with in our societies, including those rooted in religion, "*admit of* such an account and *thus may be seen as* reasonable comprehensive doctrines." *PL* 170 (emphasis supplied).

[10] See, for one twentieth-century classic, Frances Olsen, "The Family and the Market" (1983) 96 *Harvard Law Review* 1497. For Legal Realist antecedents, see, e.g., Morris R. Cohen, "Property and Sovereignty" (1927) 13 *Cornell Law Review* 9; Robert L. Hale, "Coercion and Distribution in a Supposedly Non-Coercive State" (1923) 38 *Political Science Quarterly* 470.

the liberal commitment to respect, to the limit of safety, everyone's basic liberties of conscience, thought, expression, and association. *That*, and not some consideration of whether the activity occurs in the setting, physical or social, of a home, family, business, school, church, or assembly hall—a lot of it, after all, takes place in streets, in the media, in legislatures, in election campaigns, in courtrooms—is what makes us hem and haw about shutting or locking people up for what they say, barring their meetings, banning or burning their books, closing their chat rooms, or force-feeding their educations and indoctrinations. It is just the same old bind, the same old paradox of tolerance put at the start of this chapter. It hounds the comprehensive liberalisms of, say, Mill or Kant or Popper, or of the John Rawls of *A Theory of Justice*, every bit as much as it might the political liberalism of Rawls's later work.

For suppose we all were under the current South African constitution. There is no "state action" doctrine there, no privileging for "vertical" over "horizontal" application of the constitution's bill of rights. The guarantees of the bill of rights apply to "all law," and "bind a natural or juristic person" to the extent its terms would apply to them.[11] So we bring those guarantees of individual basic liberties to the support of the applications of children against ideologically overbearing parents in their homes, of congregants against clergy in their churches, of private-academy learners against instructors in their classrooms, of the commoners against the agitators on proprietary websites. Does that work only in favor of claims on behalf of children, congregants, and plain folks against indoctrination by illiberal-minded tutors and rousers, and not in favor of claims against liberal-minded ones? Do we make the self-defensive liberal democratic state the parens patriae for the children, congregants, and plain folks, deciding what is in their best interest or the state's interest or our interest for them to hear? What does John Mill say to that? What is John Rawls saying that is any different?

It is with that question, the question of relief from the inhibitions of the liberal paradox of tolerance, that we need always to be becoming to terms. Venues for that constant exercise of the discipline of liberalism, John Rawls teaches, include the parliamentary halls and the courtrooms where lawmakers and judges apply themselves to the scheme of basic-liberties adjustments required for the least achievable detraction from anyone's

[11] Constitution of the Republic of South Africa (1996), §§ 8(1), 8(2).

enjoyment anywhere of the basic-liberty cores over an episode or span of life. The work is not easy. It will issue in mistakes and furthermore in self-sustaining bad trends crying out for interruption and correction from civil society. Political liberalism says that can be no reason to shirk the work, or pretend that the liberal paradox it addresses is dismissible by a wave of the hand or curable by an upsurge of militancy.

Bibliography

Ackerman, Bruce, *We the People: Foundations* (Harvard University Press 1991).

Ackerman, Bruce, "The Storrs Lectures: Discovering the Constitution" (1984) 93 Yale Law Journal 1013.

Alexander, Larry and Schauer, Frederick, "Defending Judicial Supremacy: A Reply" (2000) 17 Constitutional Commentary 455.

Applbaum, Arthur Isak, *Legitimacy: The Right to Rule in a Wanton World* 104 (Harvard University Press 2019).

Balkin, Jack M., *Living Originalism* (Harvard University Press 2014).

Balkin, Jack M., "History, Rights, and the Moral Reading" (2016) 96 Boston University Law Review 1425.

Barak, Aharon, "Foreword: A Judge on Judging" (2002) 116 Harvard Law Review 19.

Bellamy, Richard, *Political Constitutionalism* (Cambridge University Press 2007).

Bickel, Alexander, *The Least Dangerous Branch: The Supreme Court at the Bar of Politics* (Bobbs-Merrill 1962).

Bork, Robert H., "Neutral Principles and Some First Amendment Problems" (1971) 47 Indiana Law Journal 1.

Cohen, Morris R., "Property and Sovereignty" (1927) 13 Cornell Law Review 9.

Colón-Rios, Joel I., "The Constitution of Puerto Rico," in R. Albert, S. O'Brien, and S. Wheatle (eds.), *The Oxford Handbook of Caribbean Constitutions* (Oxford University Press 2020).

Craig, Paul, "Written and Unwritten Constitutions: The Modality of Change," in Sam Bookman, Edward Willis, Hanna Wilberg, and Max Harris (eds.), *Pragmatism, Principle, and Power in Common Law Constitutional Systems: Essays in Honour of Bruce Harris* (forthcoming).

Davis, Dennis and Klare, Karl, "Transformative Constitutionalism and the Common and Customary Law" (2010) 26 South African Journal on Human Rights 403.

Dixon, Rosalind, "Creating Dialog About Socioeconomic Rights" (2007) 5 International Journal of Constitutional Law 391.

Dworkin, Ronald, *Taking Rights Seriously* (Harvard University Press 1977).

Dworkin, Ronald, *Law's Empire* (Harvard University Press 1986).

Dworkin, Ronald, *Freedom's Law: The Moral Reading of the American Constitution* (Harvard University Press 1996).

Dworkin, Ronald, *Justice For Hedgehogs* (Harvard University Press 2011).

Dworkin, Ronald, "Hard Cases" (1975) 88 Harvard Law Review 1057.

Edmundson, William A., *John Rawls: Reticent Socialist* (Cambridge University Press 2017).

Epstein, Richard A., *The Classical Liberal Constitution: The Uncertain Quest for Limited Government* (Harvard University Press 2014).

Fallon, Richard H. Jr., "Legitimacy and the Constitution" (2005) 118 Harvard Law Review 1787.

Fallon, Richard H. Jr., "Judicially Manageable Standards and Constitutional Meaning" (2006) 19 Harvard Law Review 1275.

Fallon, Richard H. Jr., "The Core of an Uneasy Case for Judicial Review" (2008) 121 Harvard Law Review 1701.

Fallon, Richard H. Jr., "Judicial Supremacy, Departmentalism, and the Rule of Law in a Populist Age" (2018) 96 Texas Law Review 487.

Ferrara, Alessandro, *The Democratic Horizon: Hyperpluralism and the Renewal of Political Liberalism* (Cambridge University Press 2014).

Ferrara, Alessandro, "Judicial Review and Its Discontents: A Reply to Frank Michelman" (2017) 4 Rivista Internazionale di Filosofia del Diritto 61.

Ferrara, Alessandro, "Political Liberalism Revisited: A Paradigm for Liberal Democracy in the 21st Century" (2016) 24 Philosophy and Social Criticism 681.

Ferrara, Alessandro and Michelman, Frank I., *Legitimation by Constitution: A Dialogue on Political Liberalism* (Oxford University Press 2021).

Finlayson, James Gordon, *The Habermas-Rawls Debate* (Columbia University Press 2019).

Fleming, James E., *Fidelity to Our Imperfect Constitution: For Moral Readings and Against Originalism* (Oxford University Press 2015).

Foner, Eric, *Free Soil, Free Labor, Free Men: The Ideology of the Republican Party Before the Civil War* (Oxford University Press 1995).

Forst, Rainer, *The Right to Justification* (Columbia University Press 2002).

Freeman, Samuel, "Original Meaning, Democratic Interpretation, and the Constitution" (1992) 21 Philosophy and Public Affairs 3.

Friedman, Barry, "Mediated Popular Constitutionalism" (2003) 101 Michigan Law Review 2596.

Friedmann, Daniel, *The Purse and the Sword: The Trials of Israel's Legal Revolution* (Oxford University Press 2016).

Fuller, Lon L., *The Morality of Law* (Yale University Press, rev. ed. 1969).

Gardbaum, Stephen, "The 'Horizontal' Effect of Constitutional Rights" (2003) 102 Michigan Law Review 387.

Gardbaum, Stephen, "Where the (State) Action Is" (2006) 4 International Journal of Constitutional Law 4, 760.

Gardner, John, "Can There Be a Written Constitution?," in Leslie Green and Brian Leiter (eds.), *Oxford Studies in Constitutional Law, Vol. 1* (Oxford Scholarship Online: Sept. 2011).

Gerstenberg, Oliver, "Negative/Positive Constitutionalism, Fair Balance, and the Problem of Justiciability" (2012) 10 International Journal of Constitutional Law 904.

Griffith, John, "The Political Constitution" (1979) 42 Modern Law Review 1.

Grimm, Dieter, "Integration by Constitution" (2005) 3 International Journal of Constitutional Law.

Grimm, Dieter, *Constitutionalism: Past, Present, and Future* (Oxford University Press 2016).

Habermas, Jürgen, "Reconciliation Through the Public Use of Reason" (1995) 92 Journal of Philosophy 109.

Hale, Robert L., "Coercion and Distribution in a Supposedly Non-Coercive State" (1923) 38 Political Science Quarterly 470.

Hart, Henry M., Jr., and Sacks, Albert M., *The Legal Process: Basic Problems in the Making and Application of Law*, ed. William N. Eskridge, Jr. and Philip P. Frickey (Foundation Press 1995).

Hirschl, Ran, *Toward Juristocracy: The Origin and Consequences of the New Constitutionalism* (Harvard University Press 2004).
Holmes, Stephen, "Precommitment and the Paradox of Democracy," in Jon Elster and Rune Slagstad (eds.), *Constitutionalism and Democracy* (Cambridge University Press 1988) 193.
Kennedy, Duncan, "Form and Substance in Private Law Adjudication" (1976) 89 Harvard Law Review 1685.
Khosla, Madhav, *India's Founding Moment: The Constitution of a Most Surprising Democracy* (Harvard University Press 2020).
Klarman, Michael J., "Antifidelity" (1997) 70 Southern California Law Review 381.
Kramer, Larry D., *The People Themselves: Popular Constitutionalism and Judicial Review* (Oxford University Press 2004).
Langvatn, Silje Aambo, "Legitimate But Unjust; Just, But Illegitimate: Rawls on Political Legitimacy" (2016) 42 Philosophy and Social Criticism 132.
Larmore, Charles, *Patterns of Moral Complexity* (Cambridge University Press 1987).
Larmore, Charles, *The Morals of Modernity* (Cambridge University Press 1996).
Lincoln, Abraham, *Collected Works* Vol. 2, ed. Roy P. Basler (Rutgers University Press 1953).
MacCormick, Neil, "Institutional Normative Order: A Conception of Law" (1997) 82 Cornell Law Review 1051.
McCosby, Paul, "In Search of a Solution: The Centrality of History to Constitutional Interpretation as Illustrated by the 19th Century First Amendment Controversy" [2019] Liberty Lawyer 20.
Mehta, Pratap, "Constitutionalism and Nationalism" (2021) Working Paper Presented at Online Conference in Honor of Mark Tushnet's Contributions to Comparative Constitutional Law, June 25, 2021.
Michelman, Frank I., "Political Truth and the Rule of Law" (1988) 8 Tel Aviv Studies in Law 281.
Michelman, Frank I., "Review: The Subject of Liberalism" (1994) 46 Stanford Law Review 1807.
Michelman, Frank I., *Brennan and Democracy* (Princeton University Press 1999).
Michelman, Frank I., "Dilemmas of Belonging: Moral Truth, Human Rights, and Why We Might Not Want a Representative Judiciary" (1999) 47 UCLA Law Review 1221.
Michelman, Frank I., "Populist Natural Law (Reflections on Tushnet's 'Thin Constitution')" (2000) 34 University of Richmond Law Review 461.
Michelman, Frank I., "Constitutional Legitimation for Political Acts" (2003) 66 MLR 1.
Michelman, Frank I., "Faith and Obligation, or What Makes Sandy Sweat?" (2003) 38 Tulsa Law Review 651.
Michelman, Frank I., "Aida's Way" (2003) 72 Fordham Law Review 345, 347.
Michelman, Frank I., "Is the Constitution a Contract for Legitimacy?" (2003) 8 Review of Constitutional Studies 101.
Michelman, Frank I., "Living with Judicial Supremacy" (2003) 38 Wake Forest Law Review 579.
Michelman, Frank I., "Constitutionalism as Proceduralism: A Glance at the Terrain," in Emilios Christodoulidis and Stephen Tierney (eds.), *Public Law and Politics: The Scope and Limits of Constitutionalism* (Ashgate 2008) 141.
Michelman, Frank I., "Socioeconomic Rights: Explaining America Away" (2008) 6 International Journal of Constitutional Law 663.

Michelman, Frank I., "Poverty in Liberalism: A Comment on the Constitutional Essentials" (2012) 60 Drake Law Review 1001.
Michelman, Frank I., "The Priority of Liberty: Rawls and 'Tiers of Scrutiny,'" in Thom Brooks and Martha Nussbaum (eds.), *Rawls's Political Liberalism* (Columbia University Press 2012).
Michelman, Frank I., "Why Not Just Say No? An Essay on the Obduracy of Constitution Fixation" (2014) 94 Boston University Law Review 1143.
Michelman, Frank I., "Legitimacy, The Social Turn, and Constitutional Review: What Political Liberalism Suggests" [2015] Critical Quarterly for Legislation & Law 183.
Michelman, Frank I., "A Constitutional Horizon?" (2016) 47 Philosophy and Social Criticism 641.
Michelman, Frank I., "Political Liberalism's Constitutional Horizon: Some Further Thoughts" (2017) 4 Rivista Internazionale di Filosofia del Diritto 599.
Michelman, Frank I., "Human Rights and Constitutional Rights: A Proceduralizing Function for Constitutional Law," in Silja Voeneky and Gerald Neuman (eds.), *Human Rights, Democracy, and Legitimacy in a World of Disorder* (Cambridge University Press 2018) 73.
Michelman, Frank I., "Israel's Constitutional Revolution: A Thought from Political Liberalism" (2018) 19 Theoretical Inquiries in Law 745.
Michelman, Frank I., "Political-Liberal Legitimacy and the Question of Judicial Restraint" (2019) 1 Jus Cogens 59.
Michelman, Frank I., "The Question of Constitutional Fidelity: Rawls on the Reason of Constitutional Courts," in Silje A. Langvatn, Mattias Kumm, and Woiciech Sadurski (eds.), *Public Reason and Courts* (Cambridge University Press 2020) 90.
Michelman, Frank, "The Bind of Tolerance and a Call to Feminist Thought: A Reply to Gila Stopler" (2021) 19 International Journal of Constitutional Law 408.
Frank I. Michelman. "Constitutional Rights and 'Private' Legal Relations: A Note on a Rawlsian View" (2021) 23 *Ethics and Politics* 133.
Michelman, Frank I., "Civility to Graciousness: Van der Walt and Rawls" (2021) 23 Ethics and Politics 495.
Minow, Martha, "Not in the Room Where It Happens: Adversariness, Politicization, and *Little Sisters of the Poor*" [2020] The Supreme Court Review 1.
Murphy, Liam and Nagel, Thomas, *The Myth of Ownership: Taxes and Justice* (Oxford University Press 2002).
Murphy, Walter F., "Merlin's Memory: The Past and Future Imperfect of the Once and Future Polity," in Sanford Levinson (ed.), *Responding to Imperfection: The Theory and Practice of Constitutional Amendment* (Princeton University Press 1995) 163.
Neuman, Gerald L., "Human Rights and Constitutional Rights: Harmony and Dissonance" (2003) 55 Stanford Law Review 1863.
Olsen, Frances, "The Family and the Market" (1983) 96 Harvard Law Review 1497.
Popper, Karl R., *The Open Society and its Enemies, Vol. 1: The Spell of Plato* (5th ed. revised, Princeton University Press 1962).
Post, Robert, *Citizens Divided: Campaign Reform and the Constitution* (Harvard University Press 2014).
Putnam, Hilary, *Realism with a Human Face* (Harvard University Press 1990).
Rawls, John, "Two Concepts of Rules" (1955) 64 Philosophical Review 3.
Rawls, John, "Legal Obligation and the Duty of Fair Play," in Sidney Hook (ed.), *Law and Philosophy: A Symposium* (New York University Press 1964) 3.
Rawls, John, *A Theory of Justice* (Harvard University Press 1971).

Rawls, John, "Kantian Constructivism in Moral Theory" (1980) 77 Journal of Philosophy 515.
Rawls, John, "Justice as Fairness: Political not Metaphysical" (1985) 14 Philosophy and Public Affairs 231.
Rawls, John, *Political Liberalism* (Columbia University Press 1993).
Rawls, John, "Reply to Habermas" (1995) 92 Journal of Philosophy 132.
Rawls, John, "The Idea of Public Reason Revisited" (1997) 64 University of Chicago Law Review 765.
Rawls, John, "*Commonweal* Interview with John Rawls," in Samuel Freeman (ed.), *John Rawls, Collected Papers* (Harvard University Press 1998).
Rawls, John, *The Law of Peoples* (Harvard University Press 1999).
Rawls, John, *Justice as Fairness: A Restatement*, ed. Erin Kelly (Harvard University Press 2001).
Sajó, András and Uitz, Renáta (eds.), *The Constitution in Private Relations: Expanding Constitutionalism* (Eleven International Publishing 2005).
Scalia, Antonin, "The Rule of Law as a Law of Rules" (1989) 56 University Chicago Law Review 1175.
Seidman, Louis M., *On Constitutional Disobedience* (Oxford University Press 2012).
Shelby, Tommie, "Justice, Deviance, and the Dark Ghetto" (2007) 35 Philosophy and Public Affairs 1263.
Stopler, Gila, "The Personal Is Political: The Feminist Critique of Liberalism and the Challenge of Right-Wing Populism" (2021) 19 International Journal of Constitutional Law 393.
Stopler, Gila, "Patriarchal Populism: A Rejoinder" (2021) 19 International Journal of Constitutional Law _423__.
Strauss, David, "Foreword: Does the Constitution Mean What It Says?" (1985) 129 Harvard Law Review.
Sullivan, Kathleen M., "The Supreme Court, 1991 Term—Foreword: The Justices of Rules and Standards" (1992) 106 Harvard Law Review 22.
Sultany, Nimer, "The State of Progressive Constitutional Theory: The Paradox of Constitutional Democracy and the Project of Political Justification" (2012) 47 Harvard Civil Rights–Civil Liberties Law Review 371.
Thoreau, Henry David, *The Journal 1837–1861*, ed. Damion Searls (New York Review of Books 2009).
Tushnet, Mark, *Taking the Constitution Away from the Courts* (Princeton University Press 1999).
Tushnet, Mark, *Weak Courts, Strong Rights: Judicial Review and Social Welfare Rights in Comparative Constitutional Law* (Princeton University Press 2008).
Tushnet, Mark and Bugaric, Bojan, *Power to the People: Constitutionalism in the Age of Populism* (Oxford University Press 2021).
Van Alstyne, William W., "Interpreting This Constitution: The Unhelpful Contributions of Special Theories of Judicial Review" (1983) 35 University of Florida Law Review 209.
Van der Walt, AJ, *Property in the Margins* (Hart Publishing 2009).
Van der Walt, Johan, *Law and Sacrifice: A Post Apartheid Theory of Law* (Birkbeck Law Press 2006).
Van der Walt, Johan, "The Gift of Time and the Hour of Sacrifice: A Philosophical-Anthropological Analysis of the Deep Difference between Political Liberal and Populist Politics," in Brian W. Nail and Jeffrey A. Ellsworth (eds.), *Law's Sacrifice: Approaching the Problem of Sacrifice in Law, Literature, and Philosophy* (Routledge 2019).

Van der Walt, Johan, *The Concept of Liberal Democratic Law* (Routledge 2020).

Van der Walt, Johan, "Liberal Democracy and the Event of Existence, Seen from a Not-So-Rickety Bridge Between Rawls and Merleau-Ponty. Reply to My Critics" (2021) 23 Ethics and Politics 521.

Van der Walt, Johan and Botha, Henk, "Democracy and Rights in South Africa: Beyond a Culture of Justification" (2000) 7 Constellations 341.

Waldron, Jeremy, *The Right to Private Property* (Oxford University Press 1990).

Waldron, Jeremy, *Law and Disagreement* (Oxford University Press 1999).

Waldron, Jeremy, "The Core of the Case Against Judicial Review" (2006) 115 Yale Law Journal 1346.

Waldron, Jeremy, "Human Rights: Universalism or the Integrity of a Common Enterprise" (2016) New York University School of Law Public Law & Legal Theory Research Paper Series, Working Paper No. 16-48, available at http://ssrn.com/abstract=2848611.

Waldron, Jeremy, "What a Dissenting Opinion Should Have Said in Obergefell v. Hodges," in Jack M. Balkin (ed.), *What Obergefell v. Hodges Should Have Said: The Nation's Top Legal Experts Rewrite America's Same-Sex Marriage Decision* (Yale University Press 2020).

Weill, Rivka, "Reconciling Parliamentary Sovereignty and Judicial Review: On the Theoretical and Historical Origins of the Israeli Legislative Override Power" (2012) 29 Hastings Constitutional Law Quarterly 457.

West, Robin, "Constitutional Culture or Ordinary Politics: A Reply to Reva Siegel" (1996) 94 California Law Review 1465.

Winter, Steven, "'Who' or 'What' Is the Rule of Law?" (2021) Philosophy and Social Criticism <https://journals.sagepub.com/doi/abs/10.1177/01914537211021148#> accessed 17 April 2022.

Wolfe, Christopher, "Originalist Reflections on Constitutional Freedom of Speech" (2019) 72 SMU Law Review 535.

Young, Katherine G., *Constituting Economic and Social Rights* (Oxford University Press 2012) 167–91.

Cases

DeBoer v. Snyder, __ F.3d __ (U.S. Ct. of Appeals, 6th Cir., 2014).

Dred Scott v. Sandford, 60 U.S. (19 How.) (1857).

First National Bank of SA Limited t/a Wesbank v. Commissioner for the South African Revenue Services; First National Bank of Limited t/a Wesbank v. Minister of Finance 2002 4 SA 768 (CC) para. 85.

Marbury v. Madison, 5 U.S. (1 Cranch) 137 (1803).

NIFLA v. Beccera, 585 U.S. __ (2018).

Obergefell v. Hodges, 135 S. Ct. 2071 (2015).

Planned Parenthood of South-Eastern Pennsylvania. v. Casey, 505 U.S. 833, 867 (1992) (plurality opinion).

Rucho v. Common Cause, 588 U.S. ___ (2019).

United Mizrahi Bank Ltd. v. Migdal Cooperative Village, 49(4) P.D. 221 (1995) (Supreme Court of Israel).

Index

For the benefit of digital users, indexed terms that span two pages (e.g., 52–53) may, on occasion, appear on only one of those pages.

Ackerman, Bruce
and dualist conception of democracy 6, 133

basic structure
defined, as focal concern for principles of political justice and justification 28–29, 140–41
as extending to social space of 'private' ('horizontal') relations 188–89
Bickel, Alexander
on judicial review as counter-majoritarian 158n.15

civility. *See also* 'reciprocity, criterion of'
as aspect of political morality for citizens 68–69, 98–101
a motive (of passion, not reason alone) of willingness to bear with injustice 100–1
and question of application to judges construing constitutional guarantees 69–70
constitution. *See also* constitutional essentials; constitutional interpretation
as 'thick' or 'thin' xiii
as vehicle for democratic government by consent 1–3, 6, 26–27, 191
regulatory and justificatory functions of 3–6, 46–48, 66–67, 129
as basis for political justification given reasonable pluralism (liberal principle of legitimacy) 25–27, 30–31
form or medium of, when serving as Rawlsian political-justification procedure
common-law or codified? 87–88
'convention' or positive law? 38–44
observable societal regularity or publicly established directive code? 45–48
as possibly unwritten 34–37
as institution of imperfect procedural justice 29–30
but still incorporating substantive guarantees 27–28
as multi-generational 'project' 84–87
and 'four-stage sequence' 80–82
and idea of moral progress over time 82–84
constitutional essentials. *See also* constitution
as principles for a society's 'basic structure' (*which see*)
as aspect of public reason 19–20
in relation to moral perfection 66–67
as commonly, publicly legible 41–42 (*see also* publicity, principle of)
regulatory and justificatory missions of distinguished 3–6
and as shaped by duality of missions and tensions between them 8–12
as both democratically grounded and justificationally apt 59–60
as neither too thick nor too thin ('Goldilocks' problem) 42, 51–52
as 'scheme of equal liberties' subject to mutual adjustment as experience warrants, in accord with some liberal guiding aim, always preserving 'central range' of each basic liberty 52–54
as complicated by notion of liberal justice conceptions as a plural 'family' 56–58

constitutional essentials (*cont.*)
constitutional property right as example 19, 57–58
and the responsive idea of the 'at-least reasonable' 59–60, 97, 98–99
as applicable to 'private' legal relations (*see* horizontal application)
as including (or not) socioeconomic guarantees (*see* social minimum)
constitutional interpretation. *See also* judicial restraint
'originalist' versus 'philosophical' approaches 127–29
co-presence of both impulses in Rawlsian justification-by-constitution 118–21
in relation to regulatory and justificatory functions of constitutional law 129, 132–33
constitutionalism
as contested idea in democratic thought 178–79
but central in political liberalism 1–3, 7
as proceduralism 7–7n.16, 25–27, 66–67

democracy
'dualist' (or 'constitutional') conception of 6, 89
regarded as coercive power imposed by citizens on each other, requiring justification 17–18, 20–22

Fallon, Richard
on judicial supremacy in theory and practice 170–71
Fleming, James
and idea of moral progress over time in constitutional law 83n.41
on 'philosophic approach' to judicial constitutional interpretation 83n.41, 128n.3

Habermas, Jürgen
notion of proceduralism, whose, contrasted to that of Rawls 7n.16, 27
as questioning democratic credentials of political liberalism 59n.34, 80n.32, 86n.49

horizontal application (of constitutional-essential basic liberties)
the question defined, in general and for Rawls 183–85
core liberal arguments pro and con 185–88
with implication, for Rawls of horizontal application under tolerant judicial review 188–91
human rights
in relation to constitutional law 62–65

judicial restraint
democracy and legitimacy as distinct motivating values for 158–59
and a Rawlsian reconciliation of the values 168–71
and 'horizontal application' of constitutional guarantees 161–62
three aspects of 154–58
as reticence to pronounce on constitutional questions 154–59
as supreme court's acceptance of non-finality for the country of its pronouncements on constitutional questions 157–62-
as tolerance for differing, reasonable views 156–66-
judicial review. *See also* constitutional essentials; judicial restraint
and a limit on adjudicative competence ('standard worry') 139–40
in relation to democracy and legitimacy 158–59
and a 'thin' (versus 'thick') rendition of constitutional law xiii
weak form of, in relation to socioeconomic guarantees 149–51 (*see also* social minimum)
judicial supremacy. *See also* judicial restraint
in relation to parliamentary supremacy, in political liberalism 38–39, 40–41, 43–44, 122–24
in relation to (so-called) private law 190
justification (of political coercion). *See also* civility; 'liberal principle

of legitimacy'; 'reciprocity, criterion of'
as owed by citizens collectively and distributively 22–24, 107–8, 111
in relation to justice, as aim of constitutional law 28–31
'justification by constitution' 4–8, 21–22, 110. *See also* constitution; constitutionalism; constitutional essentials; 'liberal principle of legitimacy'
and 'constitution *in mente*' 35, 122–24
and institutional settlement 117–20

legitimacy (political) 2–3, 142–44. *See also* 'liberal principle of legitimacy'
in relation to justice 28–31, 142–44
in relation to government by consent 7
as test of principles to govern a society's basic structure (*which see*)
as ground of normal expectation of people's willing compliance with law 22
'liberal principle of legitimacy' ('LPL') 21–22. *See also* constitution; constitutional essentials; proceduralism; 'reciprocity, criterion of'; supreme court
placing constitution at the focus of political justification in conditions of pluralism 21–22, 27–28

people (the)
collective and distributive aspects of, in a democracy 20–21, 22–24
political liberalism
'the problem of' 2–3, 20–21
and democracy as 'dualist' ('constitutional') 6, 40–41
and democracy as government by the people 20–21, 94–95
fundamental ideas in 17–19
and liberal individualism 93–94
empirical presuppositions of (as 'realistic utopia') 90–91
social acceptance of burdens of judgment and constraint of public reason 95–96
social appreciation of 'the very great values of the political' 97, 99
and ultimate dependence on civility as willingness to bear with injustice 99–101
and question of excessive toleration for anti-liberal agitation ('paradox of tolerance') 196–97
'private sphere' ideology. *See also* horizontal application
in relation to perceived liberal toleration for illiberal political movements 195–97
repudiation of, by Rawls as proposition of liberalism 184–85
proceduralism
constitutionalism as 7–7n.16, 25–27, 66–67
in contrast to pursuit of perfect justice 77–78, 142–44
as incorporating 'substantive' terms 27–28
and government by consent 26–27
public reason
as ideal for citizens acting politically 17, 17–19
applied to claims respecting constitutional compliance 71–74
applied more strictly to courts than to citizens? 74–78, 84–87
publicity, principle of
and place of constitution in fulfilling, in Rawlsian conception 23–24, 107
with implications for positive-legal character of justification-bearing constitution 43–45, 107–8

Rawls, John. *See also* 'liberal principal of legitimacy'; political liberalism
as leading expositor of justificatory function of constitutional law 6–7
reasonability (as basis for willing compliance with law). *See also* civility; 'reciprocity, criterion of'
constitutionalism as contingent component of 19–20
as shaped within a broadly liberal political conception 24–25, 93–95
some basic elements of 24–25, 92–95

reasonable pluralism 18
encompassing tolerance for reasonable disagreement 24–25
implying a procedural basis for political justification 25–27
'reciprocity, criterion of' 105–6
observance of by citizen as ethical basis for political justification, in relation to public procedural basis 106–8, 109–13
satisfied by citizen's sincere belief in a supported law's compliance with a justification-worthy constitution-in-force, with possible guidance-taking by citizens from pronouncements of a supreme court 114, 115–20
rule of law
political distinguished from metaphysical conception of 173–75
as constitutional essential for Rawls 173, 178–79
politically not metaphysically grounded 177–75
but still with a metaphysical trace 175–76, 179–80
as compared with strong-democratic rule-of-law attachment 177, 178–79

social minimum 138. *See also* constitutional essentials; judicial review
as constitutional essential 140–44
as compared with 'fair equality of opportunity' 141–42, 146–47
as debatably problematic for strong-form judicial review 139–40, 145–46
in relation to rise and spread of ideas of 'weak-form' review 148–51
Stopler, Gila
on issue of liberal public/private distinction 184n.4
on question of excessive toleration in political liberalism 194–194–95nn.7–8
supreme court. *See also* judicial restraint; judicial review; 'liberal principle of legitimacy'
as protector of the people's higher law and arbiter of a justification-bearing constitution 22, 39–40, 73–74, 119–20, 128–30

Thoreau, Henry D. 100–1
Tushnet, Mark
and the idea of 'weak form' judicial constitutional review 141n.8, 150n.32
as putative subscriber to liberal constitutionalism (kept 'thin') xiii–xiv, 9n.18

Van der Walt, Johan
on the dependence of liberal democracy on civility beyond reasonability 91–92n.10, 99–100